Vodka with Chocolate Chasers

Dan Trelfer

LOLLIPOP MEDIA LTD.

LOLLIPOP MEDIA LTD.
21 DENMARK RD WIMBLEDON
London SW19 4PG

ISBN 0-9538421-1-8

Published by LOLLIPOP MEDIA LTD.

Designed & Produced by Off The Wall Associates

Printed in Great Britain

FOR MUM AND DAD

Arctic Ocean

MOSCOW

KAZAKHSTAN

Scale

UM, NONE. SORRY.

Key

+++++++++ — Railway Track.

■ — Water.

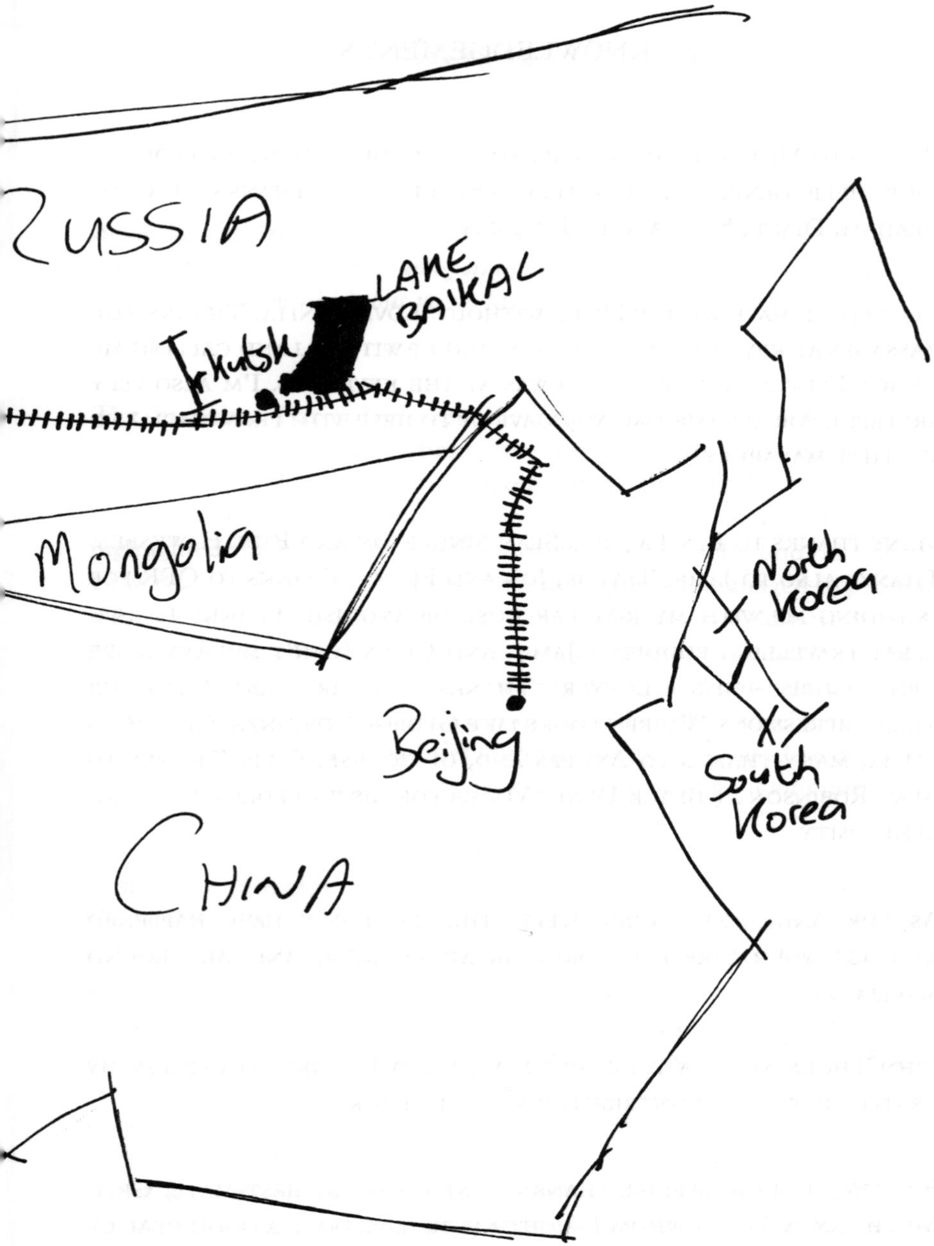
RUSSIA
LAKE BAIKAL
Irkutsk
Mongolia
North Korea
Beijing
South Korea
CHINA

way to catching their no-doubt unreasonably full train to Guangzhou or Shanghai, or, perhaps, to Moscow.

It was roughly the same scene outside now. Whole families seemed to be simply *existing* just outside the train station. Train stations in general had seemed popular places to spend the day all over China. Especially for beggars. Some of the beggars were clearly seriously ill, some were 'just' poor. Many were deceivingly clever. Edson had once risen early to catch a train at Guangzhou station, and he saw several people making their way 'to work.' One man walked carrying a wooden leg under one arm, like an old-style Englishman carrying his precious umbrella to his commuter train. Edson briefly wondered whether he had enough time to observe how this entrepreneur might arrange himself to perpetrate the illusion that he only had one real leg, but decided on balance that it was more important to catch the train.

He had queued for an hour to get a "hard seat" ticket for the sixteen hour journey to Guilin. Well, "queued" is probably the wrong word. A more correct one might be "fought" or "bundled" or, to be accurate, "pushed, jostled, elbowed and kicked" might best describe his hour-long scrap to gain an incredibly uncomfortable and cramped spot on the train. All that for a sixteen hour journey in which a carriage load of Chinese stared at his blond hair and fair skin with unceasing fascination. The trip was an unforgettable one with the highlights including an uncountable number of live chickens in (and out) of baskets, stifling humidity and stickiness, and toilets blocking within an hour. In fact it was a journey filled with everything apart from sleep, which he found to be an impossibility without the help of seven or eight huge gin and tonics. Unfortunately, this train was not equipped with modern bar facilities – the closest was a man occasionally wandering through the carriages hawking cold noodles and dried beef.

But back to the present. The expanse of people outside the station of Beijing was astounding, but once inside it was a little cooler and there were fewer beggars and more travellers. Edson had often wondered why the Chinese squatted so much or, alternatively, sat on books or large sheets of newspaper that always looked as if they had been recently pressed by a superior type of iron. He got his answer while exploring the gift shop at the end of The Forbidden City in Beijing. A lovely salesman who spoke tremendous English explained to him that the Chinese believed that the floor or a wall was too dirty to sit on directly.

He was *unable* to explain, however, why they believed an old inky fragment of newspaper would be more beneficial to their well-being than the only marginally dirtier floor. This man was in fact a rare breed in the salesmen that Edson had encountered - he did not use any pressure tactics, and seemed more interested in chatting about the Chinese way of life and the Western outlook on the world, than selling, oh, I don't know, a miniature Chinese tea set displayed in a pretty box. Although, actually, Edson *did* leave with such an item, as well as a medal with a dragon on it and a paper fan which the man had assured him was "very traditional." He failed, however, to consider exactly how the delicate china might survive all the way home to England at the bottom of his rucksack until *after* the yuan had left his super-safe, super-sweaty money belt.

II

Louis sat on the dusty floor, his backpack still on his back but with the bottom resting on the ground which took the weight off his shoulders. He fiddled with his expensive short-wave radio, trying to solve the perplexing mystery of where the World Service might reside at 7pm Beijing time. Occasionally he looked up, scanning the people crossing his path, searching for a blond head in the crowd. ". . . d Service is Sports Saturday, but before that the midday news. . ." Louis put the radio down and adjusted the aerial just slightly. The sound was still crackly, but previous experience of tortuous and futile hours manoeuvering the position of the aerial and the radio itself reminded him that it really wasn't worth the effort. Then, as a typically dull Royal story began to unfold, the signal began to fade, and was replaced by some indecipherable language. He had just started twiddling again, when a familiar green and black rucksack was rudely dumped in front of him. He looked up, "Alrt."

"Alrt."

"Wasn't gonna turn up, but I thought you might cry if I wasn't here to hold your hand,"

"Say that again, and I'll nut ya."

"Outside, now."

Louis smiled and disentangled his arms from his rucksack, which slowly toppled backwards as he rose to his feet. Edson smiled and held his hand out. Louis grabbed it with a decent grip and smiled back. It was a traditional greeting they had cultivated a couple of years before when both of them were having trouble with some wankers at school. "Alrt" meant "all right?" but with the help of an urban Kentish accent it had quickly degenerated into nothing more than a grunt that they naturally parodied. The second part of the exchange stemmed from a potentially nasty incident in their home town. They and a couple of other mates were playing pool in a moderately safe pub. It was in the middle of the Easter holidays, so there were a few others of a similar age present. It was the kind of pub that was quiet during the week, but exploded with nubile girls without tights and under-age boys with slicked back hair on Friday nights.

Towards the end of the evening, Edson, Louis and their friends were recognised by a couple of evil but harmless, skinny seventeen year old males with greasy shoulder-length hair. They threw a couple of juvenile comments over, and our protagonists replied in an equally witty way. Unfortunately, the 'harmless' seventeen-year-olds had a bigger friend, with shorter hair and the focused, sharp stare of an eagle. And that night, Edson, Louis and the rest were the frightened rodents. This guy issued several threats, which none of the group could legitimately claim to not be intimidated by. Edson's mate Billy missed his next four shots on the pool table, and soon they prudently decided to leg it. They weren't chased, but they didn't relax until the doors of the red Ford Orion were securely locked, and they had left the nearby poorly lit car park.

"Right, where's the train?" Edson asked, looking around at the great expanse of the station. There seemed to be innumerable platforms and everyone else seemed cocksure about where they were headed. Still, this was one in a very long line of strange railway stations, and it had never been much of a problem before.

"Let's have a wander," said Louis, hauling his backpack on once more. As they sauntered and chatted about the last couple of weeks, Edson marvelled for the umpteenth time about how they could be so different yet be such compatible friends and travellers. Louis was a good three inches taller than Edson, and his hair was blue-black like a character from a Marvel comic, and in contrast to Edson's straw-like hair. Louis looked considerably more weathered – his black stubble and sore neck from abrasive shaving being much more apparent than Edson's softish blond fur. Even their interests vastly differed, Edson was into the arts: cinema and the theatre, and sport - football and tennis; Louis loved the music scene, he played trombone in the local orchestra, had little or no interest in sport, and had concentrated on the sciences at school and at University.

It was easy to play spot the difference, but if you looked deeper the similarities were strong cement. Both, for example, made the effort to take an interest in the other's ventures. Edson had seen Louis in concert, Louis was good-natured when a grey Edson would mooch around after his football team had lost. Both had a growing interest in jazz, and they trusted each other's recommendations – on books, music, film, whatever. Although their tastes in films were radically different, they both knew what the other liked. And, of course, there was their mutual love of alcohol and beer in particular. But it was a similarity in thinking that made the relationship strong.

While their peers were visiting pubs on Friday nights in town, they and a couple of other mates preferred a quieter pub in the sticks. For them the contrast was stark and the choice was simple. They could go into town, which had the advantage of being more sociable, but this was the only positive amongst a host of negatives. For example, the music would be so loud in the pub that you had to literally shout in the ear of someone to have a conversation. This system of communication quickly became both annoying and boring, so in the end people just ended up nodding too much, smiling a lot, and laughing at the wrong times hoping it was the right time. Hanging in the corner was the pub equivalent to a bumper sticker saying 'My other car's a Ferrari' – a sign saying: 'If it's 2 loud, you're 2 old'. A more accurate sign might have been: 'If it's not 2 loud, you must be deaf'.

The pub would be so full that dancing was completely ruled out in case a flying elbow cracked some big bloke's jaw, or, worse, knocked the pint out of his hand. The only surefire way to enjoy yourself was to get bat-faced like everyone else, but even that was a struggle. It took a good half an hour just to get to the bar, and then the beer tasted like how you would imagine shandy to taste like if you replaced the lemonade with, well, water. The floor was sticky and studded with broken glass and the heat rose to unbearably sweaty temperatures - like a sauna packed with fully clothed people. The girls' make-up would melt and bloke's heads looked like they'd been ducked in a swimming pool. The stench of vomit would infest the area as it rapidly rotted in the heat and coats would be knocked on the floor and used as mats for people to wipe their shoes on. Edson spent long periods of such evenings looking at the floor just in case he accidentally caught the eye of some lad desperately looking for an excuse to have a fight with someone much smaller than him (so he could prove to his mates that he definitely wasn't homosexual). This, of course, ruined any chances of eye contact with the cute brunette girl in the short black skirt drinking Archers and lemonade.

At 11.30 everyone would be pushed outside by thick-necked bouncers where there would invariably be a couple of half-hearted scuffles broken up by bored policemen, who simultaneously fended off advances from drunken 16 year old girls desperate for a snog with a strong man in uniform. And the brunette girl would always vanish. Eventually Edson and Louis almost always chose the option of a quiet pub, ignoring the weak jibes of "Oh, you're going to an old man's pub again, are you?" They drank decent beer and sorted the world's problems out in three short hours. It would be comfortable, with nearly tasteful decor, and the people in the pub were of legal age. They liked to think they were ahead of their time, and to some extent they were: many of the people that had laughed at them eventually started drifting out to the sticks for a more relaxing night. The conversation was often pretty naiive, but then don't all eighteen year olds who refused to go through the tiresome manically depressed and suicidal phase believe they hold all the answers?

It was Louis who spotted the departure lounge. Well, in truth, it was an open room that led onto the platform with some hard, screwed down seats inside, but this was China, not Heathrow. Some people were already going through the glass door, having their tickets scrutinised by a smart-looking Chinese guard. In contrast to some other Chinese officials they had met on their travels, his uniform was clean and well pressed and his shoes were black and shiny. In one or two towns they had seen policemen idly picking on peasants, while wearing a tatty, unkempt uniform and flip-flops. There seemed to be little discipline in the force, but they kept order well enough – many people appeared to be quite scared of them. A shopkeeper had once tried to convince Louis that all police were experts in Kung Fu. Whether the police were just undisciplined abusers of power, or they were under-funded and neglected by the government, or even that they were doing a good job, but just didn't like the uniform, neither Louis or Edson knew. They didn't really try to find out either. Edson glanced around to see who might be accompanying them on this journey. A fair few Chinese people, a couple of other Western males with long straggly hair and dirty clothes, and, he was pleased to note, a couple of European-looking girls about their age. They joined the queue and had their tickets ripped in half.

For once, in a country bound and gagged with red tape, they got past the ticket inspector with no difficulty, and stood looking at their train, trying to work out which carriage held their cabin. It was a truly magnificent train, seemingly never-ending, the colour of British racing green, a pure picture of elegance. In a country where "restoring" sometimes translates as "knock it down and build it again" this train stood out like a twelve-ounce sirloin steak amongst a pile of floppy hamburgers. Painted in red on a cream placard on the side of the train was 'BOCTOK. MOCKBA-NEKNH,' which, they assumed, meant something like 'The train from Moscow to Beijing.' It was a sign crying out for a tourist photo session. The two girls from the waiting room were just passing, so Louis asked if they might take a photo for them, which one did, if a little unwillingly. She was the nicer looking one, black hair and dark eyebrows, dark eyes and olive skin - she looked quite Italian which Edson in particular had a well known weakness for. However, she was clearly not in the mood for a chat, and only just managed a smile when returning the camera. Louis looked at Edson and shrugged. They boarded the train.

III

The Trans-Siberian Railway has two routes, one is the Trans-Manchurian, the other the Trans-Mongolian. Edson and Louis were on the former, headed all the way to Moscow, with just a few stops each day on a journey that would include a view of the magnificent Lake Baikal at Irkutsk – the largest man-made lake in the world. Edson had considered stopping for a couple of days in Irkutsk, but the romance of a continuous six-day odyssey across the world's largest country was too hard to resist. It was a strange feeling - the excitement of a momentous journey overshadowed by the suspicion that by the following day he might be bored out of his mind, stuck in a tiny space for five more days with nothing to do except read and play cards. Louis had a favourite phrase, not entirely his own, but he couldn't remember where he had heard it: "Don't play cards. It's a waste of time." Cynical, cutting, patronising. Perhaps even true, but maybe that's the point of cards, well, unless you're playing blackjack and you've just been handed a twenty-one after betting a thousand pounds on an outlandish hunch. But, let's face it, neither of these guys had ever been to a casino, let alone had a thousand pounds to fritter away on a whim.

It was a second class carriage with four bunks to each cabin, so it seemed pretty certain that they'd be meeting a couple of new friends fairly soon. The corridor that linked the berths was beautifully old fashioned. The floor had a dark red carpet with faded gold trimmings around the outside that ran the length of the carriage. It was well-worn, thanks, no doubt, to the constant wanderings of bored passengers in search of excitement. The windows had yellow curtains attached at the top and bottom to wire-like plastic railings, when drawn they only *just* met in the middle as if someone had made a small error on the original measurement calculations, or the train company were keen to save a few pence on curtain material. At the end of the carriage was the famous samovar Edson had read so much about. Most Russian trains were equipped with one of these magnificent machines in each carriage - great silver contraptions that dished out piping hot water all day long, providing hot drinks, some warm water for washing in, and, once it was added to dried noodles, the chance of a inexpensive meal. "Ah, the samovar," said Edson, "the ultimate sign of civilisation at a cheap price."

"Yeah," agreed Louis, "The samovar has often helped to serve a thirsty congregation eager to part with their ten pences for a small polystyrene cup of tea at *our* local church."

"Or . . . or thirsty bargain hunters at a Scouts' Jumble Sale."

"Not forgetting the sterling work it can do as a vessel for home brew." Edson screwed his nose at that one, remembering the stereotypically dodgy home brew that Louis had made a year or two before. No-one who ever tasted it would have any more than that first taste, so eventually he had to stagger to a local party, carrying the juice in two enormous gallon bottles with a sticker on each reading:

"THIS BEER WAS BREWED BY LOUIS LANGLEY. IT IS A DELIGHTFULLY STRONG AND FRUITY BEER, FULL OF THE HOPPY FLAVOUR OF KENTISH HOPS. BUT DRINK AT YOUR OWN RISK. MR LANGLEY WILL ACCEPT NO RESPONSIBILITY FOR ANY AFTER-EFFECTS, EXPECTED OR OTHERWISE."

Edson smiled as he remembered one hapless guy called Adam chugging a pint of the potion, before tripping over a coffee table, spinning in the air, and fortuitously landing on a bean bag, where he remained prone for the rest of the evening. Edson had taken this opportunity to move in on Adam's gorgeous girlfriend, but failed miserably.

A moment later, they located their berth, and found themselves looking at two men, one on each of the two bunks on the right hand-side of the small cabin. There was complete silence as Edson tried to think of something to say apart from "Hi!" The man on the bottom bunk rose, holding out his hand and said "Hallo. I am Sasha," in a heavy Russian accent. Edson, wondering how he knew they were English, took his hand and said, "Hi, I'm Edson, this is Louis." Louis shook Sasha's hand also, and then smiled at the man on the top bunk.

"Hello!" he said, unimaginatively. This man looked a bit dour. While Sasha was slightly rotund, with dark brown short, straight hair, this man appeared rather wiry, his hair a dirty blond colour and a stone face that looked incapable of expression, excepting "bored," "uninterested," and "unamused." "My name is Alexander . . ." he left the sentence open as if he was about to add something, but then simply picked up an open book and started reading. Sasha grinned so widely at them that for a moment his mouth resembled a toad's broad smile. He sat on his bed and watched Edson and Louis carefully shuffle in. The berth was small, with about a single pace separating the two sets of bunk beds. The rug on the floor was thin, but it was a lovely burgundy colour that matched the carpet in the corridor, only with a large pattern of cream and light blue, roughly in the shape of a maple leaf. The bunks were dark red also, and covered with that plasticky-leathery material that is neither one nor the other. Edson sat down on the bottom bunk and admired its astounding comfort - not too soft, but not too hard, just padded perfectly like one of those couch-tables that they have in doctor's surgeries, only without the worrying connotations. At the end of each bunk was a pile of linen: a white sheet, a pillow and three blankets, two of which were of the rough and itchy variety, but the third, a blue one, was soft and downy, and, thought Edson, perfect for the blanket that would lay directly on his body at night. There was a window between the bunks, and below it was a small table that was attached to the wall of the train. A small travel clock had already been placed there, and next to it was a shot glass with a drop of clear liquid in the bottom.

Edson glanced at their Russian friends again. Alexander had his back to them, still reading, and Sasha was still smiling and watching them intently. It was very quiet. Edson and Louis both felt awkward about breaking the silence, as you do when you first walk into a new place, yet it wasn't an intimidating atmosphere, more like that uncomfortable quietness you experience in a doctor's waiting room that forces you to whisper all the time. Sasha seemed welcoming, but probably knew about as much English as they knew Russian: very little. Edson had the strange feeling that if he started talking in English, then maybe the Russians would think he was talking about them, and he didn't want to appear rude, so he just sat, glancing around the small room, trying to think of something to say. Louis, however, was already taking some bits and pieces from his backpack, and deciding where he could store the bag for the duration of the journey. "Mind if I go on top?" said Louis. Edson glanced at his friend with a bemused expression on his face, his eyes rolling and his mouth squashed to one side of his face. He shook his head slowly, pretending the weak double-entendre didn't even merit a civil answer. Louis looked back at him with his best cheeky comedian smile, and lifted his backpack onto the top bunk.

"I'm starving, did you remember the food?"

"Of course," replied Edson, "Did you?"

"*Yes*," said Louis sarcastically, bending down and pushing his face close to Edson's, attempting to be intimidating. Edson waved him away. When they last saw each other a couple of weeks previously, they agreed to bring enough food to last the entire six day trip. They had both decided that noodles were fantastic since they had been in China, and neither had any misgivings about eating them for six days running. They bought twelve packets each. Twenty-four packets in total. The two main flavours were chicken – which tasted like beef, and beef – which tasted like chicken, but there were one or two veggie packets as well. They closely resembled the Super Noodles you can get in the West, only the contents of the small silver sachets of 'flavour' were even more baffling than you'd find in England. Edson had suggested that they both bring some massive snacks of some kind, so he bought a huge tin, the size of two of those large chocolate assortment tins you can buy in supermarkets, full of Danish butter cookies that looked gorgeous on the pictures that decorated the tin. Louis bought a similar sized tin of Ritz biscuits. And, well, that was it. That was their varied diet for the following week or so. Except both had brought along a small box each of jasmine tea. So that was all right.

They surveyed the scene for a few seconds, while Sasha stood up and peered in between them on tip-toes, a beery smile on his red face. He said something incomprehensible, and Edson smiled pleasantly, hoping it was supposed to be an amusing observation. Louis pointed at the Ritz biscuits and Sasha roared with laughter. Louis took a couple out and ate them in one mouthful while Sasha calmed down. Alexander looked down at them, with an expression that could have been amusement or contempt. It was all very confusing. "I can't face dried noodles tonight," said Louis, a crumb of Ritz sticking to his bottom lip, "There is a dining car on here isn't there?"

"I guess so. . ." Edson felt slightly guilty that he had once again forgotten to read up on an important subject. Well, "forgotten" wasn't strictly true, it was more a complete unwillingness to bother with such work. He would usually pitch up at a new place and assume things would sort themselves out. And usually they did, but to Louis' occasional chagrin, it was often because he had already done the groundwork for both of them.

"Shall we fuck off then?" said Louis. He was always saying things like that: "I might just bugger off now, actually," or "I'll probably piss off at about ten." They smiled at the Russians, and wandered out, with Sasha still chuckling quietly and Alexander once again engrossed in his hardback.

As they strolled down the corridor, the train jerked slightly before slowly gliding away. They carried on walking, now following the direction of movement, hoping the dining car (if there was one) would be at the front of the train. As they passed the berths, alternately on their left and right sides with each carriage, Edson struggled to stop himself from peeking into them. It really was quite difficult - he was keen to see if there were any nice girls on the train, and it was quite frustrating when, on the odd occasion he saw a slim figure out the corner of his eye, or a girl with long dark hair just disappearing into a berth, he refused to allow himself to gape inside. He elected to look out the window instead.

They were out the station and moving into the suburbs of Beijing. Soon, he supposed, he would see the familiar paddy fields, and the large amounts of litter by the side of the track. The Chinese, he had frequently noticed, tended to clear their space of trash of all kinds: apple cores, tea leaves, take-away rubbish, and empty bottles of water; by simply chucking it, guilt-free, out of the window of their train. And although it looked fun (who hasn't enjoyed throwing an apple core out of a car window on a motorway?), Edson had had cleanliness ingrained into him at a young age. He could still remember, when he was about eight, his friends making him feel very ashamed of himself after he threw a sweet wrapper on the ground on the way home from school. A good friend of his called him a "litterbug" and he couldn't remember intentionally dropping any rubbish since. Edson was shocked the first time he saw the Chinese literally emptying handfuls of stuff out the window of a train, but Louis was quick to point out that maybe it was all part of a cycle. Maybe it was someone's job to keep the side of the tracks clean, and if this part of their culture was eradicated maybe the cleaners wouldn't have a job, and the gleaners would have nothing to glean.

In between each carriage was a darkish, breezy space, where the carpet ended. It seemed about as safe as changing carriages in mid-journey on the London Underground. The rapidly moving earth felt frighteningly close. "I bet it gets cold in these bits when we get into deepest Siberia," observed Edson,

"Mmm," mumbled Louis, clearly ever more intent on reaching the holy grail of the dining car. Finally they passed some blocked off berths, which must have been the kitchen, and walked into the dining area. It was still fairly early - around seven in the evening - and they were some of the first to arrive. There was just one table in use of the twenty or so available. There were four people at the back of the car, two men and two women, who were talking quietly over a few drinks. Edson couldn't make out their language, but they looked European or Russian. Each table was covered with a white tablecloth and all of them were next to a separate window. Either side of each table were the kind of seats that you'd normally find in booths in American-style diners or pubs, which were covered with the same material as the bunks. There was probably room to squeeze three people onto each of them. Edson and Louis sat opposite each other and looked out of the window as China tumbled away from them.

"How about a drink?" suggested Louis. It had been a good couple of weeks since they had supped a beer and had a good chat. Louis looked around for a waiter, and sure enough one appeared from the carriage behind him. He actually looked more like the chef. He was Chinese and wore a white long-sleeved top with a typically Chinese rounded collar, white trousers and a white apron covering him from his waist to near his ankles. He wasn't young, his grey-black hair was receding slightly, he had a small beard on his chin, and he walked with his back bent ever so slightly. Like virtually all Chinese people they had encountered, he looked very fit and slim – the Chinese diet was something to really behold. Edson had also noticed that many Chinese people had superbly toned calf muscles, which he attributed to the fact that Chinese people squat so much (rather than sitting), putting pressure on the calves which therefore become extremely muscly. The waiter beamed at them and bowed just a little, "Liange Tsing-Tao" said Louis, who was much better at Chinese than Edson, although he still used two fingers to indicate the number just in case he had mis-pronounced the word – an easy thing to do in a tonal language.

The happy waiter was back quickly with the beers and two glasses, and opened the bottles before shuffling off. The ritual in China is to always "wash" your glass or cup with the particular drink you are drinking before actually swallowing anything. You pour a little of the liquid into the vessel, swish it around, and then tip the liquid away. Usually, Edson and Louis liked to adhere to this rule, after all, there's nothing like a cast-iron excuse for deliberately chucking drink around, but they felt that, in the classy-ish confines of the dining car, with it's nice carpet and only slightly off-white tablecloths, it would be more sensible to just drink all the beer on this occasion. In fact, this was just one of the many instances when these two could virtually read each other's minds, and they poured slowly and in unison, no swish and tip, just a slow pour, before taking a nice long sip, savouring the amber alcohol. They both put their glasses down and smiled at themselves and each other in an exaggerated gesture of satisfaction. "So, did you make it to Yang Shuo, then?"

"Yeah, fantastic wasn't it? I'm surprised I didn't see you there, when did you pitch up?" asked Edson.

"I went there first, actually."

"Oh, I came straight to Beijing from there – you know, got the overnight train from Guilin."

"Ah, man, I had an amazing trip on that bus from Yang Shuo to Guilin, I've got to tell you about it."

"What happened?" Edson leaned forward and he could see Louis' eyes almost glowing as he remembered whatever had happened to him on that journey. Transport generally in China was amazing, it often took far too long to get anywhere, it was often dull due to these lengths of time, but it was all part of the traveller's game. Backpackers love to tell tales of hardship that they endured cheerfully without complaining, to defy the guide books' best advice, and, ultimately, to have a more gruesome story than the next person. For example, 'hard-seat' is the cheapest train travel in China, following on from 'soft-sleeper,' 'hard-sleeper,' and 'soft-seat.' In one of the guidebooks Edson had taken it recommended that backpackers should not travel on a hard seat journey that lasts longer than twelve hours if you wanted to avoid severe flat-buttock syndrome. Both Louis and Edson had beaten these twelve hours. Edson had done sixteen – it was his first journey, which made him particularly proud, and Louis had achieved a whopping thirty hours, although he later admitted that he would rather shag Mme Sante (a particularly grisly teacher from their former school who made an aardvark look like an attractive proposition) than go through that journey again.

"I'll tell you in a minute, but I've *got* to order some food." Louis could eat. Anything. He'd try anything, and even if he didn't like it (which was rare) he'd try it again, especially if it was local. At the age of seventeen he was working in a restaurant, and was already fully aware of his rights regarding meals and breaks. It wasn't the breaks he was worried about - he was a dedicated worker - his chief concern was his bottomless but unexpandable stomach. Edson later worked as a waiter in the same place, and the chefs were always remembering Louis' insistence on getting his meals at the right time. He was only exercising his rights, of course, they didn't mind that - it was more the sheer *amount* that this boy could eat. He would pile his plate up with whatever was available, and follow it all up with a large pudding. This particular restaurant, which was situated at a fairly high-brow golf club, for some unknown reason insisted that the food the staff ate should be recorded in a large, battered, hard-backed book with "MEALS" scribbled in thick black marker pen on the front cover. There never seemed to be enough room for Louis' entries. Alan, the fat head chef, (a great Irishman who talked so fast and with such a thick accent that he made Edson feel stupid and embarrassed because he always had to ask him to repeat everything he said three times) always complained that if he ate that much he would be infirm within a week.

Edson felt supremely relaxed - there just weren't any worries or responsibilities for six whole days, just scenery, food, books, and, of course, alcohol. Edson loved eating in China, you can order so many

Edson found himself agreeing to pay to go on a cormorant fishing trip that night – it's an activity that no-one leaves Yang Shuo without experiencing. A small boat takes out maybe fifteen people onto the river at night. Next to the boat in the water an old Chinese man paddles along on a primitive but flawless raft made simply from a few logs, with a basket for fish at one end. With him are about seven or eight cormorants, all of which have a rope tied around their neck. The cormorants dive off to catch fish, and when they do, the man on the boat reels in the bird. If the fish is of a size to be of use, it is kept, if not, the cormorant gets to devour it. The bird cannot eat the fish immediately because the rope around its neck impedes its ability to swallow, unless the fish is very small.

It is a very impressive night, although the cormorants looked a little scraggy, and it does seem a little torturous to the poor devils to deprive them of the food they have done so well to catch. But the man on the raft was a fantastically stereotypical Chinese character. He was completely bald, and wore an old grey shirt with only a couple of the buttons done up, and a pair of dark blue knee-length cut-off shorts, worn out and comfy-looking through toil and wear. His expression never changed, he was the personification of concentration - Linford Christie's 'tunnel vision' pales into insignificance next to this guy. On the night that Edson attended the trip, the haul wasn't particularly massive, but one cormorant did catch a fish that probably weighed about a pound and a half, which the raft-man was extremely pleased with.

Almost Yang Shuo's entire community is dedicated to looking after the backpackers who roll in when they're dog-tired of China: tired of the bureaucracy; tired of the red tape; tired of the difficulties in doing even the most simple of tasks like buying a train ticket; tired of the meat that's probably dog or lizard not beef or chicken; and tired of those Chinese people who shout "HALLO" in a mocking way at all foreigners, as if it's the only word foreigners say. In Yang Shuo they can relax: eat the Western food which the restaurants of Yang Shuo do their best to provide; watch Western videos; drink lots of beer; smoke lots of pot; eat bananas and yoghurt and muesli; sit on a clean toilet; float down the river in a rubber ring; sunbathe; climb mountains; meet plenty of other foreigners; discuss what a great experience they're having, and what a nightmare China is to travel in, while at the same time desperately trying to outdo each other with hardship stories; and spend hours in the evenings slagging off "The West" and it's capitalist values, while continually failing to recognise the fact that one of the main reasons they love Yang Shuo is *because* Coca-Cola, Kellogg's Corn Flakes, and hamburgers and chips are so readily available. The whole town is geared towards backpacking and backpackers, the entire economy seems to utterly depend on it, and everyone there loves it.

Louis returned, but Edson had to go and come back before Louis could finally start his story. "Well," said Louis, "I had to go to Guilin to book a train ticket out of there, which was a pain, because you had to do it in advance, well, you know that," Edson nodded, "Actually, it was my second trip there, I'd been the day before, queued for about four hours, then the *blahdy* woman told me that all the tickets were sold out for the train I wanted, so I'd have to come back the next day to get tickets for a train the following day. Did you try to get a ticket from Yang Shuo?"

"Yeah, but no-one could get one."

"Same with me, except one guy said he could send someone to get it, but it would just cost a load extra so I just went myself. I couldn't believe that there were only six tickets for foreigners on the whole train. Well, I can believe it. Did you have to go back twice?"

"No. Must've been lucky."

"Yeah." Louis downed the remainder of his third glass of beer and looked around to order a fourth, "Anyway, what was I saying? Yeah, so I thought I better get off the pot and make sure that I got a ticket, so I left my room at six." Louis was always saying 'get off the pot.' His own tendency to sleep a lot and enjoy lazing around with a book really frustrated him. "I've never seen a bus service like that before - did you see the way they persuaded people to get on? This was six in the morning, right, and there were only about three of us on the bus, and I wanted to get away. There was hardly anyone else around, but this real *scrubber* of a bloke walked past, just minding his own business, and our conductor just jumped off the bus, and started shouting at him, and pushing him into the bus! But this guy doesn't want to get in, you know, he's just probably out for a stroll in the morning air, or on his way to work to cook some Westerners their scrambled eggs, I dunno, but he was obviously going *some*where.

"He tried to walk away, and he was shaking his head, and looking at the floor, but our conductor wouldn't give up - they never leave town without a full bus, do they? So, after a bit more arguing, the conductor just shoved him onto the bus, and this guy just smiled in a resigned sort of way, and sat down, smiling to himself, or at the conductor, I don't know, then he stayed on the bus all the way to Guilin! He didn't even want to go there! Why did he get on? He was minding his own business, wondering what he'll have for breakfast, and then gets seduced by an ugly conductor into going to Guilin! Why? He didn't even care, he just sort of went, 'Oh well, it's easier to say yes than no, might as well I suppose, maybe I can buy a nice new pair of flip-flops.'" Louis was by now becoming more and more agitated as he threw himself into the story and the alcohol started to work its magic.

Edson also remembered his trip on the same bus service - incidentally a bargain at about 4 *kwai* or about thirty pence for an hour and a half's ride. All of the buses had such salespeople who were all true masters of their profession. There were two main methods of attack. The first was the one that Louis was describing, the hard sell. They literally forced people onto the bus when, according to all outside appearances, they simply weren't interested in going anywhere. Or maybe they were, but they were playing a canny game to try and get the price down, and once it was at an acceptable level they would admit to wanting to take the bus.

The second was a softer method, but just as effective, and it was one that Edson had fallen for in similar situations. The driver would have a gorgeous woman, dressed nicely, lovely face, full of the beauties of the Far East. She looked for all intents and purposes like a pretty face that would entice drooling men onto the bus with her seductive charm. But she was no pushover, this girl. If you walked straight past, determined to ignore her bewitching allure, she'd catch you up, touch your arm, and, standing closely, would offer a price for the bus ride. By this time most men would be unable to comprehend whether the price was reasonable or otherwise, and would follow her like sex-starved zombies to the bus. But it wasn't just the soft words or the cute accent, it was the complete air of innocence she could effortlessly maintain, further melting a man's heart, believing her to be completely unaware of her zestful appeal. Complete rubbish, of course. She was hired for the very reason that she had these amazing skills. What was surprising was that there were so many of these talented women. It wasn't as if they turned women off, either. Their charm seemed universal: innocently sexy to men, friendly and unthreatening to women, sweetness and light with kids.

Edson was a sucker for these types. Louis like to think that he was above all that, but in truth he could be worse than Edson. While in Guangzhou, one waitress took a liking to both of them, and on their last visit to that particular restaurant, Louis decided that he should give this girl his T-shirt, because she had said how much she liked the colour. So, in the middle of the restaurant, after a couple of cold drinks, naturally, he took his shirt off, and handed it to the startled waitress as he left. She put it on, and it came down to her knees. I'm off on one again, aren't I? Sorry, let's get back to the thread of the tale so far . . .

"So, I was waiting for about half an hour for this bus to fill up, and as usual a couple of old women staggered on carrying baskets with chickens in, and there were no seats left, so they found a couple of boxes for them to sit on to stop their knees from breaking, and we left. Then we stopped again, because the driver's mate was running after the bus with some important message, and after they spoke for ages, he decided that he'd come with us, so he climbed in the front. If he was blahdy coming with us I couldn't understand why he couldn't've delivered the message on the way, but there you go. Then, as we were about to go, *again*, one of the passengers decided he'd had enough, and he pushed his way to the front, and got off, but then the blahdy" - Louis always said "bloody" pronounced "*blah*dy" in imitation of a craft, design and technology teacher named Mr. Saych, who used to look skywards and say "Aaaaah, Blaaahhhdeeee 'Ell" whenever he saw someone struggling to figure out how a vice worked - ". . . but then the blahdy conductor person - well one of them, why do they need one to get people on the bus and one to collect money – wouldn't they earn more money if one person did it all? - decided that he had to try and persuade him to get back on, but he was having none of it, so they shouted at each other for a bit and the conductor pushed him back on, but he got off, and the conductor shouted louder, but he just walked off, and finally we left. More beer? I'm just off for a waz, though." Edson nodded, even though he could feel that dizzy, watery feeling starting to permeate his head. He conducted his usual test in this situation, which was to close his eyes, and see if his head felt like it was drowning in a washing machine. It wasn't too bad – the washing machine was only in that first, slow, 'getting the washing wet' stage. After a few moments Louis returned.

"Everything finally seemed okay, so I put my walkman on,"

"That's unlike you," Louis would usually advocate doing

interrupting Aretha Franklin, so I kept like, *half* standing up to see what was going on. And the baby was clearly having a nightmare – the temperature was above thirty five degrees, the bus smelt of chickens, and he had a scary old woman sitting near him on a stool."

"Then the blahdy bloke next to me started going," and Louis did a disgusting sound that people make when they want to clear phlegm from their throats, only this was a sound only created by the kind of person who would be proud to hold the world record for the 'Largest Amount of *Green* Produced, With the Loudest Sound, While Revolting the Largest Amount of People'. "And I swear to you," Louis leaned forward, his left hand vertical and rigid, up close to Edson's face – well, it *looked* close to Edson, "He smiled at me, before turning and just gobbing this great glob of *phlegm* onto the floor, without even moving from his squatting position. Then he just lit up and started smoking a really grim cigarette which made the baby cry even more, because he kept blowing the smoke forward."

"I was just about to shout 'THAT'S *QUITE* PLEASANT,' or something equally sarcastic, when I caught sight of the baby. It had one of those horrible babygrow things on, you know - the ones without a crotch so they can just pee or shit when and where they feel like it, and the mother was holding it out at arms length in front of her," Edson interrupted, anticipating the probable result,

"Oh, NOOO, NO, that's grim, ah, that's *dis*gusting, ah, man," he looked at his beer, grateful he couldn't see the no-doubt uriney colour of the liquid through the brown bottle, (by this time they'd given up on pouring their beers before drinking them) and twirled it in his fingers before taking a large gulp. He covered his eyes with his hands, and peered out at Louis' satisfied face - a face preparing to deliver a killer blow.

"Oh *yes*. In the middle of the bus the baby just started *pissing* into the gangway, and it dribbled down to the back, weaving around the grim blokes phlegm, and all the way to the back of the bus, where it made a little yellow pool. Oh, then he stopped and his Mum was kind of retrieving him he dribbled a bit, and it dropped onto the person sitting next to his Mother."

"What? She wasn't even next to the gangway?" Edson was doubling up, holding his stomach in mock disgust and real mirth. As you may know, wee and poo can become vastly more humorous, even to the most elegant and intellectual person, once a few cold drinks have been taken.

"No, just held him over the bloke sitting next to her."

"And what did he do?"

"He hardly paid any attention, just looked down at the piss staining his *nice* blue trousers, and pushed the baby back towards the mother." Louis paused and took a couple of long drinks of his beer. "I couldn't say anything - no-one else did either, so either it was a common thing for babies to piss on buses, or everyone else was as shocked as I was."

"Probably the first one."

"Yeah. Anyway, so I was looking out the window, and noticed that I hadn't seen any cars or anything pass us the other way for a while, and for a minute or two I didn't see any more either. Then we started to slow down a bit, and I was looking to see why, when suddenly he just speeded up even faster than before, and swerved off the road, onto, oh, I don't know how to describe it, like a path, but without a path there, just a stoney bit next to the road, that was sloped slightly, so he just drove on this bit, with the bus leaning *crazily* over to one side, and the squatting bloke fell into me, and I elbowed him in the ribs, and he gave me a look, but I stared him out. We were passing loads of other cars and stuff, just ignoring the whole traffic jam - we were the only ones doing it, and no-one seemed to care - maybe buses have special privileges, I don't know, but he just drove past all of them, cut in at the front, and then stopped." Edson got up quickly at this pause,

"Back in a minute."

Edson returned momentarily, looking relieved, "Go on."

"There'd been a massive crash, with two trucks involved. I don't know what exactly happened, but it looked like they had been heading for a head-on collision, and they both swerved to avoid each other, but they both crashed as a result. Everyone started to get up, and we obviously weren't going anywhere for a while, and I couldn't see much out of the window, so I pushed my way off the bus. It was amazing - there was one truck which had hit a small tree, knocked it over, and then smashed into this massive pile of rubble or gravel, or something like that, which I suppose was there to fill in the potholes or something, while the other truck had shot straight into someone's front room, and virtually the whole side of this little house had just caved in. It was so surreal," Edson, his brain fuzzy and filled with images of crazed Chinese drivers careering into houses and trees, couldn't get *Jazz Moods* out of his mind, and thought of a good joke.

"Wait, were you still listening to your walkman, and had you got to 'Pick Up the Pieces' by Average White Band, yet?" *Brilliant.*

"Er, no. I think I turned it off during 'Take Five'," in his inebriated state of mind, this actually seemed to Louis to be a reasonable question, an attempt by Edson to fully appreciate the atmosphere of the moment. "But, it wasn't only the crash," he tried to swig some beer, but most of it missed his mouth, and rolled down his whiskered chin. He wiped his face with his cuff. "In fact, that was about the most normal thing about the whole situation. I was in shock for a moment, but when I started to look around, I realised that there didn't seem to be any injured people, or any blood, or panic, or ambulances or anything. The crash must have been fairly recent, or the road wouldn't still have been blocked. There was definitely no-one trapped in the trucks, and I sort of realised that it was unlikely that they were all having a cup of char in the living room, because the truck was taking up most of the room in there. On top of that, everyone was laughing and joking around. It was unbelievable. Peasants were just sitting and pointing and laughing . . . you know, kids were jumping all over the truck that had hit the gravel, and there were some blokes trying to see if they could get in through the window of the truck that had parked in the living room. I mean, where *were* the blahdy drivers?" Edson shrugged, he finished his beer, and two more appeared in front of him; he couldn't remember ordering them, but he handed one to Louis.

"So, either it was a brilliant stoic attitude by the Chinese to make a party out of a bad situation, or I was on a bus full of lunatics that had been forced to stop over in an abandoned lunatic village who rarely got a view of the outside world. Loads of other people were coming from their cars further down the queue - no-one seemed to be in a massive hurry – a civil blahdy war probably would have broken out if it had happened in England. They were all just laughing and pointing, especially at the truck in the living room. Anyway, we obviously weren't going anywhere fast so I had a wander round. I walked around the back of the bus and I saw some Chinese businessmen - you know what they look like, men in suits with not one, but *two* pagers attached to the waist of their trousers." He tipped the beer towards his mouth, but most of it missed and splashed down his front. "There were four of them, all squatting in the dust. I mean, why are two pagers so important when you constantly ruin all your credibility by squatting in the middle of a dusty road?" With great effort, Edson summoned a shrug, and turned the corners of his mouth downwards, hoping this would sufficiently indicate an answer of, 'I don't know, but I'm in complete agreement with your sentiments, however, I'm too pissed to answer properly.'

Louis picked up his bottle, and waved it in front of himself, bubbles sprayed out and hit the window - Edson watched them dribble down and suddenly realised how dark it was outside. "They were all gathered in this circle, all looking at something, and they got more and more excited, and they kept shouting and laughing, and occasionally one of them hopped back a bit. I couldn't see what they were doing at first, so I bent forward a bit, and I saw one of them holding a lit match. At first I thought it was some bizarre experiment to burn the dust, but no!" he waved his bottle in front again, and leant forward for a moment, before realising it wasn't such a good idea, and slopped back against the seat, "No!" Then he decided to stand up to ram the point home, "There was a caterpillar there, and these fifty year old businessmen with suits and two pagers were burning the blahdy things' tail!"

Louis stepped out from the table and squatted in the gangway and started pretending to burn a caterpillar while still explaining, "First one would use a match, then another would use his cigarette, and this poor, tiny green thing was having it's body slowly burnt to a crisp, and this clear goo was dripping off it!" He jumped to his feet again, and swayed a little as the blood rushed to his head, "It was disgusting, I really should have taken a picture. You know I can almost understand these cruel bastard kids who frazzle ants with a magnifying glass – that's just part of a boy's fascination with destruction, isn't it?" He sat down again, "These were grown up blahdy businessmen with two blahdy pagers, and they were LOVING it."

Edson's eyes felt like they had lead weights attached to the eyelashes, and his head was spinning terribly. Louis grabbed his bottle and downed the second half of his beer, and they sat in silence for a moment, until Louis lay down on the seat. Edson was vaguely aware that they were the last ones in the dining car, and he felt a little lonely. Soon he'd be in the middle of bloody Siberia - how cold would it be? He had no idea about the Siberian climate at this time of year. He began to finish his beer and stared out the window, although he couldn't see anything, as it was dark outside.

The train rocked gently and he decided he needed to rest his eyes for a bit. At first he tried just shutting them tight to see if that would placate them for a while. That sometimes worked. Not today. He began to doze. At an indeterminate point later, he heard a thud. Louis had rolled off the seat onto the floor. Edson watched as he positioned himself lengthways along the gangway. "Nice story," he said, helpfully. Then he started to wonder where exactly their berth was. It had been a long walk to the dining car, and his memory seemed to be on holiday in the Bahamas. All he could recall was lots of carriages. He couldn't remember the number of their carriage let alone their berth, and Louis was clearly in a worse state than he was.

The one advantage they had was the amazing homing instinct drunk people have when they want their bed. They'll walk for miles, navigating by road-signs and gaining help from taxi-drivers, policemen and helpful hobo dogs to get them home. For a while Edson stared blankly out of the window, trying hard to summon the courage to get to his feet. As tired and pissed as he was, the lure and memory of that comfy-looking bunk was irresistible. He was at that stage where bed is all you want, at any cost, and you want to be there immediately: a taxi ride, a bus ride, or a short walk are all just too much hassle - every minute seems like an hour. He spied the Chinese waiter-chef sitting patiently at a table with a pot of tea and a small Chinese cup in front of him. Edson suddenly felt angry and wished he had stuck to tea all night, that refreshing, green, sweet tea. He felt awful. He rose, and tried to wake Louis. He pulled him up a bit, and some sticky drool dangled crazily from Louis' mouth, which snapped and fell to the floor like a broken elastic band as Edson hauled Louis to his feet with all his might. "Ed . . ." attempted Louis. But he too was feeling the call. Edson fished in his pocket and pulled out a few scruffy notes of Chinese currency and flipped them onto the table.

"Thank you, very nice, I love char," mumbled Louis as they passed the waiter-chef. Neither of them remembered the long walk back to the berth. They were both completely relaxed, knowing if they looked for long enough they'd find the right cabin. Their night was over, but the Trans-Siberian train unerringly continued its tremendous journey.

Chapter Two

Certificate: 15

Some of the heavier swear words are included in this chapter and so it is not suitable for all tastes, although the swearing is still minimal. Unfortunately, the '15' tag doesn't mean there is any sex, nudity (beyond a brief glimpse of a young man in old boxer shorts) or even any gratuitous violence.

I

Edson had no idea what time it was. It was dark, and the carriage was rolling violently, more as if he were in a cabin in a ship peaking and troughing on the high seas of the Antarctic than a supposedly smooth-riding train somewhere in Eastern Asia. But . . . *was* it the carriage that was rolling? He couldn't be sure whether it was the carriage or his own twirling head that was causing the dizziness in his skull. After much thought, which did nothing to ease his throbbing cranium, he realised that it was still night-time, and, with relief, that it *was* the train rolling and not his head. He also noted, with disgust, that his mouth tasted like, as Louis would say, 'Genghis Khan's underpants.'

Edson had forgotten to drink some water before he passed out (hardly surprising), and was now absolutely dry. He remembered, hazily, the samovar at the end of the carriage, and was thus compelled to begin a lengthy, hazardous, tortuous quest. He slowly bent his head over the side of the bunk and reached for his backpack. He quickly found his trusty tin mug that had stubbornly lasted since his often regretted Scout camp days ("Scout camp," he once explained to Louis, who had been fortunate enough to miss the sub-cadet force that has been inflicted upon millions of innocent young boys, ". . . taught you nothing more than living in a tent with other boys for 10 days gets sweaty and smelly; that the leaders only enjoy these things because they get to have a great piss-up for ten nights in a row in front of a great big fuck-off fire; and how to build a bivouac. Building a bivouac, or 'bivvy'," Edson accompanied the word 'bivvy' by sarcastically making quotation marks in the air with his fingers, "might sound like a useful skill, but if, by some astounding piece of misfortune, you find yourself in a position where you have to sleep in a wood for the night, putting some branches and some leaves together against a tree is going to be less difficult than building a small make-believe spaceship out of lego."). Edson shuffled in the pockets of his bag,[*] desperately trying not to wake his companions, which made the whole thing more difficult, and he could feel blood rushing to his dangling head with every passing second. His darkened and hazy state of mind started roaming and he found himself wondering whether if the blood kept rushing to his head, would it start to dribble out of his ears? This made him feel nauseous, so he sat back up again and rested.

Thirst, though, is a strong motivator, and the lure of a relieving cup of medicinal jasmine tea was as tempting as the devil with all his promises of guiltless sex and booze and coveting and doughnuts . . . he dangled his head again and fished some more. Around the edges of the rucksack, he felt something rectangular shaped. He forced his hand inside the bag, shoved through the clothes and gifts and books, and pulled out a box. It could have been the box with the yin and yang balls inside. Fortunately, it was the tea. He sat up a bit straighter, astonishingly remembering that the bunk above was low enough to crack his head should he sit bolt upright. He held the cup between his knees, and carefully but shakily tore open the box and the packet inside. He peered hard at his cup in the darkness, and then at the box, before aiming some leaves into the former. Some probably missed, but most seemed to go in and he was one stage further. He managed to twist his legs and plant his feet onto the uncertain floor. He got to his feet. It was freezing, but the enticement of the hot water at the end of the carriage drove him on.

He stepped out of the cabin and turned right, vaguely made out the silver samovar at the end of the train and began to stagger towards it. It was like the opening scene from *Raiders of the Lost Ark* when Indy encounters several death-threatening obstacles before obtaining the golden head . . . only much slower and without the thrills. After what seemed like about five minutes he reached the samovar and slowly poured some boiling water into his cup. There was no Indy-style quick retreat, however, just more of the same precarious plodding. He gingerly crept back into bed, petrified he would spill the tea and perhaps scald his legs. Or worse – his gonads. He wrapped the covers around himself and drank down the

---

[*] Please stop that sniggering at the back.

gorgeous liquid, straining the leaves with his teeth and silently spitting them back into the cup. Soon afterwards he was unconscious once more.

II

His slumber was short-lived as at an early hour the train slowed to a halt and Edson was woken by the sound of people alighting the train. Louis was standing in front of him, pulling on some trousers. Nice early morning viewing of Louis' boxer shorts.

"What's going on?"

"Early morning stop - I thought I'd get some breakfast in." Edson stared at him for a moment.

"Don't you get hangovers?"

"Baaarh!" replied Louis. It was his stock answer when faced with any kind of hardship. "Just get out there and get some food down you!" He added in a stereotypical regimental voice. Edson let his head fall sharply onto his pillow, and he gazed at the bottom of the bunk above him. Stepping out into possibly the remotest and least interesting outpost of China in the sharp cold of dawn didn't really appeal to him. Although, in point of fact, nothing was particularly appealing to him at that moment except for the idea of continually resting his poor head for the next six days. But this was the first real stop. Shouldn't he get out and have a look, take in the scenery?

It mildly annoyed Edson that Louis' boundless energy was so bloody contagious. He always thought of himself as being very energetic, but although Louis could sleep almost as if in hibernation, once he stirred he had the concentrated energy of a Lucozade* tablet. Edson began to haul

* Aah, Lucozade. The refreshing glucose drink. In the 1980s when I was growing up, I remember Lucozade being advertised by the virtually superhuman Daley Thompson. Kids like me believed that Lucozade was a nice fizzy drink you should have when you are ill to help you get better. In those days, of course, it was marketed in a clear bottle with a red label, and its amber colour was the colour you would imagine glucose to be. Anyway, somewhere along the line they re-invented the drink as a sports energy beverage advertised by sports people but actually drunk by fat blokes at half time of their Sunday football league matches – Lucozade in one hand, ciggy in the other. Now, of course, it's pretty ubiquitous, with different fruit flavours to try and it's available in still or sparkling like water in restaurants and it comes in cans and bottles AND in foily things that are nice to handle. And there is a Lucozade energy tablet which you can suck and eat like a rectangular Refresher for instant energy. If you don't know what Refreshers are . . . well, I haven't got time now.

himself out of his bunk. He noticed that Alexandra and Sasha were still asleep and were accompanied by assorted cans strewn across the bottom of Sasha's bunk and calmly rocking to and fro on the floor. He grabbed his jeans and fished a jumper from the very bottom of his rucksack, causing the meticulous packing he had performed when he left Beijing to be undone in one fell swoop, and ventured into the outside world.

It was damp out, but felt fresh in contrast to the confines of the train. Any views of the surrounding area were swathed in a thick mist. The landscape – what could be seen of it – seemed flat and barren, and in front of Edson was a platform and two huts – one larger than the other. There seemed to be some people queuing outside and just inside the larger one, and as Louis was nowhere to be seen, Edson guessed he had gone inside this building. He joined the queue and craned his neck to see what was inside. Fancying he could make out Louis' head - which was slightly higher than the others – he elbowed his way inside with little resistance – perhaps it was too early in the morning for the other passengers to start a full scale bundle.

Queues in China (usually for train tickets - incidentally, Edson always wondered why the queues were so long at train stations and why every train always seemed to be full to bursting point. Most of the passengers seemed to be entire families moving tremendous distances across the fantastically vast country - where were they all going? Why would heads of families decide to uproot like this? It was completely bizarre, no matter what time you were on a train it always seemed to be as crammed as a British commuter train attempting to carry all it's rush-hour passengers in a single carriage. Eventually, Edson decided that there were so many people in China that it was simply naturally crowded everywhere, and trains were the only affordable long-haul travel available. I'll start the sentence that started all this navel-gazing at the beginning again, because, no doubt, you're as lost as I am). Queues that Edson observed in China often appeared as follows: at the tail end they were completely calm, with respectful spaces between each waiting customer. As the queue neared the booth, the customers would edge a little tighter together; and as it became nearer still, everyone would be constantly trying to shuffle a couple of centimetres closer to the cursed person in front while simultaneously stretching their necks and standing on tip-toe in a desperate effort to judge how long there was left to wait; while at the very front of the line the queue vanished completely to be replaced by an astoundingly *beautiful* mêlée. Grown men – rarely women, actually – would literally jump on top of each other like out-of-control wild-eyed teenagers at some high-adrenaline rock concert.

But there was no such bundle to speak of at this more refined queue; besides, no-one really had much hope in elbowing past the truly impressive might and determination of Louis Langley. Edson watched him for a moment as he brilliantly picked and grabbed pieces of food like the biggest bird in a flock of pigeons feeding upon a discarded bag of chips. Edson pushed his way past a couple of non-plussed queuees and, not without force, knocked his shoulder into Louis' back. Louis turned round and said "Come on then!" in his mock hard boy voice. Edson wasn't pleased with the selection. There was some fresh (ish) fruit of which Louis had grabbed an armful, but apart from that it was the usual Chinese fare of dried noodles and packets of dried beef.

"Do we need any more noodles, do you think?" Edson asked.

"Hmm, no. I think twenty-four packets should see us through." It was at precisely this point of forced irony that they first registered that their food for the next five days or so was going to be a steady, but surely unhealthy diet of dried noodles, Ritz biscuits and Danish Butter Cookies.

They returned to their cabin to find both the Russians still sleeping. That looked pretty inviting, so Edson returned to bed. Louis climbed up to his bunk and read for a while but as the train left China in its wake, he too felt fatigued. It was an exhausting country to travel in. Nothing was ever simple, from booking into a cheap traveller's hotel (which required filling in enough paperwork to qualify you to take out a mortgage on the whole place yourself) to simply buying a small gift for someone back home (which required hard bargaining). Bartering was an enjoyable challenge, but at the same time it could be draining, and it was impossible to simply browse. If you so much as glanced at anything, shop owners immediately jumped on you and ask if you wanted it, how much you would pay for it, or who the gift was for. It was nice that the vendors were so keen to open a dialogue, but the pressure to buy something you'd looked at was consequently immediately heightened.

But Louis relished the challenge of taking on a vendor at their own game (He had had started referring to salespeople in the markets vend*ors*. He always emphasised the 'or' part of the word with a Northern England twang. This accentuation originated from a person Louis knew who didn't know how to pronounce the surname 'Grosvenor.' He included the 's' of the spelling to make something approaching 'Gross (to rhyme with loss) vee-*nor.*' And thus the new pronunciation of vend*or* was born). Of course, everyone always gets ripped off when they first arrive and usually on the odd occasion afterwards. It was something that everyone was always careful to guard against, if only to avoid the ignominy of discovering you've been fleeced.

We're always being told about the need for Eastern cultures such as those of China or Japan to always maintain 'face', but it's ironic that backpackers have a similar coda – particularly over the issue of bartering. It becomes essential to any self-respecting traveller to make sure they secure the right price for an item, otherwise they risk losing face and being seen as a greenhorn by other travellers who will no doubt be delighted to explain how and why the item could and should have been bought at a cheaper price.

I suspect this was originally less a matter of pride and more that travellers are usually on tight budgets – in China it was possible for Louis and Edson to live very comfortably on about £10 per day including travel, accommodation, and food. Perhaps the truth is that backpackers are constantly watching their bank balances, so any needlessly spent money really hurts. However, it's easier to explain away hard bargaining by saying it's to do with Chinese culture and your own pride rather than admitting it's because you're, well, tight. Or maybe it *was* to do purely with pride. Maybe the thought of the vendor laughing at your stupidity in paying over the odds after you've left the shop was too much for some people to bear. In Louis' more relaxed moments, usually after four beers, he reasoned that many of the vendors were relatively poor people and as it was rare to get absolutely hustled, you shouldn't feel too bad about handing over a few extra *kwai* than was absolutely necessary.

Louis still worried that this prognosis might be a condescending one. He felt that they *wanted* the argument, they *wanted* the stress and the pain of fighting for a price and that they relished the ordeal even more than he did. And Louis loved to barter – his tactics in the market area were well honed and usually effective. Most were pretty obvious and straightforward. One trick was to produce a really large note when bartering for something expensive. Often, the value of the note was not really great enough, but just the sight of it would sometimes drive the vendor wild and he would snatch it before you changed your mind. Another classic was to get a good amount of small change in one pocket, and once the vendor didn't seem to want to go any lower, to produce all that money, counting it slowly, and making it clear that it was all the money you had. Once the vendor believes he has squeezed out the maximum amount of money possible from the buyer he or she would usually relent, within reason. The key – the golden rule of bartering – was to never mention a price, no matter how many times they said "What would you pay?" Once you have mentioned a price that is agreeable with the vendor it's wrong to pull out of the deal.

Often the most effective trick was to walk away, as if completely washing your hands of the whole deal – it was amazing how quickly the price would lower after that. A vendor once chased Louis half way down the road begging him to buy a small perfume bottle painted elegantly with a typical Chinese garden design. The price became absurdly low – so low, in fact, that Louis became rather embarrassed. The vendor was so desperate for a sale that he hardly seemed to care whether he made a profit or not. Finally, the vendor stood in front of Louis and just said "Pleess" quietly, almost under his breath. Louis felt terrible, yet despite himself he still felt a sneaking satisfaction that he had won. He returned to the shop and actually paid more than the final asking price, much to the delight of the vendor. Later he told Edson that he had made a mistake – he had succumbed to a clever trick and had allowed the vendor to win – that he had "snatched defeat from the jaws of victory."

China could be one of the most infuriating places in the world at times. It had the capacity to infiltrate the mind and justify actions that would never be considered at home. Queuing for buses was another one. In their early days of city central bus-riding, Louis and Edson constantly found themselves being last onto the bus because they were being elbowed out of the way by the more cunning and experienced Chinese passengers. So they devised a way of making sure they were first to board. As the bus arrived at the stop, the two of them would walk towards it, then as it sailed past they would walk backwards, creating an impenetrable shield. That way when the bus stopped everyone else was behind them. As Louis walked backwards with his arms spread out his face was totally calm, as if he had no idea what he was doing, had no clue about the queue-cum-bundle behind him.

The amazing thing was that no-one seemed to care. In fact, they may have admired it. Edson had once boarded a bus on which there were only one or two seats left. He noticed an incredibly frail old woman, her face scrunched up with old age, her skin hanging off her like that of an elephant, slowly hobbling towards a seat. But as she was about to reach it she was denied at the last possible second by a suited young businessman who nipped in front of her with the agility and preying instincts of a panther, and bounced himself Tigger-like onto the seat. He looked up and absolutely beamed with pride at obtaining the coveted last throne. The guy was so happy he smiled for the rest of his ride on the bus as if he was receiving a round of applause from the rest of the bus for his impressively nimble speed.

China, though, was already disappearing into the distance, and the new vastness of Siberia was unfolding out in front. Louis dozed off, dizzied by the great distance behind and in front of him.

III

Edson awoke a few hours later. His previously thudding head was thankfully reduced to a mere light ache. Louis was also up and already itching to visit the dining car. The two Russians were not in their bunks, and their empty cans had been disposed of. Edson was absolutely famished, and having Louis busily chatting to him about what he would like for breakfast was not doing anything so ease his hunger. He dressed quickly and loaded himself with things he thought too valuable to leave unattended in the cabin - passport, money, walkman. Football shirt?

They arrived in the carriage and sat down at the first available table, without registering that no-one seemed to have much in the way of food in front of them. Louis opened his mouth to say something, but Edson was pointing behind him where a waiter was, well, waiting. But it wasn't the cheerful cook/waiter they had met the previous night. This man was dressed in the more traditional waiter attire of a bright white shirt with black trousers. He was tall and thin – maybe even taller than Louis – and had a very dark moustache, neither of the rampantly bushy kind or the lovingly clipped and manicured Poirot-type. His hair was the kind of hair that looks unmovable, much like women's hair looks when they wear a net (why do women do that?). It was parted, but the parting was positioned only marginally above his left ear. It was reminiscent of those pot-plants that only grow towards the light, except his hair looked as if it only grew towards his right ear: he didn't have to brush it that way, it just graduated in that direction all by itself . . . all except for a small rogue patch that tried to even things up by growing towards the left ear.

Edson, with his floppy hair that had often been the subject of ridicule, envied these people. How fantastically *easy* it would be to wake up and simply flatten your hair into its natural solid shape, rather than trying to vainly convince it to adopt the fashionable shape it seemed determined to eschew. He reasoned, though, that it must be something of a nightmare to possess hair like this guy, simply because of the complete absence of choice. This guy's hair probably looked the same when he was six and will still look similar (if not in colour) when he turned fifty-six.

He also had a peculiar way of standing. His upper body leaned slightly to the right, as if his hair was unbalancing him slightly – either that or he was built with similar foundations to that tower in Pisa. Before he even opened his mouth Edson and Louis had guessed he was Russian: the changeover must have taken place sometime during the night. "Do you have anything to eat?" asked Louis, mimicking an eating motion by pretending to spoon food into his mouth and then rubbing his stomach in mock satisfaction. Edson thought this slightly patronising.

"'Fraid not lads, not much anyway," came a distinctively English-home-counties accented reply. The waiter looked over their heads at two men sitting at the next table. The voice went on: "The selection's a bit pony. They've only got bread for breakfast; great coffee though!" and he held up the two items as he spoke before taking a gulp of the coffee and emitting an exaggerated "Aahhh!" sound in an obvious over-reaction to the refreshing taste of the drink. Edson hated people who claimed they couldn't 'function' until they'd had their 'morning coffee,' as if it was some life-giving drug – as though if they didn't have it they would just stare at the empty coffee cup like a moron all day and become incapable of movement. The other man offered a weak smile. "Hey! Lovely coffee, isn't it, Jimmy, eh?" the first man asked his companion, elbowing him in the ribs in an effort to procure some back up for his assertion.

"Yeah, great," replied Jimmy quietly, and took a sip of his coffee as if to prove it.

"Hya Hya! Come and join us you two!" Edson wasn't keen. The first guy was an immediately irritating bloke with a weird hyaena-like laugh, and 'Jimmy' just looked so depressingly . . . well, *depressed*. His face was ashen, and he had begun staring at something in his coffee cup – I mean *really staring hard*. Then he looked up and smiled at Edson expectantly. Louis uncharacteristically clambered over the seat rather than getting up and going round it, and plonked himself opposite the first guy who then introduced himself as, "Neil Bass. B-A-double S: Bass as in the *beer*, not as in the double *bass*, okay? Hya Hya!"

"Er, yeah, I'm Louis, and this is Edson."

"Nice to meet you," said Edson, holding out a hand for the new acquaintances to shake. Jimmy took his hand first, and then Neil limply passed his hand in and out of Edson's clasp quickly. It was like shaking hands with a seal's flipper. Or, at least, what Edson imagined a seal's flipper would feel like. He didn't have anything to do with touching the flippers of large sea mammals. Not since that one time in Seaworld, anyway. Louis was a staunch believer that you, "Can tell a lot from a man's handshake." He always said that in his favourite Sergeant-Major voice.

"Edson's a strange name, isn't it?" remarked Neil.

"Guess so."

"I might call you Eddie, do people call you Eddie, Eddie?"

"Not really."

"Can we have what they've got, please?" interjected Louis. The waiter, who was probably wondering how much longer he would be ignored while these foreigners finished their lengthy introductions, nodded solemnly and walked towards the kitchen.

"So whaddya guys think of the train, then? Fantastic, eh? Six days in one place, anything could happen, know what I mean? I mean, none of us knew each other before, but by . . ." Edson interrupted the soliloquy before it got out of hand,

"Well, me and Louis knew each other before . . ." but Neil jumped back in there before Edson could continue.

"Yeah, I guessed that, Eddie. But you guys don't know me, and none of us know Jim here - I only met him last night. We're sharing a cabin - it's brilliant! We got lucky and we're the only ones in it . . ." Jimmy was the next to interrupt, a bit quietly but certainly with some force.

"Yeah, but there's a lot of stops between here and Moscow - anyone could join us at any time." Edson fancied he caught a slightly camp lilt to his voice.

"I don't think that's very likely, Jim." Louis started to say something, but was stifled as Neil rolled on, "I mean, this time yesterday we hadn't even met each other and this time next week we'll probably know each other's life stories!" Neil continued unabated, clearly intent on dominating the early stages of this encounter like a boxer determined to deliver a thorough and painful message in the opening round. He was rather squat in build, and his head was the shape of a rounded-off square. He had evidently shaved his head a few days earlier as it was stubbly and stood at a length that was almost precisely the same as the whiskers growing on his jaw. It was dark stubble with the occasional patch of grey, and Edson guessed he was probably in his late 20s.

His jaw was *really* wide, so wide, in fact, that if the facial features were covered up and someone turned his face upside down, the difference might not be apparent to the naked eye. He had mad brown eyes that, in moments of excitement, seemed to almost pop out of their sockets. Edson wandered what on earth they looked like during sex, and then immediately wished he hadn't. His gaze was now riveted on the weird shape of Neil's head, but, worried that his fascination might be clocked at any moment, he blinked a couple of times and tried to concentrate on what Neil was saying.

". . . I'm a people-watcher, you see, I love watching people and speaking to them and watching their body language you can learn so much from observing, know what I mean? Like, I bet you two have been friends since you were young kids," this was not true - they had only been friends over the last two years, and Edson was about to put him straight, with no messing, when Louis got there first.

"That's amazing - how could you possibly tell that so soon?" Edson recovered his composure quickly enough to add,

"Since we were six, actually!"

"There you go! I could make some sort of career out of this, y'know! Actually I used to be an astrologer on the *Daily Star* a couple of years ago. It was a bit pony, though. Maybe I should be like a professional mystic or something, but I can't settle down. I just wanna get out in the world and meet people."

"Thanks" said Edson and Louis as the coffee and bread rolls arrived, but Louis – always mindful to think ahead where his appetite was concerned – quickly noticed the smallish portions and added, "Same again, though, please."

"I just feel so claustrophobic doing a proper job - a 'nine-to-fiver' I like to call it - I just wanna get out there!" Edson considered pointing out that being an astrologer in the *Daily Star* was hardly a proper job, but Neil was already exclaiming that he needed to visit the "Russian Trog," Edson was stupid enough to ask what that was. "It's rhyming slang for bog – I made it up this morning!" And he hopped out of his seat, over Jim's legs and strolled out of the room, laughing too loudly at his own joke.

"Thank God," muttered Jim. And things started to become clear, "I was beginning to think I'd have to talk to him all the way to Moscow, I mean, that *he'd* talk to *me* all the way to Moscow. Thank God you're here. *Jes*us Christ. By the way, my name's James, and occasionally Jim. I don't know where he got this 'Jimmy' shit from – it just makes me think of 'Jimmy Riddle.'" Edson immediately felt an affinity towards the poor guy. He plainly didn't have the wherewithal to remove himself from Neil's cruel invisible handcuffs. With a whole mouthful of bread, Louis looked up and seemed to offer a sympathetic smile, although it could have denoted any number of things. That he was enjoying the bread, for example; or that he found it quite amusing that James had been the unfortunate one to be locked away with Neil. In fact, there *was* something vaguely cruel about the smile. His mouth was full and bits of bread were popping out as he grinned while his head bobbed up and down in a sign that mixed agreement and contentment.

"Nightmare scenario," said Edson, which was the only thing he could think of saying. Even a Louis-type "Baarh" seemed disrespectful of James's miserable plight. James was now looking at something at the bottom of his coffee cup with real interest, perhaps wondering whether he could pretend to be so fascinated with whatever he was looking at that it might allow him to ignore Neil when he returned. Desperate man. "So-o" said Edson, in a searching-for-a-topic-of-conversation kind of way, "How long were you in China for?"

"Well, I've been in Hong Kong mostly, visiting my brother, but then I had a few days in Beijing doing all the sights and stuff, you know, all the usual touristy things, then I caught the train."

"By yourself?"

"Well, yeah, until . . . oh, he's back." There followed one of those really unnatural silences that happen when you have been talking about someone behind their backs and they suddenly return (it happens a lot, you may have noticed, in bad films and all soap operas). James gained renewed interest in the bottom of his cup again, and Edson followed Louis' lead in stuffing a good-sized husk of bread into his mouth.

"I tell you what, boys, there's no showers on this train! I reckon it's gonna get pretty bloody smelly round here by the end, Hya, hya!"

Edson couldn't stand people talking about how smelly they were, or how smelly they could get. Making a joke about stinking didn't make the smell funny. Or any less bearable. If anything it made it worse. And, looking at him, Edson found it easy to believe that Neil could be a pretty sweaty guy.

"You can still strip-wash."

"No need to let your standards drop just because the facilities aren't perfect - shave every day. Perform the usual ablutions thoroughly," announced Louis in his regimental voice.

"Bugger that!" Neil guffawed at an irritating volume. Edson thought he saw James's eyes roll, "Anyway, boys, I'm gonna have another coffee, who's gonna join me, eh?" he raised his eyebrows questioningly. He was the proud owner of an incredibly dark monobrow; even when his eyebrows were raised really high, in a desperate plea for someone to answer him in the positive, the eyebrows still almost joined, high up his forehead. It was astounding. All at once everyone started answering. James said he had some postcards to write. Louis made some noises about "Making a running jump at *War and Peace*" (it was a novel he had been claiming he was about to read for about a year as far as Edson could remember). But Edson suddenly found he couldn't think of any excuse, so he just grabbed his remaining scrap of bread and left quickly before Neil could attempt to persuade him to stay. As they left the carriage the waiter was returning with some more bread. Louis grabbed some while Edson asked for the cost and thrust a few hundred rubles into the waiter's hand.

IV

The three of them trooped back through the carriages in silence. Edson was consumed with the worry that they might be spending lengths of time in the company of Neil that would prove too long to bear. Neil's exuberant attempts at amiability had the very opposite effect upon him, and he found himself virtually loathing the bloke, which in turn made him feel bad because he wasn't proud of that kind of attitude. Louis was certain to find something positive about him, and Edson would be forced to keep his views to himself to avoid confrontation with his friend.

James's situation reminded Edson of a Daffy Duck cartoon where Daffy and Porky Pig try to check into a hotel. Unfortunately it is full apart from one room which they agree to share for one night.

Naturally, Daffy is an abominable room-mate, who has enough appalling habits to keep Porky awake all night. Eventually, Porky (as usual) loses his rag and tries to get rid of Daffy, who (as usual) is either too cunning or too lucky for the hapless pig.

"Have you ever seen that Daffy Duck cartoon where he shares a hotel room with Porky Pig? You know – when he gets the hiccups and Porky goes mad, and he's just the most annoying room-mate you could ever have. I think he even uses the word "Roomie" which is a word that should be outlawed, in my view."

"No," said James.

"Oh . . . there's some good comparisons in there. That's a shame . . . Have you seen it, Louis?"

"No. I don't watch television. It's the mouthpiece of the devil."

"He always says that," said Edson, looking at James and thumbing in Louis' direction. "You watched that *Beyond the Clouds* thing."

"That's different."

"You watch things like *Last of the Summer Wine!*"

"No, no!" Louis held his hand up, protecting himself from the accusation, pretending to be dead serious in the face of this childish mocking.

"And *Birds of a Feather!*"

"Noo! Shut up!" He was speaking in a voice that they both used occasionally. It was a voice that imitated a person trying to stay calm and distant from a juvenile argument, but failing miserably to do either.

"And *anything* with Robson & Jerome in it, because you love them so much, and you've bought all their records."

"Shuuut Uuuup!"

"Actually you watch loads of stuff - you only say that 'mouthpiece of the devil' thing because you think it sounds cool."

"I believe it, though. I just don't always practice what I preach. You coming in for a bit, James?"

"Neil doesn't know where you're cabin is, does he?" James asked furtively. He apparently hadn't registered Edson and Louis' comedy routine. "I mean, you haven't seen him looking in, or anything – we're only a couple of carriages down, so he must walk past here." Louis and Edson were by now sitting on the latter's bunk, and James was standing just inside the doorway. He leant backwards, his hands clasped in front of him, and peered carefully out of the cabin, as if he was playing 40-40[*] and was afraid of being seen, "Can we close the door? Just to be sure . . . you know."

"'Course," said Edson. James took a step inside and slid the door shut behind him.

"Have you got anyone else in here with you?" James asked in an ice-breaking kind of way as he sat down.

"Yeah, a couple of Russians – Sasha and Alexander. They seem all right, but they haven't said much. Although neither have we, to be fair. We haven't seen that much of them, really," explained Edson.

"I'm hoping we can try and have a chat with them because I want to ask them about vodka. I really fancy getting into the vodka-culture thing – just sitting there with a bottle of ice cold vodka, a single candle, and a couple of other people around. Perhaps with fingerless gloves or something . . . discussing Vladimir Nabokov and Dostoevsky."

"Yeah, and whether Dynamo Kiev can win the European Cup this year."

"No."

"All right. Eisenstein then."

"Who?"

"Eisenstein. You know, he invented montage and all that – he was a pioneer of cinema!"

"Film studies. What kind of *degree* is that?"

"A fun one."

"Are you two still at Uni, then?" asked James, finally smiling.

"Well, I've just finished, but this slacker," and Edson turned to push his friend on the arm, forcing him to topple slightly to his side, "Has still got a year to go."

"Yeah, well, that's mainly because I'm at Oxford and I'm doing

[*] It has come to my attention that this game might not be quite as widespread as I originally thought. It's a game I used to play when I was a kid. It's a more advanced game of hide and seek involving the seeker taking prisoner all those s/he finds. The seeker has a post, and if s/he moves away, and other players can sneak past without being seen, they can release the prisoners and/or save themselves. It's called '40-40' because you have to count to . . . 44, actually, while everyone hides. However, I will resist the temptation to make any hilariously funny observations on this game or any other childhood games for fear of sounding like one of those tired old comedians who lazily mines all his (and I mean *his*) material from his formative years.

my Masters."

"I went to Oxford as well."

"Perhaps James can get you a job Lou - what do you do, anyway, James?"

"I'm, er, I'm an accountant." There was a brief silence.

"Oh yeah?" said Edson.

"Well, if you can't get me a job in a year, I won't mind – don't worry yourself – I wouldn't ask you, anyway," Louis did a pretend nervous laugh, then a thought occurred to him, "We haven't seen many accountants out here to be honest. They've been mostly wasters like Ed."

"Like you." They never looked at each other when they traded facile insults like this. They were both looking at James and pretending to be too mature to take notice of the other's juvenile comments.

"Yeah, well, work was getting on top of me a bit, and I had the chance to come out here because my brother's working in Hong Kong, and I thought why not?"

"And now you've ended up with Neil. What a nightmare."

"He's not that bad, Ed," said Louis.

"Yeah, 's'pose."

"Try living with him," murmured James quietly, "He's the kind of guy who'd look at a the tallest, most impressive skyscraper in the world, and say, 'Imagine how much human waste comes outta that baby every day'." Louis and Edson laughed. "I should have done what you guys are doing, though. I should have done this ages ago when I could have done it with some friends – everyone just gets tied down to jobs, or gets married . . . or something." James scratched the side of his jaw. His face was smooth and it appeared that if he ever attempted to grow some whiskers they would probably end up all wispy like David Beckham's sideburns used to be.

"Then they just want to go to the *Provence* every year, don't they? Or Benidorm," noted Edson.

"Nothing wrong with Benidorm. But it's best to do this travel thing by yourself," said Louis, "I'm going to do that next year, I think. Just go somewhere, I don't know, maybe back to China again, I hardly saw any of it, and just go by myself without any blahdy tourist books, or *Rough Guides*, or *Lonely Planets*." When they first travelled a couple of years previously, the *Lonely*, as they referred to it, had been invaluable. But Louis was growing to resent the explicit instructions, how it made it so *easy* to travel in even the most remote areas. "I mean, I hate all that stuff where backpackers turn up at the same hostels and hotels just because the *Lonely* recommends them – where's the adventure in that? There's no danger – you might as well be on a package holiday."

"Depends what you're looking for, I s'pose," said James.

"Yeah, I mean, your aim might be to just have a bloody good time in a place other than blahdy *Ibeefa*."

"Yeah, but my point is that you might as well be in 'blahdy *Ibeefa*' if that's all you want."

"I guess."

"You're deluding yourself if you think you're treading some great untrodden path in a massive exploration of the Far East. You're only there because some poxy travel guide told you it was there and that you should go there . . ." Edson was about to open his mouth but changed his mind, and settled for an eye roll. James didn't notice, though. He had fished a tissue from his pocket and was giving his lenses a thoughtful polish. "I hate that kind of stuff. Travel guides always complain that remote places are being spoilt by tourism, but they're one of the major causes! They rave about it, so travellers go there, the community gets wise to that fact and starts to make money off it so *more* travellers go there who might not have risked it before, and pretty soon, you've got, well . . ."

"Another Goa on your hands?" suggested James.

"Exactly."

"But is that such a bad thing, though? Is the westernisation of these places so bad, I mean?" Edson was quite pleased at having slipped the word 'westernisation' in, "Doesn't it give them a better quality of life? Isn't their happiness and prosperity more important than what we see as the aesthetic qualities of a place, which is a pretty arbitrary thing anyway?" And 'aesthetic' and 'arbitrary'! *Superb* work! He was even getting in some of Louis' trademark hand gestures he always used to drive a point home.

"Maybe," answered Louis.

"I suppose the main point is that they might live to regret ignoring their traditional culture in favour of some ready cash," said James the Peacemaker. "It's unrealistic to expect first time backpackers to *not* use the *Lonely Planet* simply because it's too easy, though, isn't it? I mean, I found it a great help for finding cheap places to eat and stuff like that – and you could miss out on loads of stuff if you didn't read it. Not everyone's got time to just go and do a load of independent research on everything."

"No . . . I just like to see a bit of individuality, not people blindly following the advice of a single book."

"Is that why you hate the Bible?"

"I don't hate the Bible. *Jesus*. Ignore him, James."

"Where else have you been?"

"Well," started Edson, "I went to Kenya last year, and we both went to India the year before."

"And I went to Cambodia and 'Nam last year, which was superb." Louis always called Vietnam "'Nam", but he wasn't a war veteran. He was too young.

"Oh, what did you think of India? I almost went there a couple of years ago, but I changed companies and it all sort of fell through." Edson and Louis looked at each other as recollections of the trip flooded through their minds: the strange hotelier (well, the word 'hotel' is stretching it a bit. The inside of the building resembled the inside of an empty old dustbin – sticky dirt, unidentifiable fluff, and small, deadly creatures forever hoping for fresh meat to feed on. Cheap, though), who had a series of bizarre rhymes that never failed to charm his guests; when talking about whisky he sang, "Whisky is risky it makes you frisky." And when discussing a couple of Norwegian girls that were staying at the 'hotel', he proclaimed "Oh, they're not ugly, not 'cover the face, fuck the base.'" Or the time they fed wild monkeys from the door of their hotel. Or, most embarrassingly for Edson, the time when he was caught miles from a toilet with calamitous diarrhea, and was forced to run to a nearby bush. Which would have been okay, if it wasn't for the fact that it was nighttime and they had been warned about the large population of dangerous snakes in the area. Edson was terrified that his buttocks might receive a jab he didn't ask for. And they had no tissues with them, so, with tears of cruel laughter rolling down their faces, Louis and their friend Rowan tore out blank pages from their diaries so that Edson might enjoy a smidgen of comfort on the walk home.

"Well, we wished we could have had some better contact with the Indian people, to be honest – a lot of them seemed to be just interested in our money, which made it difficult to speak to them. But then, I s'pose, most travellers they met were only interested in buying things, not having a conversation." said Edson.

"It was a shame because we never knew who was being friendly and who was building up to a sales pitch. Even if you had a decent chat with someone it was sort of ruined if after a while when they tried to sell you something. It felt like the whole friendly attitude had been an act to get you to buy something."

"So in the end you just mistrusted everyone. I was probably quite rude to a few people who really were just interested in talking to people from another country."

"Was it really hard sell?"

"Well, yeah, but in a fairly friendly way – not like in Egypt where it almost feels like you're getting mugged sometimes," answered Edson.

"That's the problem, though. I know that Indians are mostly extremely nice, polite and generous people, but if you've had your fingers burnt you end up just not wanting to know. I was reading this book by a guy called Tully who's been a foreign correspondent in India for years. It really makes you think – you can't get a real *feel* for a country after travelling in it for a couple of weeks – especially when you don't stay in one place for more than a couple of days." Louis leaned right forward towards James and held his hand out vertically in front of him, characteristically forcing his point. "He was saying that many friends of his who had been out to India were obsessed with not getting ripped off – like we all are, all us slacker backpackers. But he pointed out that when you do get fleeced out there, it's usually only a matter of a few rupees – which is nothing to anyone – not even to us who travel round cheaply like a bunch of scrubbers."

"Did you ever get really turned over?" asked Jim.

"Well not really, but there was a time when we were in Jaipur that really turned us off the place," said Edson, looking towards Louis and smiling.

"Oh yeah?"

"Yeah, we arrived in Jaipur quite late at night and the next day we were trying to sort out cash and postcards and bus tickets and stuff, so we could relax for a couple of days," began Edson.

"Mmm. We didn't get up till about one in the afternoon, though, because we were knackered from the trip from Agra. Do you remember that bloke who sat next to Rowan and really stank?" Edson screwed his face up and nodded. "So when we finally got off the pot we went to the bank, and then to the post office."

"We were in good moods as well, because Jaipur looked so much nicer compared with Agra, and the hotel was about ninety times cleaner and we weren't catching some fatal disease every time we drew breath."

"Anyway, we were in this post office, and Rowan was with us because he was travelling with us then, obviously; he's a top bloke actually – really good to travel with; and you got split up from us, didn't you?"

"Yeah, weren't you looking at the post office museum round the back or something?"

"Wasn't very interesting," said Louis.

"Liar. Admit it - you *love* old post office artefacts. This building was quite big – the foyer was almost as big as some post offices back in *Blighty*. And there were loads of queues inside, all for different things, apparently, so it took me a while to find the right one, and when I did I had to wait for ages. I got my stamps and then couldn't find Louis and Rowan so I wondered out to the foyer."

"The really big one?" smiled James.

"Yes." Edson liked this guy. "And I was wondering where they could be, when these two guys came up to me and asked if I was looking for my friends. I just ignored them – I was fed up of people trying to sell me stuff, and I was just basically really wary of everyone. Also it seemed odd that they knew who I was looking for. They looked a bit weird as well – one was quite short and the other one was quite tall, and I remember that the shorter one had something wrong with his face. I don't know what it was, but his mouth was sort of bent out of shape a bit and he had a lump in his cheek, like he was putting his tongue up against it from the inside, like this," Edson illustrated his point.

"And he had one of those really wispy moustaches that I used to get when I was about thirteen, but Ed still can't grow now."

"Shows what you know. I have to shave every three days, thanks. Anyway, I looked for a bit longer, but I couldn't find them, and then one of those guys came back up to me and asked if I was looking for a tall man with black hair, which sounded like Louis, so I nodded this time, and they said they had gone into the museum."

"So I went back into the post office and glanced into the museum, but I still couldn't see them. So I went back to the foyer, thinking that I'd just wait until they left the place. I really thought those guys would be gone, 'cause it didn't look like they were actually doing anything, but they were still there! They didn't speak great English, but they told me that Louis and Rowan were still inside, but I was really wary of them by then, so I just started ignoring them again. Then they started asking me why I was ignoring them, and why no English people would ever talk to them. It made me feel a bit guilty, but . . ." Louis interjected here.

"The golden rule of travelling is not to trust anyone you don't know."

"Yeah, for all you know," Edson had been stroking his chin, but he took his hand away and pointed at James as he spoke, "This could all be some elaborate con, and we're about to lock you in and rob you."

"If it wasn't for the fact that we're on a *very* long train journey, and no-one would be dumb enough to get off in the middle of Siberia or wherever we are with the measly pickings of *one* robbery," remarked Louis in a condescending tone. James laughed, well, it was more an expulsion of air, like a 'tuh' kind of sound. But Edson wasn't beaten easily.

"We could be specialist Trans-*Sib*" (he emphasised the 'Sib' with a disgusted look on his face, as though he was a wine connoisseur who had just tasted a grim red that was being proclaimed as a great vintage by some ignoramus. He and Louis had met travellers who thought themselves very worldly and knowledgeable who called the Trans-Siberian the 'Trans-Sib' and they both hated it. "What," remarked Louis, after they had heard a particularly self-assured backpacker veteran use the term previously, "Hasn't he got enough time in his *busy schedule* of wandering *aim*lessly round China smoking joints and not washing his clothes to actually say the whole word 'Siberian?' Or is it just difficult for him to pronounce? Toss-pot." He emphasised "Toss-pot" with a harsh "T" and a flippant flourish of his right hand and he looked away, revolted. Now, where were we?) "We could be specialist Trans-*Sib* bandits, who would rob a particularly rich looking accountant – er, I mean *tourist*, then nip off at the next stop, get on the next train and rob someone else, and get off at the next stop, and so on all the way from China to Russia and back again!"

"Yerrrsss," said Louis, and, ignoring James's good-natured laughing, added, "Not sure if the trains would be frequent enough to make it worthwhile. Anyway, didn't we appear at about this point?"

"Yeah. I don't remember where from, but you were suddenly there, and we walked off and I started asking you where you'd been and all that kind of stuff, when the tall one caught up again and reminded me that he'd told me where they were. But we both ignored him. Then they started asking why we wouldn't speak to them, how all they wanted to do was have a conversation and talk about our culture and India's culture and all that kind of stuff. They were clever, you know. But we just walked on, until the one with the weird mouth stood right in front of us and asked us again why we wouldn't speak to him."

"They said they were just students and wanted to talk to us about Britain and what we thought about India. I think Rowan tried to push past them and said we had other stuff to do, which we did . . ." and Edson interrupted here,

"And no-one ever falls for that 'We're students interested in talking to you' line - it was clever once, but we're like carp who don't get caught on the same bait twice, know what I mean?"

"Er, yeah," said James, his brows furrowed, his eyes glancing at Louis for help.

"Yerrrsss . . . but as Rowan began to sort of half push past them this other bloke turned up on a moped, and they started talking to him. So we started to move away but this bloke – he was dressed much better than the other two in a sort of denim suit, and he spoke very good English – came over and said that all they wanted to do was have a chat and a cup of *chai*, and asked us again why we wouldn't talk to them."

"He was really plausible, wasn't he?"

"Yeah he was really good at drawing us in, and immediately the other two guys stood back and let him do all the talking, and they just nodded and stuff. I didn't really feel that we could just walk off when he was talking to us so civilly."

"He asked us if we were students, and we said yes. So he started a long *spiel* about how they were students as well, and they just wanted to learn good English and find out about England, and he said we couldn't discover the real India until we had spoken to Indians."

"Yeah, he kept saying, 'The Real India,' didn't he? I think that was the real killer, because that's what we were there for. I s'pose in a way you haven't got much hope, I mean what would you class as the 'real' England? All of it's 'real'. The posh, I hate that word, 'posh,' hotels in India are as 'real' as the people living on the streets."

"So what happened?"

"Well, he suggested going back to his house for *chai* and a chat. We said no straight away – it just didn't seem safe – I'd never do that in England. But he seemed really genuine and the more he made us feel guilty for ignoring them initially, the more he convinced us to make it up to them by going with them. We ended up completely agreeing with him, we all shook hands, and next thing we knew one of us was on the back of each of their mopeds, on the way to the smart guy's house. It seemed really cool as well, because we really thought we were *finally* going to find out a bit more about Indian culture, rather than just reading about it."

"So you actually went back to their house?" James sounded incredulous.

"Well, yes. But it just seemed like too good an opportunity to miss, and there *were* three of us," Edson said, desperately trying to defend himself in the most understated way as possible.

"There were three of *them*."

"Mmm," nodded Louis. "Anyway, they took us to a kind of Plaza thing, and we went up to the first floor where the smart guy showed us his family's jewellery shop. There wasn't much of a display and he told us that it wasn't a shop as such, more an export business. We walked in and used this stepladder to go up to this kind of attic. And then something weird happened which we didn't really take too much notice of at the time. The denim guy was always really charming and polite with us, but when he saw a family member he practically *ordered* them to bring us some tea, he was quite rude about it, as if it was really urgent. So we went up to the attic, which was tiny and wasn't big enough to stand up straight in."

"I thought it was quite claustrophobic," chipped in Edson.

"It was nicely decorated, though. It was more like a kind of den for the lads, you know, like an upper class indoor tree-house or something. And we started to play this game, what was it Ed?"

" . . . I can't remember what it's called now, but it was like, I dunno . . . I suppose a cross between snooker, draughts and subbuteo is about the closest I can get to it. You had to flick these draught pieces to hit other draught pieces into corners of this shiny wooden playing board . . . and you got different points for different colours."

"Did you? I don't remember that."

"I could be getting mixed up with snooker, I suppose. Maybe I'm taking the snooker comparison too far."

"I think you are. And they gave us some *chai*, but I never got used to Indian tea. All that milk and sugar, like the complete opposite of Chinese tea and it's really sickly. So we were playing this game for a while, then the smart guy took Ed downstairs to look at the jewellery."

"Yeah, they were obviously trying to split us up from our group, which I think we sort of realised at the time, but perhaps not enough to actually *do* anything about it. He was showing me all this jewellery, and I stupidly said I might be interested in buying some for my girlfriend."

"While he was down there, another one got me talking about where we had been in India, and I think I was complaining about how we hadn't had much interaction with Indians, and how it was cool to speak to someone properly, rather than haggling over the price of a small plastic marble effect model of the Taj Mahal. But I kept thinking about Ed, and I didn't like the fact that we were being split up, so in the end I just asked him where Ed was, and he took me downstairs. Which, of course, meant that Rowan was left alone upstairs, but I was more concerned about Ed at that time."

"I was in the far room downstairs, and I waved but this older bloke and the guy you were with – it was the tall one wasn't it?" Louis nodded, "Well, they sort of kept you from coming in by showing you some jewels and stuff. Then my guy started talking about exporting jewellery. He was very smooth about it all, saying that he just wanted to tell me it, and I didn't have to do it – only if I liked the sound of it – there wasn't any pressure. He told me that we were legally allowed to take something like four thousand pounds worth of jewellery back to England before we had to pay tax; whereas he would normally have to pay 250% interest on *any* jewels he exported from India.

"All I had to do was let him post the jewels to me at a London post office. There I would meet a friend of his who would pay me five thousand US dollars in cash for them, and he would sell them on for a nice profit. So paying couriers, or whatever you would call people like us, even *that* much money still meant a big profit for himself, as opposed to paying the usual tax."

"But there could be anything in that package, surely?" said James.

"Well, that was the first thing I thought of, and I asked him how he could guarantee me what would be in it, and he said that he would wrap the entire thing in front of me. I mean, I wasn't keen but that's *three thousand pounds* in cash - I wouldn't have had any money worries at Uni after that."

"And during this time," added Louis, "The other guy was suggesting the same thing to Rowan upstairs, but they weren't saying anything to me."

"I found that quite weird, actually."

"I didn't - I was obviously the most intelligent, and they didn't think they could convince me," James laughed at Louis' half-joking arrogance.

"Well, my initial reaction was to turn it down immediately - it just sounded far too dodgy to me."

"Well, yeah, I mean . . . you hear all kinds of horror stories, don't you?" began James, "Did you read about that woman who acted as some kind of courier to take something from here out to the Middle East somewhere, and the customs officers found drugs sewn into the handle of the suitcase and other places in it, and she got thrown into some horrible prison full of rats and stuff like that for about two years. She only did it for three thousand or something like that, and she didn't see her little son for *two* years. I think the people she did it for told her she was carrying some important documents."

"Exactly. I just started saying 'no' straight away. But he was really trying to convince me that it was perfectly legal. And it was quite an attractive proposition, because we didn't actually have to carry them, so at least we would feel safe going through the airports. He said he would provide us with fake receipts for the jewellery so it didn't look like we were acting as couriers. And he showed me photocopied passports of people who were doing the job for him, or had done the job for him before."

"They must have brought me and Rowan over about then, but the thing I couldn't understand was, if it was all legal, why did we need to have a fake receipt?"

"Well," said James, "It obviously *wasn't* legal, but maybe it was *almost* legal."

"Yeah," replied Louis, "But *the money* sounded so good, that we were quite keen to find a way around it. We asked about actually buying the stuff, thinking that it might give us more legality, and he said that one person had done that and was still travelling around India, but that he didn't recommend it because we might get mugged or something. More likely, I thought, we might get stung in customs."

"I remember Rowan being especially interested in it – but he was always looking for dodgy things like that, and I never know whether he's serious about them."

"He was the one who was keen to go to an Ashram in southern India – you know, one of those 'Free Love' places. He told us all about it, how you have to have an HIV test before you go in, and once you're there it's spiritual enlightenment and guilt-free sex all the way."

"I think he was mainly interested in the sex part, wasn't he?"

"Yeah," agreed Louis. James was laughing. His legs were crossed over and he really did have a slightly camp aura to him. When Edson was at school you could never cross your legs because all the 'Rugby Lads' would say you were gay because only gay men crossed their legs. Real men were supposed to sit with their legs as wide apart as possible. Edson always felt a little, well, *exposed* when he did that, though.

"So what did you do?"

"They didn't put too much pressure on, and I think none of us ever seriously believed we would do it, so we asked for a day to think about it and talk it over," explained Edson.

"They weren't too keen on letting us go, though. They kept saying that they wanted to take us on a tour around Jaipur, but we just wanted to get out of there. It just felt all ruined. We *really* thought for once that we might be able to just talk to some Indian people without having to buy something or . . ."

"Or be asked to do some small-time smuggling?" suggested James.

"Yeah, or that. So eventually they let us go and we went off to talk it over."

"I thought that Louis and Rowan would immediately say 'no' when we went outside, but they actually seemed quite keen to find a legal route through it," said Edson.

"I was just trying to look for a decent solution to a challenge, rather than just saying 'yes' or 'no.'"

"What like some kind of *case study*, you mean?" Edson said.'

"Something like that. I dunno, when you look at people like Ranulph Fiennes and see what they've achieved through sheer determination and intelligence, it just seems a waste to completely dismiss something without thoroughly dissecting it."

"Yeah, but smuggling diamonds and rubies into the country is a bit different from leading a three man expedition to the North Pole without air support, though." Edson muttered.

"That's not really the point I was trying to make, though, Ed." There was a moment of silence. "But there were too many questions we couldn't answer, like how did we know it was legal to bring in four thousand pounds worth of jewellery without it being taxed? Me and Rowan asked a guy in another shop, and he didn't think it was possible – he said we were only allowed to take about four *hundred* pounds worth of jewels back. And how could we be *really* sure that the parcel that we would watch him wrap up would be the same one that he would send to England?"

"It definitely sounds like some kind of drugs trafficking, or something," said James.

"Well, it may not have been, but the point was that we weren't even sure if the jewellery thing was legal. I mean, if we'd have got caught, that would have been it. We'd have been thrown out of University, and we'd have that on our records for the rest of our lives. Plus, how could we guarantee that we'd ever get the money from the contact in London? If he just refused or threatened us or something, we'd have nowhere to go. We wouldn't be able to sell the jewels on because it would probably look dodgy, and if he threatened us and got them off us, we couldn't really go to the police because what we were doing was almost definitely illegal." said Edson, pummelling the back of his right hand into the palm of his left.

"When it came down to it, the more we talked about it, the more we realised we just couldn't do it. We'd actually arranged to meet them the next day, but we decided against it in the end and just went sightseeing by ourselves."

"Yeah, three of us on a tiny carriage being manually pedalled by some poor bike-wallah who must have lost about three stone in sweat that day, and he probably only weighed about five stone to start with – he was skinnier than me!"

"Yeah, he *loved* it though: he got our money, commission from those gift shops he took us to, *and* a free lunch out of us."

"That's true. Oh, do you remember when we went to one craft place, and Rowan was looking at some magazines, and this really greasy *porno-wallah* came up to him and went, 'You want to see . . . *other* magazines?' Rowan nearly went for it as well."

"I bet they were really grim, though. That bike-*wallah* fancied you, didn't he?" James started laughing as Edson cringed, "We took a picture of him with Ed, and he just started snuggling up to him and trying to hold his hand."

"I'm sure it was just a cultural thing, though."

"Noooo, it wasn't - he *loved* you!" Louis was clearly enjoying himself, pointing at Edson and laughing in a maniacal way, while Edson covered his reddening face at the embarrassing memory.

V

James was grateful of the break from Neil, but he knew the cabin couldn't remain secret from Neil for the whole six days. He started fantasising about pushing Neil off the train just as they were leaving the station. Later, as they walked to lunch, James proposed this idea to Edson and Louis. As a joke, of course.

"It's fairly sound – he'd probably never find you again," said Louis.

"Can you imagine anything worse, though?" speculated Edson. "I mean, getting off the train without your passport and perhaps with only a bit of money and only the clothes you're standing in, and suddenly the train moves off and you're stuck in Siberia without knowing a single person or a word of their language. What would you do?"

"Get in touch with the British Embassy," said Louis quickly. Neil was nowhere to be seen in the dining car, but Louis and Edson spotted Alexander and Sasha at the far table with a couple of other guys. Sasha waved in a friendly way when he saw them, although there was a trace of mania about the gesture – it was just a little too . . . *eager*, maybe. He must have mentioned something to Alexander, because he turned around and managed to raise a weak smile. Our heroes waved back with some British restraint. They settled down to some more bread and coffee, and a bowl each of *borscht*. It was like beef gravy with some vegetables and a slice of what they assumed to be beef lying in wait at the bottom of the bowl, as flat and as camouflaged as a Dover Sole in the sand of the Channel. They gulped it down quickly, silently scheming to return to the relative safety of their cabin as quickly as possible. James, not wanting to outstay his welcome and only too aware he would need a friendly cabin to hide in quite a lot on this journey, said he'd better go back to his own cabin before Neil hunted him down. Edson and Louis returned to put some Stan Getz on in their cabin (Edson had speakers to go with his walkman) and they read and dozed the afternoon away.

As evening approached, Edson ventured, "James seems like a good bloke . . .?"

"Yeah, seems really sound. I hope I'm still travelling when I'm in my thirties. I really hope I don't have a job in the city, a semi-detached in the suburbs and start going to Lanzarote every year."

"I know. He seems pretty happy, though. He's not married, is he?"

"Don't think so. Anyway, fancy some dinner?"

"Thought we were going to have some dried noodles tonight instead," Edson glanced at the bottom of the bunk above him, as if he could see Louis' reaction through the solid structure.

"I was thinking that we should save them for a special . . . occasion," Louis paused between the last two words to jump down from his bunk, "Coming?"

As they entered the dining carriage Edson immediately noticed the two girls they had encountered as they boarded the train. He pretended not to notice them and scanned the carriage for an empty table. Then the voice of Neil raised itself above the atmospheric murmuring, "Hey! Where've you two been all day? Come and sit over here!" Neil was sitting with the girls. Edson was unsure as to how he had failed to see him before. The girls seemed indifferent to this suggestion – they barely looked at Edson and Louis as they approached, but they smiled pleasantly enough as they arrived at the table. Neil – the gracious host – performed the introductions, and everyone shook hands. The girls' names were Lotte and Dorte. "They're Danish," explained Neil, "And their English is absolutely superb! Much better than my Danish, which is pretty pony, to be honest! Scandinavians always speak superb English, though, don't they? I wish I was bilingual, still . . ." Neil continued his overlong introduction. Lotte was the girl that had taken the picture a day or two before. Today she had a piece of sharp-looking silver metal sticking out from the piece of flesh between her lower lip and the start of her chin. It was a thin cone-shaped stud that came to a tiny point about a centimetre and a half away from her face. From time to time, as Neil blazed on about the time he had taken a language course on Swahili while staying in Nairobi, she brushed her forefinger lightly over the point, making it wobble gently.

Louis was busy looking through the menu, but although Edson had a menu standing up in front of him he was transfixed by Lotte's piercing. He hated this – it reminded him of how respectable middle-aged men stare at goths with a look of joyous bewilderment on their faces. If you kissed Lotte, would you get a free piercing? Was it a message saying, 'Just *try* to kiss me, and see what happens' – a warning to stay away like the clacketing[*] of a rattlesnake? Or was it the opposite, a gizmo deliberately designed to make

[*] Yes, the word 'clacketing' is a made up one. But, in my opinion, it's a valid piece of onomatopoeia. Oh yeah – I did A-Level English. Anyway, if this was poetry you wouldn't have even given the word 'clacketing' a second thought. You might have even called it 'poignant'.

you look at her appetizing, brown-lipsticked mouth?

"Chicken sounds good," said Louis, and Edson was forced to start looking at the menu. Each item was in Russian with an English translation beneath it. He was about to wonder aloud, rather wittily, he thought, what 'Lulia Kebab' was – whether 'Lulia' was a Russian name, and if so, what kind of country was this that roasted members of their own species on a spit for the delectation of foreigners, when Neil stole in to ruin the moment.

"Drinks! Vodkas all round?" Everyone seemed to agree, but then Dorte spoke up.

"I'll have a beer . . ." It surprised Edson how strongly American her accent was, but before he could ponder it any further, Neil leapt in again.

"Ah! You *skunk!*" Louis and Edson gave each other a glance of derision, their eyebrows raised and their mouths lifted slightly at one corner in something approaching a sneer; '*Skunk*?' "What a fantastic idea! We'll all have beer chasers!" Dorte stared at Neil for a moment, and then took a packet of Rizlas and some tobacco from her canvas satchel and began rolling a cigarette. Without a word Lotte took a Rizla and did the same. Neil was saying, "So that's five vodkas and five beers, my man!" The waiter standing between the two tables was a tall man with mousey blond hair combed precisely into a smooth round on the top of his head. He nodded solemnly.

"Spaseeba!" said Neil, and then, looking at Louis and Edson, "That means 'Thank you.'"

"I know," replied Louis. Edson was looking at Dorte and considering whether to ask if she had studied in America, even though he was pretty sure of the answer. He was worried that it would be an obviously contrived lead-in to a conversation. She looked a bit like Velma from Scooby-Doo, only with typically Scandinavian blonde hair, and a more keen sense of style – well, it was pretty much authentic *traveller-chic*. She sported a yellowing white t-shirt with a small red symbol that he couldn't quite make out, and those trendy black sandals that sports companies make. You know, not the kind your Dad would wear – not even with his knee-length white socks, but the ones with velcro fasteners. He couldn't see her shorts or skirt under the table, only the sandals, but he suspected that she was probably wearing denim cut-offs. Most travellers apart from himself and Louis seemed to live in either denim cut-offs or very baggy, grimy cotton trousers that had a complete inability to ever return to their original colour once they'd had a few days wear.

"Where's James?" asked Louis, looking at Neil. Neil was tapping out some kind of incomprehensible drum rhythm with his two forefingers on the table, his top lip overlapping his bottom lip in a face of concentration. Dorte lit her cigarette and blew smoke in Neil's direction.

"You mean Jimmy-boy? I'm not sure, actually. He was in the cabin dozing earlier, so I came up here to see who was around, and found the girls." He spread his hands in the direction of Dorte and Lotte, so that Edson and Louis might understand who 'The Girls' were.

"Oh, you should have knocked for us!" Louis exclaimed with barely disguised sarcasm. Edson kicked him quietly under the table, then immediately panicked that he'd kicked someone else.

"Oh, man! You gotta show me where your cabin is! Give us a drag, Lotte."

"Sure." She passed a limp rolly to Neil, who took a puff and performed the same exaggerated look of pleasure he did when drinking coffee.

"So . . . did you two study in America?" Edson asked.

"Yeah, Lotte was at Boston, and Dorte was at . . . er, UCLA." Neil pointed carefully at each of the girls as he said this. The two girls smiled and nodded at Edson.

"I assume he told you that, and it wasn't some fantastic guess?" Lotte seemed about to say something when the drinks arrived and everyone said 'Spaseeba' in turn, relishing the satisfaction they got from saying the word. Go on, try it now, it's great.

"Okay, we have to down all the vodka and then . . ." Louis interrupted Neil, for a change:

"And then put out the fire with the beer!"

"Exactly." Edson looked down at his vodka. It was served in the traditional small glass, and it appeared to be hosting the best part of three shots rather than the usual derisory amount poured in English bars for ten times the price. But then Russians drank this stuff by the canful, so it was hardly surprising that the shots would be larger.

"Right, bang the glass on the table three times, then chug it! ONE, TWO, THREE!" Edson threw it back and felt the fire in the back of his throat, and then the redness creeping with abandon across his face. A mixture of groans and sighs emanated from the other four, and then loud laughter from another table. Edson looked up and saw Sasha and Alexander a few tables down – they were roaring and pointing at him, and when they saw him looking at them they held their shot glasses up in his honour and guffawed harder. It seemed unusual behaviour for Alexander, but then Edson wasn't fully aware just how red his face had become.

"I think you better have some beer," said the calm-faced Louis, "Put out that fire." Edson took a large gulp and felt the burning slowly recede.

The waiter that served them in the morning sidled up and looked at them expectantly. "Chicken?" said Edson.

"Stroganoff." The waiter's voice was very low and serious, like the voices of old men who sing in church choirs.

"Sorry?"

"Stroganoff."

"How about the roast pork?"

"Stroganoff." Edson heard barely stifled giggles from the others.

"Could you show us what we *can* have?" asked Edson, offering the menu.

"Stroganoff," and he pointed at the Russian word with the English translation – stroganoff.

"Only stroganoff?" said Louis, helpfully, and the waiter nodded, "Well . . . five stroganoffs?" Louis glanced at the others and everyone nodded, "Yeah, five stroganoffs. Spaseeba."

"Why do they give us menus if there's no actual choice?" remarked Edson obviously.

"Looks good, dunnit? Hya, hya!" replied Neil.

"Does it mean we've got stroganoff every night?" asked Lotte.

"Suddenly noodles don't sound so bad after all," added Neil.

"We bought twenty-four packets with us," explained Edson. This caused an outburst of loud laughter from Neil.

"Didn't you know there was a dining car on board?" and he laughed some more, conspiratorially looking at the two girls; although they didn't seem to find it so funny. "Who on earth booked your tickets for you - didn't they give you *any* information? Ah dear," and he wiped an invisible teardrop from his eye.

"Does anyone fancy another *wodka*?" Louis said it in the Russian way. He waved the waiter and ordered five more. "I really am keen to get into this *wodka* culture." Everyone performed their ritual again when the drinks arrived, only this time Edson didn't feel his face go red. He looked up at Sasha and Alexander and waved his glass – and they laughed hard again.

"Have you been travelling long?" asked Louis, and took a sip of beer. It was the stock question when travelling. It often turned into a competition: who's been travelling the longest? Who's used the least money? Who's carrying the least luggage? Who's endured the longest bus journey? Who's eaten the strangest animal?

"Six weeks, but we are going back to Denmark now," said Lotte, who possessed a more noticeably Scandinavian accent than Dorte.

"Oh, yeah, where've you been?" Louis spoke slightly slower than usual, but Edson worried that speaking too slowly might seem somewhat patronising. Lotte fingered at her pointed stud and looked at Dorte.

"Well, we were in Australia for maybe more than three weeks, then a week in Hong Kong, then we flew to Beijing."

"That must have cost a lot of money – to fly to Beijing, I mean," said Neil.

"Not really," Dorte was concentrating on rolling her next cigarette, and didn't look up as she spoke, "We got a good deal." There was a pause.

"What was Australia like? . . . I keep meaning to go there," asked Edson. But before they could answer, Neil started laughing too hard and shouting out random stereotypical Australian phrases.

"How about another shrimp on the ba-arby? Fancy another tinny? You great galah!" The girls looked baffled. Frightened, even. Dorte smiled and took a long suck of her flimsy cigarette. It looked like she'd only put about three strands of tobacco in it. Neil reached over and took it from her, uninvited, while still looking around at the boys, expecting to see real mirth in full swing. Then, looking back at Dorte he said, "Hey, you know they're just a load of old cons, don't you? Hya Hya!" Dorte took her cigarette back.

"I thought it was a really friendly country."

"Oh, yeah, I bet the lifeguards on the beach were really welcoming, eh? Nudge, nudge, wink, wink." Neil turned and beamed at the boys. All lads together. Edson had to admit to himself that he'd been down the path of flirting-by-insult – perhaps by inferring that a girl is nothing but a hooker masquerading as a nice-girl-next-door type. But this was something that could only be done with girls that liked that kind of humour, or were willing to fight back with some quips that perhaps focused on penis-size.

"I think that they hated the English though," said Lotte quietly, and forcefully stubbed her cigarette out in a small saucer near Dorte. At that moment, the waiter without the moustache approached with a plate of brown stroganoff in each hand.

"Ah, the grub!" Neil exclaimed. "Stroganoff and *wodka* - we have *truly* entered Russia." The waiter quickly returned with three more – one expertly balanced on his forearm. Edson examined his food – it didn't look too bad – perhaps not as appetizing as their Chinese marathon the night before, but not too bad. He took a first tentative mouthful. By this time Louis was already on his fourth shovel-full, a smile beaming through full cheeks. Lotte pushed some stroganoff into the rice and made little grooves between the food with her fork. Eventually she ate a small amount – most of it rice.

As they chatted and ate, a young man walked in alone. His hair was cropped short, and his hairline was clearly receding, although the short cut style accentuated this perhaps more than he deserved. His expression was one of indifference. He did not look around him, but made his way smoothly to an empty table a couple of tables down from where our little group was seated. He wore an extremely dirty long-sleeved top, possibly made of hemp, and its cream colouring was slowly being replaced by a darker, grimier shade that was closer to a grey-beige. It resembled the colour of that grime that men get around their shirt collars – the kind of dirt washing powder commercials are always at pains to claim their product can remove. (Whenever they bring out a 'New Formula' – maybe an 'Ultra' or a 'Best Ever' – they make that claim, don't they? Either they've been lying for years and it's only the latest one which can actually get rid of the troublesome grime, or they're just pretending that they've never said it would rid your collars of grime before – either way we've been duped at some point).

His trousers stopped half way between his knees and his feet, they were extremely baggy (they almost looked like a sarong) and again very dirty. There might have been a radiant light blue under there somewhere, if only he'd invest in some Vanish stain remover (or any other similar reputable product). He wore the same style of sandals as Dorte. What a surprise, thought Edson – perhaps there's a special traveller's shop somewhere where you can buy a backpack that comes complete with a white tin mug with a blue rim, those sports sandals, a squash ball to plug any sinks you might want to block (pretty much vital if you believe the *Lonely*), and a really grimy T-shirt that didn't need breaking in. But the stranger's most distinguishing feature was his poncho and cigar . . . wait, that's Clint Eastwood – sorry – *this* stranger's most distinguishing feature was a small beard. It was about the same length as his hair, but it resembled nothing so much as a small dark hamster clinging to his chin. Edson wondered whether he ever reached up to pet it a little, which then made him wonder why Lenny had never thought of growing a soft beard to pet instead of killing all those animals.

"Yo! Damon! How's it going, my man?" Neil, apparently, knew everyone. With almost shocking indifference Damon lifted a hand to acknowledge him, which caused the waiter to hurry over to him. Damon spoke quietly to him, without seeming to experience any of the problems Edson's group had encountered.

"Do you think he'll have the stroganoff?" Edson smirked.

"Hey! Dame-o! We recommend the stroganoff! Hya Hya!" Yeah, very original, Neil. Edson was well on the way to developing a pathological hatred of Neil's rasping laugh. It echoed the marvellous laugh of Sid James, only with absolutely none of the dirty charm, rendering it just plain, well, *shit*, in Edson's eyes. Or ears. Damon smiled, sardonically, thought Edson, although he may have been looking a little too hard for it. Neil abandoned the long-distance non-conversation – or rather he was forced to stop as Damon had taken out a large hardback, and was quickly engrossed, occasionally using his finger to follow a passage. "It's just like that *Python* sketch here, isn't it? Hya Hya!" and he twisted his head slightly to one side and hit each appendage on his left hand with his right forefinger as, with a high pitched voice, he reeled off an approximation of the famous sketch: "*We got spam, spam and eggs, spam and spam, spam, spam, spam and spam, spam and cheese, spam sandwich, spam and chips, spam . . .*" and there was more, but there's no need to put you through the whole thing. No-one likes someone who's spent half their life learning *Python* sketches, unless his name's Michael Palin.

Everyone had left a few pieces of gristly beef at the side of their plate but Lotte was still making grooves in her meal. Dorte had already started rolling up again. "Oh, roll us one, sweetheart," said Neil in a cockney accent.

"Sure."

Sasha and Alexander left the carriage, waving merrily as they passed. Sasha was wearing the kind of incredibly red-face that the word 'beery' was invented for, only in this case it was vodka that had given him the glow of a *Ready-Brek* kid who'd mixed his oats with liquor instead of milk. Damon followed them out, probably for the bathroom. Louis shoved his plate to one side and nestled his beer snugly between his hands. Jerking his head in the direction of Damon's exit, he asked, "So, you know him then, Neil?"

"Well, I spoke to him a few days ago – I met him on the Great Wall, and he told me he was getting this train. I suggested that we share a cabin, actually, but the skunk said he'd already booked a single one. He's Scots, you know. I think he might be a Buddhist or something. Nice bloke – bit on the quiet side, maybe. He did mention loads of countries, though – I reckon he might be as well travelled as I am! Hya Hya!" Stop it. "I spoke to another guy at the Wall and he reckoned that Dame-o had told him that he'd been travelling for *four* years! You'd think he'd be a bit happier, wouldn't you, eh? Carefree life, wandering the earth, getting spiritual and all that pony."

"Maybe he just didn't feel like talking," said Dorte with feeling, and blew some smoke in Neil's direction.

"Hey! As Bobby Hoskins says: 'It's good to talk!'" For a cockney, his accent was appalling – as bad as Edson's Russian impression.

"I dunno. I wouldn't talk much or be that happy if my clothes were that grimy," remarked Edson. And then he felt stupid for sounding like his Nan.

VI

Later, Edson and Louis were walking back to the carriage. "What d'you think of the food?"

"Good stodge, get it down there, replace lost energy! Baarh!" boomed Louis. It was roughly what he always said when the food was edible, filling, but not exactly of the subtlest quality.

"I thought it was a bit like school dinners. Do you think it *was* beef?"

"Probably."

"Bit, er, bit *chewy* in places, wasn't it?"

"Nothing wrong with that! Good for the teeth!"

"Did it taste like dog?" Louis claimed to have eaten dog on a few occasions while in China. Don't wince at the back there – it's no more or less disgusting than eating a pig. Think of little *Babe* if you're thinking of poor *Lassie*.

"A bit. But dog does taste like beef, so . . ."

"Do you know what the exact time is for where we are?"

"Nope."

"Do you think we've crossed any time zones? Must've done, I s'pose."

Back in the cabin Sasha and Alexander were continuing their drinking session. On the small table leaning against the side of the carriage was a large bar of chocolate with the wrapping undone at one end. The wrapping was orange and brown (always an ill-advised colour scheme for some reason), and the orange was so bright that it was almost fluorescent. Sasha was beaming. And I mean *beaming*, he was smiling, yes, but his *Ready-Brek* face had taken on an even deeper red hue that seemed to radiate the area around his head. They cheered in a drunken sort of way, and both swilled a huge mouthful of drink from their cans and shoved a jagged chunk of very dark chocolate into their mouths. Louis and Edson sat down on Edson's bunk, and after Sasha had replaced his can on the table, Louis reached towards it, his eyes squinting in curiosity, "Mind if I . . . ?" he muttered, and took the can in his hands. Edson had assumed it was beer, but Louis exclaimed, "Jesus! This is *wodka*!" Louis passed the can to Edson.

"What?" The can was mostly black, but on the front was a large white skull wearing a black top hat with some red Russian writing. "I wonder if they ask for a shot of coke and then get a can of *wodka* as a mixer?"

Louis looked up at Alexander on the top bunk. "What does this mean?" He asked, pointing at the large writing.

"In English I think it mean Black Death Wodka."

"Er, right, thanks," replied Louis. "Sounds nice."

"Catchy name."

"I think I might have heard of it back in England, actually," mused Louis. Alexander swung a hand down, tapped Sasha's head and said something quickly. It sounded somewhat slurry, but it was difficult to tell for sure. Sasha laughed – there was a lot of laughter here – maybe there always is when foreigners are around. People sometimes make more of an effort to be cheerful in the presence of a virtually insurmountable language barrier – an insistence, a reassurance, maybe, that everyone is having a good time despite the elongated silences. It's like that first date scenario where neither person speaks for a while, then someone says something like, 'Are you having a good time?' and the other replies, 'Yeah! Of course! Great!' with more forced zeal than the question merits, just to make sure the other person feels comfortable. Sasha pointed at the can of Black Death and then at the two Englishmen.

"He would like for you to have some *wodka*," explained Alexander. Edson had to admire Sasha's willingness to attempt to communicate without using or knowing a single English word. Would the English do the same in a similar situation? Maybe. If they were as inebriated as the beetroot-faced Sasha, perhaps.

"Heh, Heh! Excellent," laughed Louis, nodding his head in amusement and pleasure, and gently stroking his chin with his thumb and forefinger. He hadn't shaved since they'd been on the train, and his black whiskers were quickly darkening his jaw. When Louis did shave he did so without care. His neck and the area under his chin would be red raw where he had scraped so harshly at his beard with his dull razor. He even forsook shaving foam – he just used lather from an ordinary bar of soap.

Edson vividly recalled the thumping state of his head only a few hours earlier. Unfortunately, neither Louis nor Sasha looked particularly likely to take 'no' for an answer and the last thing he wanted to do was offend his cabin-mates. In fact, Sasha was already pouring some unfeasibly large shots into a couple of large plastic red mugs. He handed a mug each to Louis and Edson, then gave them both a piece of dark chocolate.

"You must first drink, then eat," slurred Alexander from his bunk, and he held his can of wodka aloft.

"Spaseeba!" said Louis, raising his mug.

"Spaseeba!" said Edson, doing likewise, although not as high. Everyone slammed back their drink. Immediately Edson felt the force of the liquid fire. At first it felt like someone had poured detergent down his throat; it tasted tremendously clean, yet simultaneously poisonous. It felt like the airwaves in his throat and nose were being stripped bare, as if he had just swallowed some kind of concentrated Vicks solution. Then he felt an intense burning in his throat, like someone had thrown a lighted match on the alcohol he had swallowed. He felt his face start to go red again, so he shoved the chocolate in quickly, and it soothed the burning – sweet ointment applied to the scald.

"*Wodka* with chocolate chasers, not bad!" said Louis, jabbing a finger at Edson.

"Not bad at all," Edson managed to croak. Sasha was already pouring some more large shots. He said something in Russian to Alexander, and Alexander translated.

"Do you like this drink?" Louis nodded his head vigorously and laughed, and he spoke slowly back.

"Do . . . you . . . know . . . where . . . we . . . can . . . buy . . . good . . . *wodka* . . . in . . . *Mockba*?" Always one to slip in a foreign word if possible. *Mockba* was already becoming a fabled land in their minds. It stood for so much, food not made on a train; sleeping on a bed that didn't rock; having a better chance of avoiding Neil. Alexander shrugged and pushed his lips out from his long face.

"It is easy to buy," he raised his can once more, and Sasha distributed the chocolate. Down went the firewater again, although this time it didn't have the same startling effect. Edson realised that it helped if the liquid didn't actually touch the inside of his mouth. As Edson gulped it down he heard the metallic cracking of cans being crushed. He looked up and saw the two Russians joyfully squeezing the life out of their empty wodka vessels with great smiles on their faces. They all ate their chocolate – Louis crunching it and sending it down quickly, Edson savouring it by sucking it like a toffee.

The previous night's session had been one of slow inebriation. The beer that they drank took time to infuse their bodies and they became slowly more drunk as the evening wore on. As you know, drinking sessions have many varieties but all are boring if retold to someone who wasn't there. Whenever anyone comes up to you and says, "Right, this one time I was on holiday/in the union bar/at this club (delete as appropriate), right, and I was *so* pissed, right, you'll never believe what I did . . ." I think you're probably like me and your eyes glaze over. The story will no-doubt be as dull-a story as you can possibly imagine, and will inevitably involve either snogging someone ugly; taking too many items of clothing off; or barfing in a swimming pool/someone's garden/down someone's throat whilst unerotically tongueing them. Occasionally the story will be a combination of all three. These are dull stories for two reasons. The first is that they are all highly believable stories, mainly because you have either heard them a million times before, or, more likely, done it yourself*. The second is that they *simply aren't funny.* Many of them *could* be funny if the person wasn't actually drunk at the time. For example, if one day you were on your way to work, suddenly got all wobbly, took out your knob or your tits, and barfed in the nearest person's briefcase for no obvious reason, it could be highly amusing, or, at the very least, disturbing. If you are drunk at the time of all these events the *predictability* of the whole occurrence makes it lifeless and decidedly unamusing.

Anyway, as I was saying, there are many types of drinking sessions. Some start loudly and hopefully, but peter out as everyone gets tired and goes home. Others start boisterously and end in fights or other jolly entertainment. And some (and these are the best) start as a quiet drink and end up being a fantastic night full of laughs and reminiscences and old friends who you haven't seen for ages turning up in your pub completely unannounced and totally by chance. On nights like those, I feel sorry for teetotallers. But vodka nights can end very quickly. Sasha was proving to be a man who had clearly never heard of a shot measuring twenty-five

* I'm being honest here, although I can't claim to have ever chundered down a girl's throat – just on her shoes.

millilitres. He'd probably never even heard of 'shots' or 'millilitres,' actually. All he knew was pouring and swigging. The greatest bartender on earth. And here he was again; passing another can of Black Death Wodka to Alexander from a stash under his bunk, and cracking a new one for himself like an Australian snapping open a can of lager.

Edson could already feel his head going, but he was enjoying this cultural experience of interaction with the two Russians. As Sasha was about to pour into his cup, he reached out his hand and shook it, saying "Spaseeba, spaseeba," hoping to stop Sasha from adding to his deteriorating state. Sasha stopped and looked up, his fat lips were turned downwards; his glee interrupted.

"Oh, come on, mate! Just one or two more!" said Louis, elbowing Edson in the ribs, full of only half-mocking peer-pressure.

"Oh, oh, I'm, er, I'm not a lightweight . . . I'm driving."

"Yeah, right. We're on a train."

"Come on, please join us in one more drink," said Alexander, and lifted his can in the air, which, yes, he was doing rather a lot.

"Okay," he said with exaggerated weariness, and nodded his head. The smile instantly returned to Sasha's face and he liberally poured another vodka. And down went the clear liquid that was so cunning it disguised itself as harmless water – the fluid equivalent of one of those deadly poisonous stonefish. Fortunately, Edson's tolerance was building, and the burning sensation was lessening. He wondered whether Sasha and Alexander hardly tasted this stuff at all thanks to years of drinking it. That's probably why they bought it in cans. He was so busy pondering this, and hearing Louis ask Alexander something about what he did for a living somewhere in the distance that he barely noticed Sasha remove his mug from his hand and place it back again a few seconds later.

And then suddenly it was morning.

Chapter 3

Certificate 12

No sex, violence or nudity I'm afraid. Young men and women in swimwear are briefly on view, although there are no actual pictures, you have to use your imaginations. The stronger swearwords are in use once again, although I reckon 12 year olds will probably be all right as long as there's an adult nearby.

I

Six days is a long time to do nothing but drink coffee and read *War & Peace*, you know. Six days is a long time to do virtually anything. Unless you have reached total spiritual enlightenment. But let's face it – neither you nor I have reached that stage of nirvana yet. Chances are we're both stuck in a job that underpays and undervalues us, and the odds of our being perfectly content in the foreseeable future are pretty long.

Ambition, you see, is at the root of all unhappiness. It's considered a great thing to have ambition. But if it is always part of your personality, then surely you will never be satisfied, and, ultimately, never fulfilled. What I'm saying is that . . . it's best to . . . well, you'll always . . . end up drinking a lot if you're not fulfilled – if you have ambition, I mean. The difference with spiritual enlightenment is that there actually is a *final* goal. If your ambition is to make a million, and you eventually achieve this goal, you won't find satisfaction, because it won't be enough – your tastes will have become more expensive; your luxuries will have become essentials. So don't frown upon these poor drunks – they're just like you and me really. (If you were not frowning upon their drunken squalor, I apologise – I am glad you agree).

II

As with the first morning on the train, they were once again woken early. This time, though, it was to cross the Russian border. And this time it was *very* early. Of course, due to the disorienting changes of time as they randomly crossed (and maybe *re*-crossed) time lines, neither Edson nor Louis could exactly say *how* early. Although, admittedly, any time before lunchtime would have been too early. They were snapped awake by a guard, who stood barking at a furious rate at the opening of the cabin. Edson awoke and sat up immediately, impressing himself once more that he had managed to avoid cracking his head into the bottom of Louis' bunk. He opened his eyelids a crack and closed them again quickly as the harsh light burnt his previously cosy eyeballs. "They must want to change to broad gauge," said Louis authoritatively, as Edson strained his eyes open long enough to see the bottom half of Louis' bare, hairy legs dangling down from the bunk above.

"Can't they do it while we're still on the train?" whined Edson, but he was already hauling himself to his feet, and trying to remember where he kept his clothes. He noticed that the Russians' bunks were neatly folded; even their bags had been partially and neatly packed, and five black empty cans of Black Death Wodka were neatly stacked next to each other on the lean-to table. What *did* the Russian prose underneath the skull mean, he wondered. "*We thought this sign might be a suitable symbol for people not familiar with this vodka to stay away.*" Or, "*Do not accept sweets or vodka from strangers.*"

The guard was still waiting at the door, at them to hurry up and then demanding to see their passports. Edson found his in his money belt and handed it over as Louis did likewise. The guard studied them hard, like a kid learning to read who thinks it'll help if he looks closer at the words. This worried Edson, but Louis seemed nonchalant, "I wonder if there's a cafe round here - fancy some more stroganoff?" he said. Edson was nearly too ill from the previous night's entertainment to answer.

"Cup of tea would be good," he mumbled. The guard handed the passports back and stalked off only to return seconds later, waiting impatiently and looking big in his tight uniform and cap, which was pulled down right over his eyes. It was amazing that he could even see that there was anyone in the cabin, it was tugged down so low.

"Jesus! I need to get changed! Get out!" Louis stared maniacally at the guard. It was his special look of complete seriousness that oscillated somewhere between anger and lunacy. It was his blue eyes – like Henry Fonda's in *Once Upon a Time in the West* – that helped him carry it off. Without warning he lurched forward and pushed the guard out of the doorway and slammed it shut. It was surprising his show of defiance worked, actually. Louis was wearing only his "Hallo Banana!"[*] T-shirt and his boxer shorts. His hair was sticking up in the wrong

[*] "Hallo Banana!" incidentally, if you are unaware of this phenomenon, is a phrase well known to backpackers experienced in the Far East area. There is, if she is still alive, a

woman who lives in a small town that dedicates its economy to the tourist trade – in particular the backpacker custom. She is old and wanders the small town in the early evening trying to sell her fruit (*Noooo*, I mean *really* fruit, as in apples and oranges - your dirty mind disgusts me). She goes from cafe to restaurant, shouting "Hallo! Banana!" But she isn't hoping that her mute yellow friends will answer her back, instead she is saying "Hallo" to attract attention and proffering the backpackers' favourite safe food as bait. There she waddled, a long flowery dress covering her superbly stout figure, with a great wooden plate of goodies resting on her stomach with one arm surrounding it for balance.

directions. His eyes were red and bleary. It was hardly an intimidating sight. Edson, meanwhile, was so hungover he was failing to even attempt an outward appearance of dignity. It would have proved a near-impossible task anyway – his skinny white frame was standing in just a pair of stripy football shorts two sizes too big that that hung limply from his hips like a rapper's trousers.

So they emerged, still blinking like moles in the morning sunshine, with the angry guard's words still running round their heads like so much gobbledegook. To their right, as they alighted the train[*] was a large building, like an aircraft hanger for trains. It was the building in which the entire Trans-Siberian train might be lifted and replaced with wheels to fit the broad gauge track still used in Russia. To their left was another building with a large clock on the outside, resembling a kind of town hall.

"It's very bright," said Edson, shielding his squinting eyes with his hand.

"Mmm."

"I'm knackered. I might just sleep on that wall over there," and he pointed at a low brick wall, built in a square around a sparse garden of sorry-looking grasses.

"Could do with a coffee, actually. Do a bit of reading." Do people *ever* talk to each other in the morning, or do they just talk aloud

[*] It came to my attention while writing this book that Canadians, and possibly Americans use the term 'de-'plane' to denote alighting, or getting off an aeroplane. Why have they invented a totally new word that means the same as 'alight' or 'disembark'? Because the former is associated with trains and the latter with boats? I don't know. And who thought of it? The same person who decided 'pro-active' was a proper word I suppose. The same person who I once heard say in an office meeting: "We're shooting at an open hole here, we haven't got time to play percentage golf". Twat, whoever he is.

in a series of statements about what they themselves are going to do? "Did you bring your book out?" Edson had bought *Crime and Punishment* from a bookshop in Beijing, which he had been told could be quite heavy going (at least it's got a *plot*, I can hear you saying).   At the moment, though, he was still on John Irving's *The World According to Garp*, which had been recommended by his brother. Why he was taking his brother's advice on such issues he wasn't sure. This brother, named Charlie, was a great Terry Pratchett and Robert Rankin fan, which didn't really appeal to Edson's tastes – a bit too similar to the kind of thing people who work in *The Games Workshop* read.   Nothing wrong in that at all, you understand, but still . . . Charlie had certainly improved his tastes with a gem like *Garp*, though – a bit of a turn-up for a George Lucas fanatic.

"Er, yeah," he said, accidentally dropping *Garp* to the floor and bending very . . . slowly to pick it up, "How's, er, how's *War and Peace* going?"

"Not bad, I'm getting into it a bit more now."

"Where're we going then?" Edson glanced at the wall. When you are tired any surface can look incredibly comfortable. Come on, you were always doing it at school. You were in a really dull science lesson with a science teacher who either found it all so fascinating that his undying enthusiasm became intensely irritating; or he found the subject, his job, and especially you and the entire class, incredibly dull and a complete waste of his time. You'd been up late the night before watching *The Sweeney*, or *Minder*, or reading *magazines* when everyone else was asleep. You were bored and knackered, and the second hand on the classroom clock kept sticking and generally failing to proceed at anything like the correct rate. You looked at that lovely long wooden work surface that ran the width of the classroom. You rested your elbows on it, then your forearms, then, like some kind of perverse masochist, you laid your heavy head on your forearms, just for a moment, just to see what it felt like. Then you dreamed of just getting up onto that hard wooden surface, lying full length and just dozing, maybe with your big winter coat draped on you for warmth. It looked so inviting, didn't it? School days? Best of your life.

"How about that building? Must be able to get a coffee or something there," Louis strode off, but it wasn't his usual purposeful gait. So even he could suffer the after-effects of a vodka night.

They emerged soon enough with a polystyrene cup each of strong black coffee.

"I reckon we should go and look at the train's gauge being changed, it might be quite interesting." Louis was refusing to sit on the wall, which made Edson feel a little uncomfortable. Louis held his cup next to his mouth, and craned his neck, indeed, his entire frame, in an effort to see what was going on in the hanger.

"If you're into that kind of thing . . . Neil might be down there . . . I bet he is, actually." Louis looked down at Edson and laughed.

"Yeah . . . Hmm," he took a sip and then put his thumb and forefinger on his chin in his classic thinking pose, "I'll just see what's going on."

"Let me know if it's interesting."

Edson tried to get comfortable on the wall but it wasn't quite as inviting as his tired brain had convinced him it was. Over a period of, oh, a minute or two, he experimented with several different positions none of which were comfy and all of which made him look like he was performing Yoga. Eventually, he placed his cup on the floor, lay down on the wall and tried to read the book by simultaneously using it as a shield from the sun. Garp was about to lay the babysitter – a great part of the book* – but at the end of the next paragraph he rested the book on his chest and closed his eyes.

Louis later returned accompanied by Neil and James. James had explained that he hadn't bothered with dinner the night before because, "I didn't really *feel* like it. Must have something to do with being in *motion* all the time, you know?"

"Little bit delicate, our Jimmy-boy," Neil explained while resting his hand paternally on James's shoulder. They stood in front of the dozing Edson, although Louis was sure that on one or two occasions he saw him flinch when Neil laughed.

"Hey! What's up with Eddie? Long day was it yesterday? Hya Hya!"

"We had a bit of a *wodka* session with our Russian cabin-buddies last night."

"What, actual *interaction*?" said James quietly, sarcasm dripping from his tongue like blood from a wolf's canines. As he said it he parodied that irritating sign for communication that office jobsworths love to use. You know – when they wave their hands back and forth in front of their chest as if wafting away a smell.

"Wow! You *skunk*! How were they – I bet they drank like a couple

---

* Sorry about the lack of sex in this particular book.

of goldfish, eh? Hya Hya!" Why Neil had to laugh after everything he said was still unclear to all present. Except for Neil, presumably.

"Well," Louis started, using a passable cockney accent while putting his hands up to some imaginary collars on his T-shirt and cocking his head forward and back a couple of times, "I like to think I 'eld me own, know what I mean?"

"Hya Hya! I bet you were out and on the floor before they'd even got numb lips!"

"We ate chocolate as chasers, have you heard of that before?" asked Louis, as if he didn't know what Neil's answer would be.

"No," said James.

"Yeah! Of course! Common practice, innit? Have you guys *really* never heard of it?"

"I used gin and tonics as chasers, once," said James, leaning forward slightly to see Neil's reaction. Louis tried hard to conceal a smile.

"Oh, don't get me started on the time I did that, man, that was *sordid*! Hya Hya!"

A little later the train began to return with all its new bits and pieces. Louis decided it was time to wake Edson. He grabbed him by the side and started to roll him off the wall, but Edson woke up in time to put his feet down before he fell. He was squinting again.

"Time to get back on in a minute, mate."

"You sure? I was in the middle of sleeping, you know."

"Yeah, any minute."

"Bastard. I could have slept for half an hour longer," said Edson half an hour later as they remained on the wall.

"Sorry . . . You're a lazy git, anyway."

III

After 're-training' Edson fell back into a glorious sleep for about thirty minutes, until Louis informed him they were making their first stop inside Russia. It was a large station with at least four platforms, and there were lots of people milling around selling food and drink. Did their livelihoods depend totally on the Trans-Siberian, wondered Edson, or did they receive custom from different trains all day? "Come on, let's see if we can get some breakfast," said Louis.

"Could do with a fry-up. That would really sort me out."

"Yeah, that would be a winner. Not very likely, though." They left their carriage and immediately noticed a throng of about fifteen local Russians jostling with each other at the front of the train. Once there they saw the waiter with the moustache and an older woman who they had never seen before (the cook?) who effortlessly personified the word 'dowdy.' It sounds like a terrible stereotype (and as you know, I'm quite good at terrible stereotypes), but her reddish face and short, unkempt curly, dirty brown-grey hair made her resemble a fabled farmer's wife, only without the motherly charm. And there they were, with a bundle of clothes behind them, handing them out to eager Russian hands, and receiving fistfuls of cash in return. They handed out shell suits and leather jackets, tight-looking denim jeans, big woollen jumpers, and sundry other items of fashion that most Westerners gave up wearing in 1986.

"Is that legal?" asked Edson.

"It's like their commission, I s'pose . . . I bet they don't get paid very much," Louis considered for a moment, "They probably work two weeks on and two weeks off, so they don't see their families for half the year."

"So, what, do they buy all this stuff in China, come over the border and then flog it all for a profit?"

"I guess so. I wonder how much of this kind of stuff is available in Russia at the moment. I'm not very up on Russia's social problems." They were still staring at the throng in front.

"I remember watching *Blue Peter* in, I dunno, the late eighties I s'pose, and they went to Russia for their annual summer holiday . . ."

"I've always hated *Blue Peter*."

"Yeah, me too . . . But I remember all the Russians in Red Square gathering around them – was it John Leslie, then, I can't remember - it was after John Noakes, but . . . well, it doesn't matter, but they were all staring at the cameras because they had never seen them before, and there was no food available and the shops were virtually empty." There was a pause.

"Alright girls? There's some fresh Russian bread going over there – looks pretty good. I'm going in to try and get a coffee. I *really* need my morning coffee, know what I mean? Hya Hya!" Neil had appeared behind them. Where did he come from? Edson hadn't met anyone who needed coffee as much, or drank so much of it, since observing teachers at secondary school. "You coming Jimmy?" he shouted. James was standing at the bread stall.

"Er, I'll be there in a few minutes."

"You two come and join us as well, all right? I'll try and find the girls and maybe Dame-o as well, if he's feeling up to it. He's a miserable sod that one. I think he needs a bit of company. We can play cards or something."

"Don't play cards. It's a waste of time." Louis muttered. Edson started to laugh, and then tried to cover it by putting his hand in front of his mouth and scratching a pretend itch on his nose.

"What?"

"Nothing."

"Oh! Hya Hya! You *skunk*! Hya Hya!" and he clapped Louis on his upper arm and walked off to the train.

James was paying for his bread. "Does anyone know what kind of exchange rate is going on here?"

"No idea at all. I got my rubles from US dollar traveller cheques, which is a bastard because I have to remember what the exchange rate from pounds to dollars was before I can work out pounds to rubles, and I can't even remember what the dollars to rubles was, either . . . does that make sense?" said Louis.

"I don't know," said Edson weakly.

"Well, I *think* the bread is pretty cheap."

"I thought you were the one that should know about money and stuff, you know, being an accountant n'all," said Edson.

"What's that got to do with exchange rates?" asked Louis.

"Oh, yeah . . . Let's get some bread. You going to go and see Neil?"

"I don't know. I don't want to. What about you guys?"

"Probably. He's got some *cards*!" said Edson with false excitement.

"Well, in *that* case . . . !" James looked skywards, and held out his upturned palms. Louis was already ordering four bread rolls from a wrinkly woman with a table crammed with different shapes of bread.

"I got four. Three for me and one for you, because you're fat." James looked at Edson's thin frame. A few pounds less and he'd look emaciated. He laughed and pushed his forefinger into Edson's hard stomach a few times.

"Podgy!"

"Look, I'm very sensitive about my weight, thanks. You don't know what it's like – always having to play the fat parts in school plays. I had to play the elephant when we did *The Enormous Crocodile* by Roald Dahl. And then I had to play the three little pig's big fat pig mother. They made me eat swill made of cold porridge," and then he did his

Homer Simpson impression, "*Mmmm, cold porridge.* And everyone called me 'Fat-boy.'"

Moments later they entered the dining car to a cry of glee from Neil. "Guys! The girls are here! Couldn't find Dame-o, though. You know, the other day I heard him tell some Russian guy that he'd been on the Trans-Sib three times already! Pretty impressive!"

"Yeah, pretty," mumbled Edson. Lotte and Dorte were sitting silently at the table, and smiled as their guests joined them. Dorte was next to the window. She had a dark blue cardigan on which was all bobbly with age, as if a cat had clawed at it to make a comfortable bed. Her hair was down and needed washing. (Although, Edson himself hadn't washed his own hair since that communal shower in that dodgy hostel in Beijing. Even then he'd been forced to keep his eyes painfully open during the lathering operation because every time he looked around he was sure that at least two of the four Chinese men present were looking at him. He couldn't understand why they weren't looking at the other Westerner – *he* was the one with, well, with . . . a particularly *large* penis). Lotte, meanwhile, looked nice in her oversized white wool jumper with the cuffs hanging just past her wrists - something Edson found strangely alluring.

"Oh, come on, guys, we can all squeeze in here, can't we?" Neil was saying, "We can't play cards across the gangway!" He was all excitable like a small child about to get ice cream. Edson reluctantly dragged his thoughts away from Lotte and her jumper and on to the sticky situation that had suddenly presented itself. Where was he going to sit? Would Lotte feel uncomfortable if he sat next to her – would she think he was coming on to her? He didn't want to sit next to Neil for several obvious reasons, ranging from mere dislike to the fact that he probably hadn't washed in weeks. Although, he realised, he hadn't had his daily strip-wash yet; which was another strong reason to avoid sitting next to Lotte. On the other hand, James had already sat next to Neil enough times to last the whole week, and it was surely unfair, not to mention cruel, to make him do it again. The prime position was definitely opposite whoever was next to Lotte, and next to whoever was next to Neil. But before he could formulate an effective plan to ensure he obtained that position, James settled next to Lotte, who smiled and made room for him as he sat down. Edson smiled at Louis as they stood dumbly in the gangway.

"After you," said Edson.

"No, please."

"But I insist!" he replied, heaping on the melodrama, and clinched victory before Neil could become suspicious.

"I can't wait for a coffee. When are they going to come round?" Neil half stood up and looked behind him for the waiters, but they were still busy clearing up the produce they hadn't managed to sell to their eager punters. The train started. "I can't start this bread until I've had a drink, my mouth's too dry." He began shuffling the cards by stacking them in two piles and then using a corner on each pile like a flick book. He was bent right over the cards, his monobrow gathering together angrily as he concentrated.

For a moment everyone tried to be interested in looking out of the window. This was impossible. There was simply nothing to see. Edson and Louis had talked excitedly before the trip about great countryside, magnificent mountains, torrential rivers. In fact it was pretty barren, lit up only by huge swathes of silver birch trees whose attractiveness wore out pretty quickly with so little with which to juxtapose them. Louis turned his roll over and over in his hands. "Ah, waiter!" said Neil suddenly, "What do we want, guys? No vodkas, okay? You skunks! Coffees all round? Yeah? Okay six," and he held out one open hand and a single thumb. Hairy arms, thought Edson. "Six coffees."

The coffees arrived quickly in oldish china cups and saucers. Edson braced himself for Neil's boringly inevitable reactionary gasp of pleasure. "Aaaahhhhh! I *love* my morning coffee . . . *J'adore mon café dans le matin! Ich lieber mein Kaffee in der Morgen!* Right. Who knows how to play *Cheat Shithead?*" Louis said he did, the others didn't. "Okay, it's going to be difficult to play with six, but I'll explain the rules . . ." but before he could proceed he was interrupted by Dorte.

"I don't want to play."

"You sure?"

"Yes. Well, I will help Lotte."

"Okay, let's get on with the rules. Best thing might be if I deal out the cards. I'll be," and he said the next bit in a Hollywood trailer voice, "*The Dealer*. Hya Hya! Okay, as I deal, lay the first three cards out in a row in front of you *face down*. No, face down, here, I'll take that card back and you can have a *virgin* one," he took back Lotte's valuable King of Clubs with a slight leer, and handed over a mystery card. "Okay, now lay the next three face up, one on each of the face down cards." He dealt rapidly and from time to time his tongue licked his lower lip as he strove for accuracy. "Now, just pick up the rest of your cards," he said as he finished dealing the deck.

"Oh, is it like *Slam*?" asked Edson.

"Not really, Eddie." *Eddie*. "Right, the object of this game is to get rid of all your cards. Now, you always have to lay cards higher than the last person, but you can only lay more than one card if they're the same number. But this *is Cheat Shithead*, and everyone puts their cards in the centre face down, so you can cheat. For example, if I laid two Queens, Hya Hya! If I laid two Queens I'd be bisexual, Hya Hya!" Ah, innuendo: so versatile. The Danes didn't laugh. Dorte was still looking out the window, and Lotte was rearranging her cards. "Well, then Lotte could only lay Kings, Aces, *or* twos which will start the cycle again, *or* she could lay a ten which clears the whole pile away and she has another turn where she can get rid of her low cards. But if she didn't have any of those cards, she could cheat with some lower cards, and hope to get away with it. Lots of bluffing in this game, boys."

"Bit like poker, then, in that respect?" asked Edson.

"Not really, Eddie." *Eddie*. "Right, Lotte, you start, remember, it's a good chance to get rid of your lowest cards. And remember to say what you are laying down – hey, boys, wouldn't mind seeing 'er being laid down, eh?" Dorte looked at him, and then fished in her canvas satchel for something. Within seconds she was rolling a cigarette.

"Er, two fours."

"Okay, now you're turn Jimmy."

"One five."

"You can lie if you want to Jim, cheating literally is the name of the game, you know."

"I don't want to yet . . . or maybe I just have."

"Aha! You wily skunk! Oh, I didn't explain what happens if you think someone cheated. Well, if you do, say cheat, or bollocks or whatever, and if they have, they take all the cards in the pile, but if they haven't you have to take them. Okay, Eddie!" *Eddie*. "Your turn."

"One ten, and then a thre . . ."

"Wait! Do you want to get rid of your ten *now*, Eddie? Bit early!" *Eddie*.

"Er, yes," and then in an attempt at a Wild West accent that came out as a baffling amalgamation of Western drawl, New Yorker and Australian (he was no Bobby Davro), Eddie, er, I mean *Edson*, countered, "Why? You wanna challenge me, Slim?"

"Why d'ya call me Slim?" It went a quiet. Dorte blew some smoke across the table. Some of her tobacco dislodged from her packet and rolled in a ball across the table accompanied by a light *whoosh* of wind (not really, but how cool would that have been?).

"All Western characters are called Slim, aren't they?"

"Are they, Eddie?"

Louis won the first match, with James just edging out Lotte in the sudden death style encounter that occurs when only two players remain. As a result everyone charitably changed their "Shithead! Shithead!" chants to a variety of kind commiseration: "James was really lucky there," (Louis); "You're last three cards didn't help – nothing you can do about that," (Edson); "Sorry," (James); "Hey! You're a girl, we don't expect you to win!" (Neil).

As the second match started, James took his third bite out of his roll, and then suddenly made a sound that transcribes as something like, "Uurrghh!" although that doesn't do it full justice. It was like some fantastic concoction of surprise, disgust and horror all whisked together. He dexterously managed not to spit directly at anyone, although there were a few grey flecks of food on the back of Louis' hand of cards. He showed everyone his roll. It had two fish running the length of the roll inside, like two small sprats. This wasn't a sandwich, mind, the sprats, or whatever they were, had been kindly baked *inside* the bread by a thoughtful Russian baker. A cold fish roll first thing in the morning when James was expecting a simple piece of bread. Grim.

Louis contrived to lose the second match, and Edson was at the forefront of the chanting, leaning right over his friend and jabbing his forefinger towards him as he sang jubilantly. "You're a real skunk, Eddie," commented Neil joyously. Of course, it all backfired when Edson lost the next round. Louis' retaliation was inevitably merciless – and everyone else was similarly Ming-like: in between squinting eyelids in the face of the barrage of insults, Edson noticed even Dorte joining in the fun. At least it made Lotte look right at him for a while. These shenanigans went on for a good while, up until lunchtime, actually. At which point Edson was getting literally itchy for a wash and desperate for a clean of his by now uncomfortably furry teeth.

Lunch was borscht. Again. But, in the face of no apparent alternative on the menu, the lure of a thin sliver of meat at the bottom of a silver tin bowl of minutely chopped vegetables floating in a greasy thin gravy was still more of an attractive proposition than the dried noodles. It was getting close, though.

IV

The two Russians were not in the cabin when Edson and Louis returned from lunch. "They're not here very much, are they?" said Edson.

"They must have some friends on the train somewhere or something like that."

"What time is it?"

"No idea."

"I'm going to have a wash," Edson had been fishing around for his black washbag for a moment, and he now held it slightly out in front of him in a detached kind of way, as if worried that it might look like he owned a ladies' handbag. "Do you wanna go in first?"

"Erm, nah, go on."

The bathroom possessed nothing more than a metal toilet and a metal sink. The floor was red, and the window was misted and patterned to ensure the wilderness didn't get a peek of a different kind of nature. Edson gazed absent-mindedly at the mirror for a moment, and then tackled his teeth with his blue bicarbonate of soda Colgate toothpaste. The brush worked hard to remove the fur, the vodka, the bread, the borscht – in short, the sorts of things you would probably unearth in Genghis Khan's underpants. Bored with his reflection, he read the instructions on the back of the toothpaste tube:

For a child, use a pea-sized amount of paste and clean the teeth lightly but thoroughly.

The words 'pea-sized amount' seemed odd. It reminded him of the instructions on a bottle of hair conditioner that he had once used where it said something like:

Pour an amount of cream onto your palm that is the size of a ten pence piece.

It was so *exact*. And the size of a ten pence piece had changed since he last read those guidelines. Did they change the instruction?

Pour an amount of cream onto your palm that is smaller than a two pence piece, but marginally larger than a new ten pence piece.

Such are the wonderings of a man cleaning his teeth. And why not? Cleaning your teeth is something that you cannot combine with any other meaningful task. You cannot even read a book for fear of dropping a great globule of blindingly white toothpaste spit onto the pages.* Or you'd be running off every few seconds to spit and rinse. Totally ruins the flow of the book, like an author who can't stick to the subject matter. A quick scrub of the tongue now, *just in case*, and he was ready for the next stage. Edson was always having a go at Louis, actually, for his teeth cleaning methods. Louis cleaned his teeth with the same violent vigour and force that most people reserve for scrubbing a stubborn burnt tomato sauce stain off a gas hob. Louis just didn't care – raw gums and a skinned neck from scrapy shaving were things he didn't think were worth worrying about.

It wasn't warm in the bathroom, but it wasn't freezing either, which would have been okay if there had been hot water. But there wasn't. There wasn't even a hot water tap. He would have to shave in cold water. He lathered up the blue gel and smeared it on his face. He never knew how much was enough – there were no specific instructions on these cans as regards to which vegetable-size amount to spray into the palm. As he shaved his longish whiskers, some blond, some black, and, worryingly, some *ginger*, the razor made a real rasping sound, like that of a car moving across gravel.

Bracing himself, he whipped off his black sweatshirt and Great Wall of China T-shirt, and he filled the sink with cold water. He made the flannel wet in the water, squeezed it slightly and then held it in front of him for a moment. He could feel a worrying draught of cold air wafting up from the freezing water, and the fine blond hairs on his arm were sticking up, doing their flimsy best to conserve warmth. He held his breath and flung the flannel all around his upper body. He gasped as

*Toothpaste white is, of course, the only kind of white that can actually stain your clothing forever – even if that item of clothing is white itself. So, what I want to know is, why on those sick-inducing poor washing powder adverts do they always use blood or blackcurrant (or just common-or-garden grime) as examples of what their product can 'shift' (they love that word, have you noticed?). When will they finally get to grips with a real stain? Toothpaste spit. One day I want to hear that phrase muttered by an actress-housewife: 'Yes, the trial has been excellent. I even accidentally dropped a glob of *toothpaste spit* on my best little black number and it even got that out! Kevin was pleased he didn't have to shell out for a new one!' (She glances at him with pathetic maternal smile, he looks up from his paper briefly with bored expression in brilliant stereotypical family life cameo) he returned the flannel to the sink, but bravely carried on at a brisk pace. He lathered his Imperial Leather (cheap and not girly) and made sure he was well washed in his armpits but didn't make much of an effort with his back. Then he flung the freezing flannel around his body again before gratefully towelling off and replacing his T-shirt, still warmish from his former body-heat. Now, below the waistline, or leave it until courage returns, or until someone notices a smell, or until a way of obtaining hot water provides itself? The third option sounded like a decent compromise under the freezing circumstances.

Back in the cabin Louis had put Miles Davis' *Sketches of Spain* on. They weren't experts in jazz but their appreciation was similar. Louis did this face when he was pretending to be a cool jazzman listening to the music. He closed his eyes, without screwing them up, and squashed his closed mouth in ever so slightly, and out just a fraction, and then nodded his head up and down, just quietly bobbing, not head-banging.

Earlier on in this trip, Edson and Louis had stayed together in Guangzhou. Louis knew a couple of girls who lived on the other side of town so, on hired bicycles, they set off to meet them at their place. It was a good night, fuelled by cheap Chinese beer. It was late as they returned to their ridiculously cheap but possibly disease-infested hostel. The streets were pretty much deserted, so they rode at leisure, free from the maddening traffic they had experienced on the way. For some reason Edson was looking at the back of Louis' bike when it suddenly punctured. He actually saw a puff of chalky air blow abruptly out of the tyre, like you would expect to see in a cartoon. Louis dismounted (de-biked) and they were forced to walk the last two or three miles to their beds.

Ordinarily, there would be hundreds of oil-covered bike-vendors at the sides of the roads eking out a living fixing people's old bikes following punctures, or chains falling off, or trousers getting embarrassingly caught up in the pedals or something. But not at two in the morning. Then Louis started to sing,

"*Let there be you,*" and immediately Edson joined in with the Nat King Cole classic.

"*Let there be me. Let there be oysters, under the tree.*"

And so on. So there they were, singing Nat King Cole at two in the morning on the deserted and oddly hushed streets of Guangzhou. And sure, a couple of times one or the other got the words in the wrong order, but on the whole it didn't detract from the experience.

V

Edson awoke a while later. "Louis?"

"Mmm?"

"What time is it?"

"No idea." Edson listened for a while. From time to time he could hear the sound of a page turning, but he could also hear a loud crunching noise.

"Are you eating?"

"Mmm".

"What, those Ritz biscuits again?"

"No, I didn't want to waste the noodles, and I didn't fancy them cooked, so I'm eating them raw. You probably still get all the main nutrients." Edson propped himself up on his elbows.

"You're eating them *raw*?"

"Yeah, not bad actually," crunch, crunch.

"That's grim. Have you squeezed the sauce over?"

"Nah. I'm not too bothered about wasting them, I've got no idea what they put in them." The sachets that accompanied these noodles were not sachets of powder like you might get in your average packet of Western Super Noodles, it was a thick clearish sauce – light if it was chicken, slightly darker if it was beef. And they had different coloured tiny *bits* in them, as if someone had crunched up a variety of autumn leaves into the mixture.

"What's it like?"

"Bit dry."

"Mmm . . . Fancy a jasmine tea, then?"

"Yeah, that'd be a winner - my mug's on the table."

Louis had started playing some Sarah Vaughan now, and her sultry summer voice diffused the cabin air with some fantastic beauty. "What do you think we'll have for dinner tonight? Or do you want to stick to the dried noodles?"

"Stroganoff," said Louis in his deep Russian voice.

"Hope not . . . I've never seen those waiters smile, you know."

"I've seen them laughing and stuff actually. When the two waiters and *Olga*,"

"Who's *Olga*?" They were both starting to say every vaguely Russian word in a deep vaguely Russian voice.

"That cook-woman, her name must be Olga something . . . *Olga Notsothinski.*" Edson laughed at this cruel attack.

"Yeah, or *Olga Nodresssenseski.*" Well, you know. You had to be there to enjoy the slightly jingoistic sense of humour. But as Danny Baker says, "Foreigners, like monkeys, were put on earth to make us laugh." How very true. The Chinese, for example, often seemed to find Edson and Louis hilarious.

"Well, I saw all three of them sitting on that bottom table nearest the kitchen this morning all laughing and smiling, but as soon as the moustache man stood up to serve us he went all sombre again."

"I didn't notice that."

"Yeah, it was weird. It could be the way you are supposed to serve people in Russia, I'm not sure . . . But they just look so pissed off about it all. Can't blame them I s'pose. I wouldn't want to serve *you* for five days." At that point Sasha and Alexander walked in.

"Hallo," said Sasha. Alexander just smiled briefly and climbed onto his bunk. Sasha said something in Russian, and Alexander sighed and said,

"We will soon be leaving at Irkutsk."

"Oh," said Edson.

"We will miss you. Thank you for the *wodka* last night – my head hurts a bit," said Louis carefully, and he put his hand to his head and exaggerated the hangover pain. Alexander laughed . . . briefly.

Soon, the great expanse of water that is Lake Baikal swam into view. After almost two days of pretty dull views, this magnificent oasis came as sharp relief for all on board. Nearly everyone left their cabins to stand in the passageways and quench their thirst for something different. It was amazing what an effect the lake had; everyone seemed to be a notch happier and the air was filled with excitable chatter from the passengers, as if the end of the journey was nigh for everyone rather than just a few. The size of it was breathtaking. It is, as you may know, the largest man-made lake on earth.

Edson and Louis had been staring at it for about ten minutes when James, Neil, Dorte and Lotte came up the corridor.

"Hey guys, I've got a tremendous idea. Jimmy-boy reckons that legend has it that if you swim in the lake it adds an extra twenty-five years to your life! So I propose we should all go for a dip! Whaddya reckon?"

"Yes!" exclaimed Louis, pumping the air with his fist, "It'll be the only chance we get for a proper wash for the next few days, as well. How long have we got to do it? How long's the train stopping at *Irkutsk* for?"

"Well, I've been looking at the timetable at the end of my carriage, and if I've understood it properly, and I probably have, I'm a bit of a linguist in my spare time, it's about twenty minutes. If we get our swimming stuff on ready, with towels and cameras, we can leg it out, jump in, frolic around a bit, take some pictures, and then leg it back in – there and back in ten minutes, no probs!"

"Okay, well, let me have a look at the timetable too. See what it looks like," said Louis. They all gathered round, and although they couldn't understand most of the names, they managed to find Irkutsk, and there was a number twenty after it. "That'll do me," said Louis.

"Are all you guys doing it?" asked Edson.

"Well, Jamie-boy says he's not going to, but I reckon I might be able to persuade him, and the girls are definitely doing it!" Edson looked at them. They had huge smiles on their faces. His immediate thought was that this was a golden and very possibly unique opportunity to see Lotte in nothing more than a (hopefully very) small swimsuit. It crossed his mind that maybe this was some bizarre plot hatched by James, and maybe the girls too, to abandon *Neily* without clothes in Siberia, thus ensuring a more pleasant journey to Moscow. Ingenuous if it was, he thought. "There's no way you're getting me out there," said James.

"Yeah, I don't think I'm going to risk it either – what if the train left early – you'd be fucked. You'd be standing in the middle of Siberia with only swimming trunks and a towel and possibly a camera. Apart from that, it's blahdy freezing out there, and the water's probably even colder – I don't fancy putting my gonads through that kind of pain." Edson was acting all light-hearted but he really couldn't believe they were seriously contemplating this cockamamie notion.

"Ah, come on, Ed, you might never get the chance to extend your life for twenty-five years again!" laughed Louis.

"It's not *The Fountain of Youth*, Lou, it's not the fucking *Holy Grail*, it's a bloody cold piece of water in the middle of a piece of land famous all over the world for being bloody freezing! If any bloke steps in that water past his waist, he'd probably lose the ability to father a child!"

"Well, why don't the rest of us go and get changed and meet back here in a minute?" said Neil, and everyone wandered off. If Edson had been Charlie Brown, his facial expression would have been a wavy line.

Back in the cabin, Louis was putting on his swimming shorts on the top bunk. Sasha and Alexander were sort of half-watching; trying not to look but occasionally glancing up to fathom what on earth he was doing.

"You're not really going to do it, are you?"

"Yeah – come on, Ed, you'll regret it if you don't."

"No, I quite clearly won't." He lay on his bed and started reading, but he couldn't concentrate. True, there was a tiny part of him that fancied this trip. It was the part that relished danger, the same part that had made him eat chicken feet in China just to see what they tasted like. But eating chicken feet did not run the risk of genital frostbite.

Minutes later, James and Neil returned. James was still dressed in black jeans and his yellow shirt with a T-shirt underneath, which made Neil look ludicrously under-dressed in white adidas T-shirt, his black adidas swimming shorts that just peered out from under his T-shirt, and a pair of white Nike Air trainers with blue flashes. Despite the lamentable state of Neil's various white T-shirts, his Nikes remained virtually spotless. He had swung a light blue (with the odd white-ish stain on it) towel around his neck – like a boxer does before a fight – and in his hand he held a camera in a case. Sasha looked a little confused. Alexander barely seemed to notice.

"You not changed your mind, Eddie?" Edson was becoming just a little annoyed by all this – it was a stupid idea that he didn't want any part of, and people indiscriminately calling him 'Eddie' was not helping the situation. He lowered the book that he was unable to concentrate on reading.

"Nah," he put it up to his face again. Above him Louis shrugged at Neil. Neil looked at the two Russians and raised his hand in greeting. Sasha smiled back and said something in Russian to Alexander, who didn't reply.

"Mind if I sit down, Eddie?" and Neil sat down before Edson could answer 'plenty of space on the floor, Neily' or something equally as witty. James sat next to him, and then Lotte and Dorte arrived. There was no clothing hanging from under their T-shirts, giving the impression that they were naked underneath. Maybe they were. Edson tried not to stare at Lotte.

"Girls! Come in!" said Neil. They walked in gingerly, as there was little room left in the cabin. It was becoming extremely cramped and they were forced to stand awkwardly on the floor in between the bunks for a moment, resembling models on a catwalk.

"Here, sit down," said James, and got up and stood in the doorway. Dorte sat down next to Edson.

"Yes, sorry ladies, have a seat," and Neil stood with James.

Louis belatedly introduced everyone to the Russians, but it wasn't a comfortable scene. Alexander was not in one of his talking moods, so Sasha, although enthusiastic, was rendered without a translator. Eventually, everyone except for Edson stood out in the corridor, watching the enormous lake and talking about nothing in particular. A couple of times James sat with Edson, and they incredulously discussed the ludicrous idea.

"Think about it," Edson explained, "You'd have no passport, no money, and you can't speak the language. What're you gonna do? Sell your swimming trunks? When would the next train be along? How would you get on it anyway? You'd have no ticket, no proof of identification. Nothing. You'd be *absolutely* freezing. It's not even as if we're close to a British embassy, is it? It's about four blahdy days away by train!" Soon, in the late afternoon – well that's just an estimate* – as I keep saying, no-one was ever sure of the correct time, but it felt like late afternoon – the train drew into Irkutsk station. Neil started jumping around excitedly in his Nikes.

"Come on! Come on! Only twenty minutes, let's go!" He, Dorte and Lotte looked expectantly at Louis. The two Russians were taking their matching green suitcases and were about to leave the cabin. Louis and Edson stood up and shook their hands.

"Thank you very much for the *wodka* – it was nice to meet you!" Edson said, slowly.

"Yes, thank you!" Louis smiled a huge smile, showing all his teeth, and Sasha laughed loudly and warmly, and shook both hands hard. Even Alexander smiled.

"It was nice knowing you," he said in a very deep voice. And then they left.

"We should have got them a present, or something," whispered Louis. But before Edson could answer, perhaps to point out that no-one on the train was handily running a small gift emporium out of their cabin, he had already joined the other three intrepid explorers in the corridor.

---

* Incidentally, does anyone out there know why people say 'guesstimate'? What's the point in it? It's not like 'Chunnel' for Channel Tunnel, which actually and fairly cleverly *shortens* two words into one is it? Because they're so goddamned *wacky*, that's why.

"Be careful, and get back here quickly," Edson shouted after them, but none of them turned round. He and James watched out of the window as the four rushed past, holding on tightly to cameras and towels. Sasha and Alexander waved as they walked past.

"I hope they make it back," mumbled Edson.

"Yeah, I don't fancy trying to tell the driver of this train to wait five minutes."

So they stood there, like two parents waiting for their children to come home after their first night out on the town. They both pretended to be interested in the activity outside, but both looked at their watches every couple of minutes. They might not be showing the right time but they could still time twenty minutes. Plenty of people were leaving the train, and a few were boarding. James wondered aloud whether someone else might be joining him in his cabin.

"Do they segregate men and women?" asked Edson.

"I assume so. Be a bit dodgy otherwise."

"They don't on sleepers in England, though, do they?"

"I dunno. I don't think I've ever been on a sleeper in England."

"I did once. I was going up to look at Glasgow University when I was eighteen. I was in a two-bunk sleeper. And there was a Scottish businessman on the bottom bunk, quite a young guy. He asked me where I was going, and when I told him he said, well, I won't do a Scottish accent, because I'm crap, but he said, 'Yeah, it's good crack up there.' And being the young innocent that I was in those days I thought he meant crack as in the drug! It was only later I realised it was an Irish thing – you know good *craiq*."

After about fifteen minutes, they began to worry more openly. They still weren't back, and the flow of people de-training and re-training had slowed to a trickle.

"They better hurry up," said James, quietly. They both leaned forwards and scanned the small crowds outside for any sign of them. A moment later, Edson spotted Louis weaving through the crowds like an expert winger in a football match, his T-shirt in his hand and his towel wrapped around his back and shoulders.

"There's Louis!"

"Where?"

"Look – just there . . ." and he pointed, "Neil's just behind him."

"Oh yeah I see . . . Where are the girls then?"

"Can't see them. They'll be along in a minute." Louis' hair was black with wetness, Neil's wasn't, obviously, as he didn't have any hair. Edson wondered whether he had a lot of chest hair. From his limited experience, bald or balding men always seemed to possess extraordinary body hair.

"I feel twenty-five years younger!" they heard Louis shout from outside.

"They should get warm as quickly as possible," said James, and then, "Do I sound like my Mum?"

"I don't know. Did she have a kind of deepish man's voice like yours?" Louis and Neil came strutting down the corridor, glowing in their triumph. A bluish, fridge-like glow, you understand, but a glow nonetheless.

"Where're the others?" asked James.

"Oh I think Dorte tripped."

"What? Didn't you wait for them?" cried Edson incredulously.

"Well, we went back, but Lotte just told us to go on and said they'd be right behind us," replied Louis. "I thought they *were* just behind us, actually." He peered out the window with Edson and James. "I could've *sworn* they were right behind us."

"They probably just got on further up the train guys, don't worry about it. Anyway, I'm off to get dressed, it's a bit chilly in that lake." Neil stalked off, but no-one was paying too much attention.

"He's probably right guys," reasoned Louis.

"Well, probably isn't much good is it?" replied Edson irritably, and he glanced at his watch. "That's got to be twenty minutes now . . . what if Dorte hurt herself or something. I can't believe you didn't wait for her, Lou. *Jesus*."

"They said they were fine – she was getting up when I last looked." Edson looked worriedly at his watch again.

"Maybe I should go out and find them," he murmured.

"Ed, that's a dumb idea – what if the train goes? It's going to go any second now," said James.

"Well, I'll stay close to the train, take my ticket out with me to make sure I can get back on. I'm gonna do it."

"Come on Ed, they're probably already in their cabin – it's not worth the risk," reasoned Louis.

"Well, I'll only be a sec, I won't go far." He leant into the cabin and grabbed his trusty old money belt which contained his passport, his ticket and a few dollars.

"Right, I'll just be a minute."

"This is stupid Ed, stop trying to be a hero," said Louis finally, but Edson was already halfway down the corridor.

He turned left off the train and jogged up towards where James was looking up at the window. He looked through the crowd, then he jumped up to try and see over it, and then he dodged his head in all sorts of directions as he tried to see past people who were waving off friends and relatives. He carried on half-running along the side of the train. A quick glance at his watch showed that they had now been at the stop for over twenty minutes and he began to feel rather panicky in his stomach. It was a little bit like musical chairs. You know, when you have to run past the sections that are without chairs in case the music stops at an inopportune moment – Edson was now running between the doors of the train in case it suddenly decided to move off as he was stuck half way between two entries.

"Lotte!" he finally shouted in desperation. "Dorte!" But his voice was never going to carry over the mini-throng gathered on the platform. Finally he stopped next to one of the last doors, the one that was just before the dining car, in fact. He stood on tiptoe and looked around some more. Then he started to hear a couple of the train doors slamming. And then a couple more. Still no sign. He took one last look, felt a touch of almost complete horror as he watched the surreal scene of people on the platform waving merrily, blissfully unaware of the disaster that had befallen these two Scandinavian girls. He tried to get on the train, but there was a guard there unwilling to let him on. All the doors were slamming and Edson was suddenly struggling to pull out his ticket. For one or two brief seconds he felt utter and helpless panic as he experienced visions of the great guard refusing to let him on the train just because he couldn't dig his ticket out in time. Finally he pulled it dramatically out of his money belt, flashed it at the guard and pushed his way past.

In the first corridor with windows looking back out onto the platform Edson stopped and looked out again, but they weren't there. He jogged back to the cabin, praying for some kind of miracle, and wondering what on earth they were going to do. Could they pull an emergency cord? Was there even an emergency cord to pull? He felt like shouting at Louis. He couldn't believe his friend could be so stupid.

But as he neared his carriage, James came running the other way. "I didn't find them James," he called. "Those two are the biggest two twats I've ever known. I can't believe they left them there." He felt his eyes watering which annoyed him because he wanted to be angry.

"Ed, it's all right. We got them. I don't know how you missed them – they got on a couple of minutes after you went out for them."

"What? Why didn't someone come out and get me?"

"Well, no-one wanted to get caught out there and we knew you'd get back on."

"Gee thanks. I've been shitting my pants here. I really thought they'd gone."

"Nah – just a bit slow. You know what women are like."

They arrived back at the cabin and Edson saw Lotte and Dorte standing in the corridor. Lotte's lips were tinged blue.

"Jesus you guys!" was all he could think of to say.

"Thanks for looking for us Edson," smiled Dorte.

"Yeah, that was very sweet." Edson's anger dissipated almost immediately.

"Hey, it's the least a guy could do," and he looked in at Louis, who was sitting on the Edson's bunk drying his legs vigorously.

"I told you they'd be fine, Ed. You just overreacted."

"So how was it?" he asked the two women.

"Freeeezing," said Lotte.

"Yes, very cold," agreed Dorte, "But it was wonderful!"

"You should've come, Ed!" called Louis, but one look at him shivering in his cabin convinced Edson that he had made the right decision. At that moment Neil came bounding back up the corridor wearing a t-shirt, jeans and no socks.

"Ah! There you are girls. I was a bit worried there. Knew you'd be all right though. It's a shame you didn't come, mate. Just think, us four will have twenty-five more Trans-Siberian re-unions than you two!" he cried Neil. He was now standing just behind Lotte and Dorte with his elbows resting presumptuously on their shoulders.

"Never mind," replied Edson, fancying that he saw a few wisps of thick chest hair protruding from the neck of Neil's t-shirt. 'As I thought,' he said to himself.

"Yeah, well, now I know you girls are okay I'm gonna have a nice lie down," Neil stated.

"Yeah, I'm going to get dressed, too." And Dorte moved off in the opposite direction.

"Thanks again, Edson," said Lotte over her shoulder. Edson watched them go, taking the chance to have a good look at Lotte's legs, but unfortunately it wasn't a very erotic sight. If she'd been shivering any more vigorously she would have looked blurred.

"Lou, you know I would've hated it," said Edson as he stepped into the cabin with James. "I used to get so cold in the school swimming pool that I had to get special permission to leave ten minutes early while everyone else got their fun time at the end of the lesson. Getting a verruka for about the last year of primary school was the greatest gift God has ever sent me."

"So, no new *cabinsky's*, then?" wondered Louis aloud as he scanned the cabin for extra baggage.

"What?"

"No new guests for our cabin?"

"Oh, no. We've just got a lot more space."

"Well, anyway, if you two don't mind I'd like a bit of privacy so I can get changed."

"Cold water not done you any favours, Lou?"

"Shut it!"

James decided that he better return to his cabin to see whether he had any new arrivals. Edson noticed that James seemed to have worked out a kind of plan to keep on the move as much as possible in order to avoid his natural predator: Neil. It made him think about the Kenneth Anderson books he liked to read. They are mainly about hunting man-eating tigers in Indian jungles. The trackers described in the books were fantastic at spotting the tiniest signs when following the spoor of a tiger, or a human, or whatever. He imagined Neil stalking the corridors, sniffing the curtains, analysing door handles, and cursing the guards for hoovering the thin carpet on the corridor floor thus eliminating vital signs and odours. He was about to imagine Neil pouncing on an unsuspecting James, when Louis shouted out that he was now 'decent,' so he went back inside and put his mind to more commendable uses.

The room felt a bit empty, a bit quiet. "Let's have a bit of *Louis*," Edon said, pronouncing 'Louis' 'Lewis' – the way Louis Armstrong always referred to himself.

"Yeah, lets get some tunes on, nice idea. What you got?"

"I got a bit of *Louis* playing WC Handy. This is superb, I love it. Hang on . . ." Edson fiddled with a tape in his walkman and attached his little speakers. They listened to Louis playing his horn, and both danced around the cabin playing air-trumpet and air-saxophone. At one point, Louis leapt onto Edson's bunk, squatted, screwed his face up and then played the air trumpet in the most bizarre position, as if physically trying to show how the music was twisting his body up.

"D'you wanna get some dinner then?" said Louis, inevitably, when the album had finished.

"Yeah, might as well. Any idea what the time is?"

"No, but it must be about that time, the sun's going down."

"God, it would have been easier to bring a sundial with us."

The buffet car was quite empty when they arrived, and Edson remarked that it might be too early for dinner. The waiter with the moustache was sitting quietly at the bottom table, immaculately turned out as usual.

"Louis, my man! Eddie! How the *hell* are you guys?" Neil had somehow approached silently from behind them, and he proceeded to slap Louis' back, making a loud crack. James was in tow.

"You all right, James?" asked Edson. James was looking a little off-colour.

"Hey! He just needs a good feed, don't you Jimmy! Hya Hya!" Like a footballer or a cricketer, he seemed to feel compelled to call everyone by a name that ended with an 'ee' or an 'o' sound: Jimmy, Eddie, Dame-o. Louis was lucky. After all, Louis-o would have been quite ludicrous. "Anyone seen my matey Damon lately? He's a bit of a strange one. Maybe it's drugs . . . but hey, we've all been there haven't we gentlemen, eh?" Neil looked all about him for support, and then, more seriously, as if speaking from a clichéd film script where characters are always repeating key cheesy lines (If only you knew (sigh) . . . If only you knew.") ". . . Haven't we, guys?" His three companions looked at each other blankly.

Have you ever noticed how people are more and more frequently talking in movie clichés? I'm not exempt – I've probably done it a thousand times in this cock-and-bull story already – but it does seem as if the lines are blurring between film and TV scripts that strive for realism and the rest of us who strive for a life 'like it is in the movies' (there you go, I did it there, only I cheated and put quotation marks round it so it looked I was being ironic. Is this postmodern, or not?). People routinely adopt words, phrases, accents and inflections from sounds they hear on television, as naturally as young children imitating their parents as they learn to talk. I'm not talking about people going round witlessly quoting Harry Enfield at anyone who'll listen, I'm talking about actual integration into speech patterns. For example, certain phrases from Australian soaps first assimilated into British speech through ironic imitation by kids at school. Typical Aussie phrases used in these soaps like, "Aw, Rack off!" or "You Dobber!" are sarcastically copied in an Australian accent at schools by kids to such an extent that they are eventually 'normalised' and become part of everyday speech.

British kids of today virtually live in parallel world soap operas: people in this country actually name their children 'Kylie,' 'Shannon,' 'Tiffany,' and 'Brad' after various characters or actresses. On top of that, various plot lines end up in some newspapers as 'news'! I'm not talking about 'feature' articles that are legitimate spin-offs using a current story line as a basis for an investigation. I'm talking about instances where vital upcoming events are leaked to the press and are reported as a news story. Someone's going to kill someone/get married to someone who is the same sex but doesn't realise/have a baby that might be the spawn of the devil. Whatever. And then these stories are picked up and discussed endlessly on most radio stations as if they're genuinely important.

The same people who 'report' these stories and make livings writing features off the back of them probably piss themselves laughing at some of the American soap operas like *Sunset Beach*, but at least *Sunset Beach* and their cousins (including their second cousins that appeared as a result of their cousins mating – the *World Wrestling Federation*) are honest. They don't pretend the plots are realistic, they don't pretend the dialogue is typical, and most importantly Americans don't lavish the 'actors' and 'actresses' with countless awards for their performances (although that doesn't stop them from spreadeagling themselves at the feet of people like Calista Flockhart). The British and Australian soaps are to some extent parodies or at least exaggerations of everyday life, but they are copied by us over and over, so we end up endlessly exaggerating our original exaggerations and parodies. So I ask myself, where will it all end? *Where will it all end?*

Right, it was dinnertime wasn't it? Ah, yes, and Neil was

wondering about Damon.

"Haven't seen him since yesterday," said Edson, "What about the, er, girls?" he asked, as casually as possible.

"They'll probably be along later – no-one can resist the Neil Bass charm, know what I mean? Hya Hya!"

"Look!" whispered Louis to Edson, "They're doing it now!" Louis pointed to the two waiters and Olga sharing a joke. It was the first time Edson had seen any expression on their faces apart from concerned, bored, or serious. The waiter with the moustache was jigging up and down slightly as he laughed, but his moustache still obscured much of the shape of his mouth and his teeth weren't showing. The blond waiter, however, had a massive smile, not so much long, but high with big teeth, and the hitherto stern and seemingly unapproachable Olga was giggling away, her dark eyes suddenly wide open as she listened to the blond waiter. It was like watching rare birds copulating.

"What's going on? Ah, the waiters have arrived . . . Sir!" the whole scene was lost on Neil who signalled with his hand for the waiter to approach. The birds had been disturbed. The blond waiter looked over and his high smile withered. He walked up to them in his professional-but-bored kind of way, and gave the four men two menus. Did he long to be the customer? Did he yearn to toss away his conventional waiter hat and do some children's entertaining? Maybe wow the customers with some juggling or fancy cocktail bar tricks?

"It's still a bit early, isn't it? Shall we just get four beers as an appetiser, lads?" said Neil. Edson was staring at his monobrow again. Why *was* there so much hair there, but so little on his actual head? If he grew his hair into a kind of lush but slightly receding side parting would he start to look like Verloc out of Hitchcock's *Sabotage*? Now *there* was an excellent example of the monobrow in all its shifty glory.

"Er, I was quite . . ." Louis was cut off as the waiter mumbled 'four beers' under his moustache and turned to fetch them. Edson was still looking at the menu. He had noticed the day before that none of the main dishes had a price denoted except for the stroganoff, which had the cost written almost illegibly with a blunt, faint pencil next to it. He hadn't thought much of it at the time, but this evening the price next to the stroganoff had been rubbed out and instead there was a number next to 'Lulia Kebab.' Belatedly putting two and two together, Edson showed the menu to Louis and explained his theory.

"Anyone know what *Lulia* Kebab is?" Edson asked.

"Well, it's er, it's probably yer typical, er, typical Russian meat dish – just pork or something, and a few veggies – it's just a colloquial name, innit?" Louis was shrugging his shoulders, looking a little indignant, but it was all a game, enhanced by a favourite know-it-all southern market trader kind of accent.

"So, just meat and vegetables, then?"

"Shut iiiit!"

"What if *Lulia*," James was joining in with the deep pseudo-Russian accent now, "really means rat or, I dunno . . ."

"Or skunk?" said Edson, looking at Neil.

"Doubt it, Eddie," said Neil, looking up from the menu with a perplexed look on his face, "They're natives of Northern America, I'm afraid. They're not exactly going to fly a few succulent youngsters out just for some flimsy Trans-Sib menu, are they? Hya, hya!"

"No, I, er, I s'pose not." The beer arrived, and Louis started to point to the menu, as if to ask what Lulia Kebab might be, but the waiter was already returning to his table.

They made a couple of toasts and discussed cuisine for a while: what they cooked as students ("I was the master," said Neil humbly, "I could make superb and healthy meals every night of the week for thirty quid a month from the local *Netto* – and it wasn't just baked beans all day. You know that old saying? The way to a man's heart and all that – bollocks. The way to a woman's heart, or at least up her skirt, is through a bloody good home-cooked meal, know what I mean?"); which country had the best food (Neil preferred Indian, "I'm the master of the balti," he claimed); and Louis ranted on about how he couldn't understand why grown adults loved to eat burgers at fast food joints ("In a local pub back home you could get this huge roast beef sandwich, with massive doorstep bread and gorgeous gravy dripping from the sides and about six layers of prime thinly cut beef *and* a salad for about two-fifty. So why do people go and eat that horrible crap they give you in those places?"[*]).

Their beers were disappearing fast, and soon the waiter returned. "Do you have *Lulia* Kebab?" asked Edson.

"Yes."

[*] As a caveat to this outburst, I would just like to make it plain that the views expressed by certain maverick characters within this book are not necessarily the views of the author. Many thanks for your attention.

"Okay, four Lulia Kebabs, please. Spaseeba. Does anyone want another beer?" Everyone did, except James, who had only sipped about a third of his.

"Not for me," he said, "It's embarrassing, but I've, er, I've got a bit of a weak, er, bladder."

"Hya Hya! Poor old Jimmy-boy can't hold it in, eh? Hya Hya! You should get the op, geezer! Hya Hya!"

"And three beers then, spaseeba," said Edson, mentally trying to block his ears to the laugh, and trying not to wonder whether that was some kind of reference to getting a vasectomy, and if it was how that could possibly help a weak bladder.

There still wasn't any sign of many other people in the carriage when the Lulia Kebab turned up about ten minutes later, and Edson started wondering what exactly everyone else ate and where. Was there another dining car they didn't know of, that sold something apart from Lulia Kebab and borscht? After all, although there had been times when the dining car was pretty full, that surely couldn't have been *everyone* who was on the train. "So, where is everyone then? Why don't they come to dinner?"

"Maybe they've bought something else to eat," said Louis.

"What, like noodles?"

"Maybe."

"So, what, they just stay in their cabins for the entire journey, gorging themselves on noodles, Ritz biscuits and chocolate while reading *War and Peace*?"

"Maybe."

"*Oh God*!" squealed James, violently breaking up the exchange that was going nowhere anyway, "Have you tasted this *Lulia* Kebab? It's grimsky, oh *God* it tastes really dodgy." James screwed his face up, and stuck his tongue out to give it an airing from the taste. At the same time he shovelled the kebab as far to the side of his plate as possible, leaving him with just some mushyish rice and some cabbage. The kebab itself did not look much like a kebab. It was more like a pork-chop shaped piece of meat, but with the strong impression that some random meat had been processed and then carefully moulded into a meat-cut-shape. Orangey in colour, it was stubbornly unwilling to offer any kind of hint as to what animal or animals it originated from. Louis and Neil tucked in regardless. Neil screwed his face up a little, but immediately tried to hide it with a quick cough. Louis said,

"Aah, it's not too bad," and then, "Good stodge, get it down you, replace lost energy."

"Yeah, come on Jamie-lad, get it down you, what did you expect – a gourmet meal in deepest Siberia? Hya Hya! There ain't no Marco Pierre-White working on this train, matey! Not even a Delia!"

"What do you think, Ed?" asked James. Edson was looking at the piece of pinky-orange meat on the end of his fork, wishing he was vegetarian so he would have a valid excuse. It had been there for a few seconds now, waiting to be eaten while Edson, like a paranoid monarch watching his taster test his food, observed everyone else's reaction. Finally, he put it in his mouth. He chewed a little. It was definitely a pork kind of flavour, but not as strong as bacon. It was a little chewier than he had anticipated, and the salt content rivalled that of that crisp in a Salt n' Shake packet that always manages to bear the overwhelming brunt of the salt sachet. It wasn't great, but he'd tasted worse.

"It's pretty bad . . . but I'm pretty starving," said Edson, acting like a Liberal Democrat, as he ate another piece of the salted meat. James continued to pick uncertainly at his rice, and later even ate another of mouthful of the kebab, but his opinion of its quality only worsened.

VI

"Do you want that?" Louis asked James after it was clear he had finished eating. Louis' vulture-like fork was poised in mid air, ready to swoop on the grim remains of the kebab.

"Oh, you're not going to eat that, are you, Lou?" said Edson, disgust in his voice, and his hands covering his face, "It looks all congealed now." Louis was brilliant at not-quite keeping a straight face in situations like this, but Edson could see him clearly striving to keep his lips in a straight line.

"Hmm," Louis looked closer and poked at it with his fork, like a child poking a dead animal with a stick*, then sat back, "Yeah . . . probably best not to."

"Why do you think there's not many people in here tonight?" asked Edson.

---

* Back in my primary school days I used to go to an excellent after school club run by the wonderful Mrs. Hastings. It was called Animal Club, and we'd learn about animals and nature and stuff. Anyway, one week was particularly odd. Some person came in and laid

out newspaper on all our tables, then he gave us all some owl shit to sort through with some small fork utensils. The idea was to find things that the owl had eaten, so we excitedly found various skulls and bones and, of course, a Florida license plate. Anyway, our picky actions with the fork were pretty similar to Louis' prodding of the Lulia Kebab. Oh yeah, I paint pictures with words, me.

"Probably knew about the *Lulia* Kebab," said James, and he pushed his plate another couple of centimetres away from him, as if it was contagious.

"I tell you what, why don't we get a few beers from here and go back to our cabin and have a chat there? It'll be a bit more comfortable?" said Neil.

"Yeah, I'll go for that," smiled Louis, then, "I'll bring some Ritz biscuits down and those Danish Butter Cookies."

"Right, let's get the bill." Neil looked around for the waiter, but there was no-one to be seen, "When I was a waiter at the Savoy in London, I never let anything like this happen – you just don't *ever* make customers wait for anything. Repeat custom is the key to any successful restaurant, know what I mean?"

"You were a waiter at the *Savoy*?" asked James, a little incredulous, but doing his best to mask it.

"'Course – I'm sure I've mentioned it before, haven't I?"

"No. You said you used to be an astrologer," Edson wasn't impressed by people who thought themselves so *interesting*, so *complex*, that they felt the need to pretend to forget what they had and hadn't said over the previous twenty-four hours. The waiter did return, and Neil asked for the bill. When he had gone Neil said,

"So sorry. He's from Barcelona. Hya Hya!"

Ten minutes later they were gathered in Neil and James's cabin with seven bottles of beer (James only wanted one) and two massive tins of biscuits. Edson sat on one bunk next to Louis, who was chain-eating Ritz biscuits from the huge tin that had settled snugly between his thighs. He ate two at a time, crunching loudly, in a seemingly endless cycle. Occasionally he looked at everyone and pointed at the tin in an offer to share in the delights of the cheese biscuit, but Neil was the only one who ever took him up on his offer.

"So, whaddya reckon about our pad, then?" enquired Neil between chews of Ritz. "If I was an Estate Agent, and I spent a bit of time in that game at one point – it's bloody good money if you're any good, and if you're bad the money's even better, know what I mean? Hya, hya! But if I was an Estate Agent I'd describe this place as 'spacious, room for four, would suit two bachelors,' Hya, hya! Get a couple of rich City-types in, you know?" and he elbowed James – fellow bachelor and confirmed City-type.

"I've stayed in much worse places, anyway," munched Louis, and then with a Yorkshire accent, "It's bloody luxury, really, isn't it?"

"What's the worst place you've ever stayed in, then?" asked James.

"I dunno . . . that place I just stayed in in Beijing was pretty bad. It was called the Jing Ho, or something like that."

"What was it like, then?"

"It looked all right from the outside, actually, but I s'pose it was dark. Even the reception area was really nice with great sofas and it had this glass counter where they sold chocolate and condoms – nothing else – says something about backpackers, doesn't it?" He stopped here and opened the Danish cookies and offered them around. The pictures on the outside of the oversize tin made them look like big, lush, light cookies, but they were in fact tiny biscuits with a hard texture and they left a greasy smear on everyone's fingers. They tasted as if they had been cooked for too long, as if they had been whipped out of the oven just before they were burnt black. Louis chucked a couple into his mouth and crunched for a moment. "They'd built underground to get more rooms into the place and got some backpackers to do some stupid signs saying stuff like, '*You don't have to be poor to stay here, but why else would you want to?*' and '*Hallo Banana!*' and, er, oh what was that other one . . ." he ate another cookie, and chewed thoughtfully for a moment.

"It wasn't, '*I usually stay in The Hilton*' was it?" asked Edson. Louis laughed and said,

"No, oh I know, '*Why work when you can travel?*' and there were loads of drawings of cannabis leaves on the walls," at the mention of cannabis he was instantaneously interrupted here by Neil.

"Oh, man, I haven't had any *ganj* for ages. I tried to bring some on the train, but I couldn't get any,"

"I'm glad you didn't, those Russian soldiers searched some of the cabins when we crossed the border, and they're not exactly the most understanding guards in the world," James looked a bit horrified, and he shook his head in incredulity and wonderment as he spoke. Neil ignored him.

"I've gotta get me a ciggy," and he produced some tobacco and a wrinkly packet of Rizlas from his backpack, "Sorry, matey, carry on."

"Well, they'd obviously only just built this underground place. It had about twelve rooms all on one level, with four beds in each one. So there could be forty-eight people there at any time, but there were only two toilets and one washbasin between the lot of us. And to get to the showers you had to go outside into this yard and walk about fifty metres, and there were some communal showers – Christ knows where the womens' ones were – which was fine except that they only opened for a couple of hours each day, and they were different hours each day, so in just under a week I only had one shower because they were always blahdy closed . . ." Neil interrupted again.

"I need a light, I'll be back in a minute, I'll go find the girls," and he was off. The remainder looked at each other for a moment.

"Right. And that shower I had was at about three in the afternoon because that day they were opened from two until four, which I never worked out, I mean, is that the normal time to shower in China? The actual rooms looked quite clean, with a bed in each corner and nothing else. Some people had chained their bags to the bed, but I didn't quite get how that was stopping anyone from taking anything out of the bag."

"Maybe the chain was attached to some kind of zip, or something, or like, the clasp to open the bag," mooted Edson.

"Possibly," said Louis unconvincingly. That was another of his favourite words. If he didn't agree with a hypothesis and wanted to offer an alternative, he would try to soften the blow by saying 'possibly' instead of 'no, that's wrong'. "I don't know, seemed a bit useless to me. Anyway, the beds were just boards with a sheet, no mattress or anything like that, but that was fine with me because most Chinese sleep like that, and I'd been doing it for a while anyway, because it helps your back. There were only two tiny lights in the room, and one wasn't working, so you could barely see anything. But after I looked round for a while I could see things crawling here and there, and the whole place had loads of cockroaches in it!" James and Edson made the kind of noise that James had made earlier when he had bitten into his fish roll.

"Grim*sky*!" said James.

"I don't actually know why cockroaches are so grim, actually, do they bite or something? Only, in a Squeeze song, there's a line that goes,

'Misunderstood like a cockroach,'" asked Edson.

"They smell, don't they?" said James.

"Yeah, and they eat everything, books, paper, dead insects, everything, and I think they spread disease with their excrement."

"Oh. So not misunderstood at all, then."

"Well, maybe. Maybe, what's his name: Glenn something?"

"No, Chris Difford does the lyrics."

"Well, maybe Chris meant something a bit deeper like the cockroach isn't an evil insect, determined on murder and destruction, but that's just the way it lives – it's just nature."

"Possibly," said Edson.

"We got pretty good at killing them with our paperbacks, though. There was this Scots guy and a couple of Americans sharing the room, and it'd all be quiet as we tried to read or whatever in the really dim light, and you'd suddenly here this," Louis moved his right hand towards his left and then clapped his hands together and made a "wwwhhhishhh-crack" noise with his mouth, "And then usually a cheer, as his guidebook squashed the cockroach. It was pretty grim, though, because you'd find them in your sheets and in your clothes, ah, it was pretty horrible, and it was obviously because this place was just a converted basement, so the cockroaches loved it. When you woke up it was always pitch dark inside because there were no windows – it was like living in a blahdy underground cave or something."

"So how come you ended up there? Why didn't you move?"

"Well, I couldn't be arsed to move – it was only for a few days and it was pretty cheap. But I was kind of forced into staying there because I didn't arrive in Beijing until about six in the evening and every hotel I looked at was full – I must've gone to about four, I suppose. The cost of driving round in those bread van taxis from hostel to hostel was getting a bit too much, so I started phoning round a few places. And this place was, oh I dunno, it was probably the fifth place I phoned and they said that they had a few places left, so I headed over there before those spaces went. Bit of a mare, really."

"I had to stay in a hostel in Hong Kong for a night."

"I thought you stayed with your brother," pointed out Edson.

"Well, yeah, but my flight to Beijing was really early in the morning, and my brother lived and worked out of town so he couldn't take me to the airport, and it actually worked out cheaper to stay in this hostel for a night than get a cab all the way from my brother's house. So, you know, I thought I'd have a few beers in the city in the evening, and stay there, because it would just be a lot easier and my brother wouldn't have to worry. So I stayed in a place called the Elizabeth Hostel . . . or something like that, and it was really cheap. My thinking was that all I needed was a bed – I'd be leaving first thing in the morning so it didn't need to be a palace or . . ." and suddenly Neil returned, lit cigarette in hand.

"I just found that old dog Dame-o talking to Dorte and Lotte in a carriage back there. He was telling them about the time he went to Denmark. He reckons he's been everywhere, that bloke. The girls didn't seem that interested, though, they looked a bit pissed off when I arrived. I told them to join us later, but they said they hadn't had dinner yet, and they were tired and stuff. It *is* a bit knackering just being on a train, though, isn't it? Don't know why. And Dame-o said he had some postcards to write. Don't know where he thinks he's gonna post them round here, though. Oh, I was just remembering this nightmare place that I stayed once, it was in China and . . ."

"Actually," said Louis, loudly, "James was just telling us about a place in Kong Kong," he wasn't rude about it, he was even friendly, but it was enough to knock Neil out of his stride and shut him up for a second.

"Oh, sorry, Jimmy-boy . . . where're me manners, eh?"

"Don't worry. So, it was in a street that looked a bit dodgy anyway, and when we eventually found it, my brother just dropped me off and we said our goodbyes. There was a sign at the door saying that the hostel was on the fifth floor, which sounded a bit strange, and then the lift was out of order, so I had to lug all my stuff up five floors. And as I walked up I noticed all the wiring all the way up was just totally exposed everywhere, it just looked really shoddy. I started having second thoughts about staying there, and when I got to the third floor I looked out to see if my brother was still there, but he'd already gone."

"Shitting your pants, were you, Jimmy-boy? Hya Hya!"

"A little bit, yeah. So I got to the fifth floor, and found the reception being manned by a couple of really greasy looking blokes, so I signed in and they took me upstairs to the room. Basically the whole hostel had one room for sleeping in which had seven bunk beds squeezed into it, so there was enough room for fourteen people. They did have a kind of living room as well, with a load of student-types in there – Christ knows if they did anything else all day. They were watching *The Simpsons* on the TV – it was that episode where Bart's class go to the box factory."

"Oh yeah," interjected Edson, "Great episode. Bart becomes Krusty's assistant, and Krusty throws him a towel and Bart goes, '*Wow! An oversized clown hankie!*' and Krusty goes, '*That's not a hanky, kid, that's a towel! Now go clean my car!*' Superb."

"Yeah, that one. The sofa was just falling to bits with loads of stains on it. The bathroom looked okay, but I think that was because the shower floor was the floor of the whole bathroom, so it washed itself every time someone took a shower. I didn't sleep that well, either. I just kept my wallet and passport underneath my pillow, and even then I kept waking up to check it was still there."

"Yeah," agreed Louis, "It does sound like the kind of place where you'd wake up dead with a knife in your back."

"Well, exactly," said James. Edson decided to get in quickly with the story he had been itching to tell ever since the conversation began.

"I slept in a tent for two weeks on the coast of Kenya. We were surrounded by jungle and a couple of times we found massive spiders in our tent. One time one was crawling up the inside of it, and it crawled to the roof, but we batted it outside with some paper. And that wasn't as simple as it sounds because I can't stand spiders. And another time, well we had these pockets in the sides of the tents on the inside and we kept our torches and books and stuff in there. One day I was going to grab a pen or something from this pocket, and just before I put my hand in, I suddenly thought, 'what if there's a spider in there?' so I looked, and there was this huge brown spider just sitting inside, *waiting*. I couldn't believe it. I hate it when I see big ones, I can really feel my toes curling up. We got a Kenyan we knew to take it out in the end, but it was so fast, he was chasing it around our tent for ages trying to catch it."

"Was it poisonous?" asked James.

"No – well, he said it wasn't, anyway. But then he also said to make sure we wore shoes if we were walking around at night or at dusk because of spiders and snakes."

"What did you make of Kenya, then, Eddie?"

"It was pretty amazing – we had one absolutely bizarre day once, but I'll tell you about that another time – it takes ages. I think the worse place I stayed in was in India – on Abu Road – remember that, Louis?"

"Oh . . . yeah, that place was the scummiest place on earth. We were with our mate Rowan, and we were going up Mount Abu to go to the headquarters of a spiritual group called the Brahma Kumaris – they've actually got branches of it in England. But we arrived late at Abu Road, and the buses had stopped going up the mountain."

"So we had to stay in Abu Road. At first it didn't look like this place would even have anywhere to stay, because you couldn't imagine anyone living there, let alone come for a holiday or something. I mean, an hour or so up the mountain was supposedly some beautiful town that the British had built as some kind of holiday getaway where the weather was cooler, so why would anyone live at the bottom there? The main road was scummy, and that was all there was, that and a few side roads – their whole economy seemed to be the bus station that took people up and down the mountain and to other places away from there.

"So we walked down this road, it would have looked a bit like a road out of a Western, if there hadn't been so many neon lights everywhere. Then this young Indian guy with a lame attempt at a moustache came up out of the blue and asked if we were looking for somewhere to stay. So we followed him down a couple of side streets, and saw a few pigs rooting around all the rubbish and tipping it over and stuff. I tried to take a picture but they legged it."

"Notoriously camera-shy, pigs are," interjected Louis.

"Yeah. Eventually he showed us this room, and it was the grimiest place I've ever seen. There was only one bed, but it was quite big, and I was actually quite glad because I didn't fancy sleeping there alone 'cause it looked well dodgy. So there were three of us on one bed. I kept most of my clothes on and didn't use their pillow, just my own towel, because it looked like you could pick up an infection or some nasty disease in there just by breathing. The mattress was old and had hundreds of stains on it, the shower was a rubber hose, and the shower floor was covered in dirt and grime. You know how those soap adverts talk about 'ground-in dirt'? Well, the dirt was so ground in that it had started to actually *grow into* everything and started to live in the floor and walls, I think. I would say that the place was probably full of rats and cockroaches, but I doubt even they could have survived it to be honest." Everyone was screwing their noses up.

"And when we went out for some food, we had omelette and naan bread, but the omelette was a horrible green colour and it was just swimming in grease on a silver tin plate. Even the naan tasted old – that must have been the only naan I ate in India that wasn't delicious."

"I hardly ate anything that night. When we got back to the room there were two blokes sitting outside our window. We were on the fourth floor or something, and the corridor to our room was like a balcony at the front of the building, and they were just milling around there, outside our window. And one of them, this really greasy bloke who was chain-smoking, was constantly staring at us. He just couldn't look away. Eventually we wanted to get changed, so we asked him what he wanted, but he just smiled and said something to his friend that we didn't understand, and carried on staring through the window. I'm not joking, he was looking at us like a really greasy grim leering bloke would look at a stripper in a really seedy club. We couldn't even close the shutters because there was a huge piece of machinery bigger than a . . . a washing machine, that was supposed to provide air-conditioning – obviously it didn't work – that blocked the shutters. So the three of us had to manhandle this thing away from the shutters, and then Lou slammed them in the guy's face.

"The door didn't have a lock, either, so Rowan put this tiny padlock on it that he had for his backpack. But in the end we were so worried about this guy that we wedged a chair up against the door as well." Edson shook his head, a look of disgust on his face at the memory of it, "It was the kind of place that as soon as you walk into it, you start itching all over because it feels like there are tiny insects crawling all over you."

"I get that when I do coke," said Neil. "But I stayed in this place once, and I promise you, it was ten times worse than that, it was absolutely diabolical." Pause. Edson and Louis looked at each other, then back at Neil. Neil took a drag on his rolly and closed his eyes, savouring the cancerous smoke-taste for a moment. Then he looked at the other three, and took another drag. James smiled.

"So?" he challenged Neil.

"Well, I'd been on this bus from Chengdu to Jinjiang in China, you know, but the bloody thing took over twelve hours longer than it should have done. Basically, we were motoring along quite nicely and I had some mad hash in my pocket that I had bought off some crazy middle-aged Israeli woman in Chengdu who smoked the stuff constantly. I couldn't wait to get off the damn thing so I could have a puff or ten. It was bloody boiling as well – like travelling in a mobile sauna or something. Anyway, this massive truck came the other way and slowed right down, and then for some reason we stopped and the driver of the truck started talking to our driver. They talked for about twenty minutes, and I was getting a bit pissed off with the waiting, but luckily I'd already learnt there's no use getting uptight about anything in China – you'll just kill yourself with stress, so I sat back and made up a rolly. Then suddenly we did a u-ey and started going back the way we came, then after ten miles of going in the opposite direction to Jinjiang we did a left and drove down some track – if you'd have seen it in England you'd have thought it led to a farm or something. Anyway, there was this Westerner further up the bus who had been talking to a few of the Chinese, so I asked him if he spoke English and he said he did as he was American, so I said he couldn't *really* speak English then, hya hya! He told me that the truck driver had told our driver that there was a police checkpoint ahead on the road we had been travelling on, and our driver hadn't got a driving license, so he decided not to risk it and had taken some massive bloody detour."

He took a large puff on his cigarette and blew the smoke upward in the air and away from his face. "I reckon the whole detour cost us four hours or something, and you always have to add on at least two hours to these journeys from what the Chinese tell you, so we were running bloody late by now, especially as we'd left an hour late too. I went back to my seat and fell asleep, despite the smell of the bloke sitting next to me, thinking when I woke up we'd finally be in Jinjiang. But guess what?" he stopped, searching the faces of his acquaintances.

"You still hadn't arrived?" said Edson, with more than a hint of sarcasm.

"Yes!" and he jabbed his the small remaining butt of his cigarette in Edson's direction "Eddie's right! *We still hadn't arrived!* I can't remember what time we were s'posed to get in – about one in the afternoon I think, but it was really dark outside. Chuck us a beer, Eddie." 'Eddie' picked one up and lobbed it over.

"There you go," and then contemptuously and almost under his breath, "Neily."

"Beauty! So, cut a long journey short, as it were, hya hya, I didn't get to Jinjiang until about ten or eleven at night. I was supposed to get a bus to Lijiang from there, but I didn't because obviously all the bastard buses had stopped running for the night. So I was stranded in this tiny little town with absolutely nothing in it, know what I mean? It might as well have been a fucking bus terminal and nothing else for all the bloody use it was . . . Come to think of it, maybe it *was* only there because it was part of the bus route. I dunno. Anyway, everyone else on the bus seemed to disappear into nowhere, although about three of them stayed sleeping on the bus and the driver had to go and kick the buggers out.

"So I started wandering around, looking for a place to stay. It was dark and there was only a couple of buildings around. I couldn't even see what the damn place looked like properly," he took a quick swig from his beer bottle, made his aaahhh sound and wiped away some imaginary beer froth from his mouth with the back of his cuff. He leant forward. "Then this old guy just, like, walked out of the shadows – and I mean old – you know, like one of the 'Old Gits' on Harry Enfield, you know, like," and he scrunched himself up and did his impersonation, "Eee, I 'ate bloody everything, especially little sweet kittens – burn 'em I say – a dog's not just for Christmas? It bloody is after I've had it as a bloody starter to me turkey!" and he laughed hard at his mediocre impression. "Honestly, he was so old I was going to ask him if he helped build the Forbidden City! Anyway, he had a walking stick, and he hobbled up to me and asked me in Chinese if I needed a place to stay."

"Do you speak Chinese, then?" asked Louis.

"Yeah, he does," piped up James.

"Yeah – I've already told Jim-bob about a couple of the mad things I did in China, haven't I Jamie? Hya hya! So I said I did and he asked me to follow him – but he was so bloody slow I was getting a bit irritated – I didn't even know where he was taking me – it could have been an ambush or something."

"I thought you said he was really old and decrepit?" said Edson.

"I did – I mean that he might have been leading me to someone else, see? Anyway, we came to this tiny hotel – it was so small it could just have been his house with a spare room, but he did have a small reception bit. That was the only place I stayed in China where I didn't have to fill in about six hundred forms before I went to the room. Crafty beggar was probably trying to avoid tax or something." Another swig, "So I followed him to this room upstairs. When we got there I just couldn't believe my eyes. The room was quite small, with a wooden bed at one end, but the mattress on it was, like, stained *yellow* with darker patches all over it. The whole room smelt like shit. There was no electricity – the guy had brought a candle with him and put it on the ledge, and I was half-glad I couldn't see the whole place because I wasn't sure if I wanted to know what the smell was. But that sheet was disgusting!"

"Sounds like our bed in Abu Road," suggested Edson.

"No it was much worse than that," replied Neil with authority. "I asked how much it was, and he said five kwai, so at least it was cheap. Then I asked about a toilet and a shower but he just shook his head. I asked if he had any water at all, and he shook his head again. I wasn't a hundred per cent sure he knew what I was saying, so I asked about a bed, and he pointed at the wooden thing behind me. So no electricity, no water, no toilet and a disgusting bed, but I realised there was nowhere else to stay so I had to take it.

"After he left me for a bit I went out to find some food. It was pretty late, but I reckoned I could find some stall nearby that would at least give me some noodles and veg or something. But I asked the old man and he said there wasn't anywhere. So I asked whether he would sell me any food, and he nodded and told me to wait there. I waited about five minutes and he came back with a bowl that had soup in it. But it was more like some kind of watery gravy with some strange meat floating about in it. It was a kind of yellowy green colour, but I was bloody starving so I ate it all."

"I remember some of my students telling me that they'd chased and caught a frog one day and made frog soup," said Louis.

"Could have been that I s'pose. I'm sure I've had that before though, and it didn't taste like that."

"You've had frog soup?" asked James.

"Course I have Jim! You haven't lived until you've had a bit of liquidised Kermit."

"What colour is it?" asked Louis.

"What? Oh, green. Anyway, so I drank it down, paid him some money and went back up to my cesspit. God! It smelled so much! I thought I'd just put a sheet I had in my bag on the bed and just get to sleep, and wake up early to get out of there. But as soon as I started going to sleep I heard little scratching and scuffling sounds, and they got louder, and then there was just a constant scurrying sound," he paused for effect, and drank down some more beer.

"What was it?" asked James.

"*Ratssss*," he hissed. "Bloody *rats*. I threw my shoe at the sounds at one point and I heard a squealing and it went quiet for a moment, but only for a moment. I hardly slept all night. The window was broken and mozzies were coming in and biting me because there wasn't a mosquito net there, and whenever I did get to sleep I had nightmares about rats eating me alive, gnawing at my toes and stuff."

"Sounds really bad," offered Louis.

"It was. When I woke up, I saw rat shit in little piles on the floor, and I realised then what the smell had been. And the sheet under mine was revolting, I think it had rat shit on it as well. I had huge bloody bites all over my legs and arms, and one on my face, just under my eye from a mozzie, and it really swelled up, you know? I just got out of there and waited on the road for the bus."

"Gee," said Louis.

"Nightmare," said Edson.

The chat continued for a while longer, but as Neil's boasts grew, Edson's tolerance of his bravado was shrinking fast. Within another half an hour he had made his excuses, admitted to being a lightweight, and headed back to bed, closely followed by Louis, who knew a chance for escape when he saw one. For poor James, however, there was no such escape route.

Chapter Four

Certificate: 15

There's not much here to preclude younger readers from reading this chapter. If they've got this far they're probably desensitised to casual swearing anyway. True, they wouldn't be desensitised to sex and violence, but it doesn't matter, because, disappointingly once again, there's none here. However, there are some rants about train travel, and I wouldn't recommend it to youngsters simply because none of them like trains any more. They wouldn't understand. It's all spaceships and micro-scooters nowadays.

I

Everything about China fascinated Louis: the cuisine, the opera, the karaoke, the squatting, the spitting, the architecture, the language. He had lived in Guangzhou for a few months, teaching English to Chinese students. His flat was situated just a couple of hundred metres away from the school's male dormitories and these places sounded like an absolute nightmare. The students were squeezed into small rooms on triple bunk beds. Their personal space was no more than their bed and a small locker – no bigger than those small lockers that schools provide for pupils in Britain. In an age where many kids in Britain have TVs, videos, Dreamcasts, music systems, en-suite bathrooms, virtual reality helmets and sometimes even a book or two in their comfy 12 foot by 10 foot bedrooms, this sounds like some kind of jail-term in comparison. Indeed, their morning routine wasn't too dissimilar to the kind you might expect those serving their time at our own overflowing prisons (At the time of writing, Birmingham prison (Winson Green) has a capacity of 734 inmates, but is holding 1,100. Even worse, Leeds (Armley) has a capacity of 786 but currently houses 1,234).

The students were woken early for their morning's hard exercise – always held outside, however cold. It involved lots of star jumps and squat-thrusts and other tiresome exertions that made them look like space invaders from the computer games of the good old days – you know, just before *Pacman* made a decent fist of world domination. In short, the kind of physical punishment that no-one would appreciate doing at such an early time of day . . . well, apart from people who enjoy that kind of thing, anyway. Health freaks and the like.

But the most vivid description of this hellish place must be reserved for the showers. Even on the coldest and bitterest of cold and bitter winter days it was always the same – the water was absolutely freezing, and Louis could hear the screams from his flat. Clearly the screams were a psychological method of attempting to blot out the shocking numbness of this pneumonia-trap – so they probably weren't quite as warranted as their shrillness suggested, but what had these poor kids done to deserve something like this? It's the same the world over, though. Here in the UK we expect our own children to sit on horribly hard wooden chairs every day – something we would never stand for at our work places – we'd all be suing for back injury within two weeks and begging to have those nice comfy computer chairs back. We make them do homework – I appreciate that some people bring work home from the office, but, really, don't most of us yearn for home so we can forget about working? Yet home time at school is just the creation of a gap between work at school and some more work at home half the time.

And if the kids start working hard and obtaining good exam results, what happens? We get a load of old jealous bastards and bored politicians bleating on about how easy exams are nowadays. Sixteen year olds are an easy target, you see, they don't answer back with marches and campaigns like fox-hunters, pensioners and people who think that it costs too much to pollute the world with their cars. A year of youngsters achieve excellent academic results at the age of sixteen, but instead of the congratulations they might rightly expect, they're toasted with headlines saying they only achieved success because the exams are too easy. Either that or someone complains that the balance between exams and coursework has gone too far in the direction of the latter, which again makes it 'too easy'. As if grown-up life consists of endless exam-like situations. Really? If you write a report for your boss (or a similar task) are you locked in a room in absolute silence with nothing but a pen and paper, or do you have as many resources as possible at your fingertips to do the best job you can?

We make kids sit on cold dusty floors in assembly rooms to have prayers and hymns thrust upon them in an attempt to ensure they grow up with only a single religious viewpoint planted in their impressionable heads. And we make them do projects on *apples*. Is it really so different? Some schools seem to be positively *modelled* on prisons. I went to a

Grammar that was all walled off with vivid red-orange bricks so you could never climb out. A few years later when I went to Wandsworth and walked past the prison I had a strong sense of déjà vu. There were big sixth formers (that's 'Year 13ers' if you're a few years younger than me) guarding the school's front gates (Oh, yes. We had gates. They would have built a drawbridge too if they'd been able to afford the moat with a stock of happy-snappy crocodiles back in the 16th Century) at break times in case you decided to, quite literally, make a break for it (I hope you liked that clever little pun, there). I don't know where they thought we'd go. And on the last day of term (after we'd been released for our brief parole), particularly before Christmas, one or two teachers – the biggest, maddest ones with hair that stood out fluffily from their heads in a variety of trajectories – strode about the town in search of anyone who dared to loiter outside Burger King or harass innocent civvies.

Anyway, the plan for the section above was supposed to be a short lead-in to saying that old habits seem to die rather hard with some people. Edson awoke with an earache because the pillow didn't have as much give in it as he would have liked, and those delicate ear bones (or is it cartilage? Or both? – I really should do some more thorough research) had taken a bit of a hammering during the night. He looked at the other bunk expecting to see Sasha's frog-like mouth, but he had gone, and the cabin felt a little hollow. Outside he could hear a gentle banging that was elevating itself above the noise of the moving carriage. It became louder and louder. Then it faded again. Then it became louder. Then it faded. "What is that noise?"

"Come and have a look," replied Louis in an oddly hushed voice. Edson swung his feet round and planted them on the floor. He looked up and saw Louis on all fours at the bottom of his bed peering out of a small gap in the door. His hair still needed its morning pat-down.

"What is it?" In the corridor he saw an oldish Chinese man, probably well into his fifties with shaved – probably a grade four – grey hair, performing his morning exercise. Old habits die hard, you see. He was wearing a brown button up cotton shirt with short sleeves like my Granddad used to wear, and beige shorts that stopped just above his knees. Naturally, he wore flip-flops. And there he was doing a kind of strange jog at a mightily slow pace, slower, perhaps, than slow motion itself. The paces he took were very short, and although he lifted his feet higher than he would if he were walking, his thighs were never raised. It was his heavy footsteps that Edson had heard, for this perplexing exercise was not doing an incredible amount for his physique. "Is running that slowly really going to help you get fit?" Edson wondered aloud. For a moment, in silent awe, they observed the slow motion roll of his belly as he lolloped up the corridor.

"Doe-sn't look like it," murmured Louis.

Edson reluctantly withdrew his gaze from the mesmerising floppy bulk, sat on his bunk, and inspected his toenails for any abnormal or excessive growth. They seemed okay, although the nail of the big toe of the right foot looked too thick and white and he began pulling at it with the nail of his forefinger. It was a tough one and it stubbornly refused to yield to his patient attempts at peeling the top off a little. As he considered heaving his entire foot up to his teeth in an effort to give the process a little kick-start, Louis interrupted from above, "I'm blahdy starving!" Edson looked up at the bottom of Louis' bunk and then back at his toe.

"Yeah. I wouldn't mind a bite of breakfast," he admitted, and then, sarcastically and in Neil's faux-cockney, "And you know how I can't function without my morning caffeine, Guv'nor." He couldn't recall Neil ever actually using the word "Guv'nor" but it seemed to fit his speech quite well. With the toenail receiving a stay of execution, Edson dropped his foot to the floor, and looked at the empty bunks. "Looks like we might have the place to ourselves for a while, then?"

"Don't tell Neil. He'll probably suggest him and Jim should move in."

"I wouldn't mind if Jim did,"

"Or Lotte!"

"Goes without saying . . . Do you think there's any way of saving *Jimmy-boy*, though?"

"Dunno. It'd look pretty blahdy obvious, wouldn't it?"

And so they made their way to the dining car, without saying too much. Backpacking is a strange sport in many ways. Apart from co-habitation, for what other reason would you choose to spend vast hours, days, and weeks living your life with one or two other people – even to the point of sharing the same room every night, possibly even in the same *bed*? The close proximity you share is astounding when you consider all the elements: eating meals together; sitting next to each other on every twelve hour train ride; sharing the same water bottles; abandoning most privacies. Perhaps most importantly, joint decisions have to be made on just about *every*thing, from which restaurant to eat at, to which place to visit next, to what time to wake up in the morning. Who could endure such a journey without the occasional tense moment?

Louis was striding again. Even on a train ride lasting six days, thought Edson as he trotted along just behind him, he had to attack every tiny chore with great outward purpose. The carriage was already fairly full when they arrived. Louis swung around the edge of a free table and sat down hard on the lightly padded seat, beaming like a madman as Edson followed suit. "Maybe this train is some kind of obscure health farm," remarked Edson out of nowhere. Louis smiled wider and snorted an intrigued-sounding laugh,

"What do you mean?"

"Well, it's obvious isn't it?" answered Edson, leaning back and folding his arms, with a self-satisfied cheeky smile on his face, "Rich and fat Chinese people come on board for six days. They eat *Lulia Kebab*," of course, pronounced in the by now obligatory Russian accent, like the English idiot out of *'Allo 'Allo*, "They eat and then repeatedly eject the *Lulia Kebab*, they run very slowly up and down some corridors, they eat more noodles and less *Dove* chocolate, and by the time they reach *Mockba* Central Station, they've lost three stone and got their magnificent calf muscles back after all the squatting following their healthy dose of *Lulia Kebab* dysentery. Then they get on a plane and fly home. It's a marvellous idea. I wish I'd thought of it."

"Pure genius . . . Er yeah, coffee and a roll," said Louis as the moustachioed waiter hovered uncertainly at an angle near their table.

"Make that two," said Edson, holding up two fingers. "Spaseeba."

"I suppose the added bonus of this train is that there's no escape. In the ones back home there's always those people who leg it off to the nearest town for a kebab or a sneaky Mars bar. Maybe we should market it. Sell it over the internet or something. The internet's got to be the way forward, I reckon." As Louis finished his sentence a man, probably in his mid-60s, stopped at their table.

"Excuse me chaps. Mind if I join you?"

"Of course," said Louis with a friendly smile, and he shifted up to make room.

"Aah. Thank you. Very kind. The name's Thornley. John Thornley," and offered his hand across the table.

"I'm Edson Shepherd."

"Louis Langley. Nice to meet you." They all shook hands, except for Louis and Edson – they already knew each other. Louis and Edson looked at each other with raised eyebrows. Louis continued, "Were you staying at Irkutsk?"

"Yes, I stayed with a family there for three days."

"How was it? I kept thinking about doing it, but we both went for the straight six days across Asia in the end," asked Louis, motioning to Edson as he spoke.

"They were *absolutely* lovely people, you know, *most* welcoming," he closed his eyes tightly to emphasise the point as he made it, and then propped his chin on his hand. "I mean it was fascinating to taste their life. A whole er," and he made a kind of cupped rounding sign with his hands, "A whole *comm*unity, just built up and living off this huge lake. It's remarkable."

"Yeah, I couldn't believe just how big that lake is," said Edson, and both Louis and John murmured their agreement.

"Astounding," said Louis. The coffee and bread arrived, and John ordered a breakfast of the same. "What do you make of the train, then?"

"Very comfortable, yes. Staff are a bit long-faced, maybe, but it must be a jolly demanding job looking after the likes of us all day and night eh?"

"Bathrooms are a bit chilly," pointed out Edson, immediately wishing he'd made more of a positive contribution.

"They're not that bad – I've been in a lot worse," said Louis predictably.

"Yes, quite," agreed John, before adding conspiratorially with an embarrassed laugh, "They can get bloody nippy, though." Edson smiled at this: an honest reaction in opposition to what Edson saw as the sometimes pointless nature of Louis' calculated stoical stances. "Food's not too bad either – it can't be easy to buy for an indeterminate amount of people for six or seven days."

"Did you have the *Lulia Kebab* when you were on before?" asked Louis, with a hint of a smile, before popping a piece of parched bread into his mouth and chewing awkwardly.

"No, I don't think I've . . ."

"You were one of the lucky ones," said Edson in a deep dark tone.

"What exactly is, what did you call it?"

"*Lulia* Kebab," replied Louis.

"We don't know."

"And we don't think we want to, either." John laughed, and then said, "Still, I've been quite impressed with the borscht, though."

"Oh yeah . . . we'd never knock the borscht!" replied Edson,

"The borscht has been a real life-saver. Before we got on the train we had some feeble plan to live totally on noodles and Ritz biscuits, you know, but I got bored of the noodles after a day, and so did Lou, although he keeps eating them raw which is disturbing me a bit now."

John laughed again, and Edson looked at Louis who was plainly as pleased as he was that this excellent man had deigned to join them for the second half of their trip. John chewed slowly with a similarly delighted look on his face. His eyes, tired, wrinkled and weighed down with age, were almost closed, and his body gently bounced as he laughed quietly. There was something about him that compelled both Edson and Louis to imagine they were in the presence of some kind of *legend*; he exuded a quality that made them feel privileged to have him there, addressing all his attention to *them*. In addition he appeared to be the very embodiment of the personality they had been discussing, imagining, developing over the last few weeks: the British hero, the gentleman abroad, the stoic. The man who had seen the empire drift away, but instead of becoming xenophobic, bitter, and angry, appreciated the right to independence and embraced change, entrepeneurship, individuality. A man of intelligence and a man, in short, fascinated by the world. Everything about him, from his elephant-like face with the large ears and grand, noble nose, to his still-flourishing silvery hair neatly parted on the right hand side, to his elegantly simple checked shirt and slacks, exuded kindness, worldly knowledge, and, well, *comfort*. He gave the kind of amazingly positive first impression you might only experience once or twice in your entire life.

Most of the morning passed as the triumvirate chatted about their travels. Edson and Louis strove to extract as much information as possible from their new friend, finding at each turn that he somehow matched up to their projected idol. But I'm keen that you don't misunderstand me, here. Don't think this was some kind of post-modern appreciation where their perceived admiration amounted to little more than ironic deference or cleverly disguised condescension being exerted by our two heroes. Don't compare it to 'Old Adult at Party Syndrome.' If you are not familiar with OAPS, then let me explain.[*]
OAPS is when an old guy turns up at a party or perhaps in a pub full of

[*] And it's very possible that you haven't heard of OAPS because I made that name up myself, just now, firstly to help illustrate the point and secondly for a bit of comic value. I hope you are as impressed as I am that I've somehow managed to work a clever pun into an acronym.

young people. Despite the fact that under normal circumstances most people at the party wouldn't be in the least bit interested in some random old bloke, the conditions are such that his differences (bigger ears, wrinkly skin, slacks, silver hair) instantly make him 'cool'. Before he knows what is happening, he's surrounded by people chatting to him. Girls fawn over him and flirt with him – affording him the kind of attention many of the boys present would slay dragons for, thereby driving them wild. Which, of course, is exactly why they're doing it. Boys, keen not to be left out of the novelty, rap casually with him about fishing. But at the same time many of the boys and girls will be secretly looking at each other with evil smiles: "Look! He actually thinks we're *interested*!" This is a deplorable practice, if not a particularly regular one, and I'm not saying that any 'young' person who speaks to an 'old' person is taking the piss and exacting some strange perverse pleasure in pretending to like someone they don't. All I'm saying is that our heroes really *were* interested in John Thornley.

Like James, John had relatives in Hong Kong – his son had emigrated there and was working as an accountant for some multinational. John and his wife Jennifer had been visiting him for his birthday. When Louis asked where Jennifer was, John charismatically replied that they both agreed she probably wouldn't enjoy this particular trip, "So I sent her back home on a plane from Beijing. No sense me dragging her half way across the world when she'd rather be at home is there?" If this sounds a touch old-fashioned somehow, it didn't when John said it. His manner was so confident, so sure, and he spoke of his wife with such obvious admiration and love. (Of their long eleven hour haul from the Paris changeover to Hong Kong airport, he said, "I'm not a great fan of flying, but do you know? It was wonderful. Jennifer and I talked the whole way about everything, you know, I couldn't tell you exactly what, but the time just seemed to go. After all these years I'm still stimulated by our conversation. I've been rather lucky, I think!") His honesty and openness, quite the opposite of what you might expect – we're always being told about how closed and emotionless the British, particularly the older members of society, are – was wondrously touching. There wasn't a hint of him believing it was too much for a woman, or her place was back at the house – it was as simple as his explanation – it just wasn't something she wanted to do, so he went alone.

John further endeared himself to Edson when the subject of

football finally arose – as it inevitably does in any decent conversation. John had been a keen Ipswich Town fan while living in Suffolk in the seventies and early eighties. From his conversation, it became obvious that he possessed an impressive wealth of connections in various areas. Yet the recognisable names of people he knew appeared in conversation only in passing (the Dean of the University of East Anglia, and the Chairman of Anglia Television, for example) and it was precisely in this matter of fact way that he mentioned Bobby Robson.

For those of you not interested in football, and don't worry if you're not – Louis went very quiet during this part of the conversation – Bobby Robson is, at the time of writing, manager of Newcastle United, but has been manager (or coach) of Barcelona, PSV Eindhoven, Sporting Lisbon and, of course, England amongst others. However, before he became England manager he was in charge at Ipswich Town, a then-smallish club in the East of England. Whilst there he turned Ipswich from Second Division under-achievers into First Division runners-up (they were only stopped from winning the League by the phenomenal Liverpool side of that era) and brought them glory in European competition. He was responsible for making two of the first foreign signings that are so prevalent in English football today – two masterful midfield players: Arnold Muhren and Frans Thijssen, both from Holland.

Robson is a legend in today's game, and John was now casually reporting what a nice chap he was and what enthusiasm he had for the game. "Absolutely amazing enthusiasm," he said, squeezing his eyes shut again as he emphasised his words, "I mean he was *so* passionate, and approachable too. I think some managers are intimidated by their best players . . . their talent frightens them somehow. Whether they find it difficult to rectify in their minds that the player's talent might be greater than their own, I don't know. But not Robson. He loved working with these players. I mean he *loved* it," and he clamped his eyes again, "I don't whether you've heard of these players, but Muhren, Thijssen, Wark, Butcher . . ."

"Yes! Of course, Mariner as well," Edson replied, eager to make John aware of his own football knowledge.

"Ah, you have! Well, Robson was so *excited* by them. And he was brilliant at spotting their potential. If they were good he could make them better; if they were great he'd make them greater . . . such motivation. You couldn't help but like him."

"So did you meet him a lot?"

"Well, I wasn't great friends with him by any means, but I had a few chats with him after a couple of games, you know. Fascinating." Edson had the distinct impression they'd had more than just a few chats.

"Do you still go now?"

"No, well, we live nearer Norwich now, so I occasionally go down to Carrow Road – sample Delia's pies, you know!"

"I thought Ipswich hated Norwich?" John laughed at this.

"Yes, well, I think I'm past all that now!"

So sparse are the activities on the Trans-Siberian railway that it is dangerously easy to simply while away the hours between meals chatting to fellow travellers in the dining car. In a situation where the only 'real' times of the day are related to either food or sleep, it becomes a case of merely finding the most interesting way of getting from one time to the next. The staff, though, need their space, and so at a couple of indeterminate points during the day Olga and her friends kicked out any loitering, gassing travellers so they could prepare their carriages for the next meal. One of those indeterminate points had now arisen and the blond waiter ushered them out so he could stare out of the window for a bit in peace.

Outside Edson and Louis' room, John suggested that they might meet for dinner later. "Sounds good," agreed Edson.

"Good plan," said Louis, "What kind of cabin are you in?"

"Same as yours," and he bent his head round the door as if to confirm it for himself, "Mmm, four bunks. I thought I'd prefer it with a bit of company."

"Good idea. Have you met anyone interesting?" asked Edson.

"Well, before Irkutsk I was with a couple of guys around your age. One was from Holland, but he spoke pretty good English – a lot of the Dutch do speak excellent English I find – he was going to be a sports teacher I think. Called Iwan. And he was with a friend of his from Holland. Interesting chaps, but er," and he smiled with a hint of embarrassment, or perhaps relish, "They did have an eye for the women – tried very hard with one lovely English girl called Alex, but I don't know whether she was interested."

"And now?" asked Louis.

"Well, I'm with another couple of chaps – James and Neil. James seems like a great chap but Neil's rather strange – I don't like to say it, you know, but he is, a bit." Louis and Edson smiled.

"Oh yeah, we know them. Neil is a bit weird!"

II

Picture the scene. There I am, on a Friday night after work and I'm waiting at Wandsworth Town station, South London, for my train. I'm going to Kingston to meet some friends in a pub called, with a certain obvious cleverness, The Kings Tun[*]. The Tun is part of a chain of those large cavernous pubs that have started to dominate England recently (not that I'm complaining – any place that can offer such incredibly cheap beer is fine by me. I once spent an intoxicating afternoon reading *The Independent* in The Tun when I was supposed to be out delivering leaflets). The rise of these pubs in Britain corresponds directly with the diminishing number of branches of banks and building societies. One day, however, people will be able to buy drinks over the internet like they do their banking nowadays – instantly and at any time. Instead of actual human contact they'll order their pint by email and it'll be delivered immediately by an incredibly efficient courier service (there'll be no traffic to worry about, as everyone's at home!), and they'll chat over the internet using webcams and webmicrophones.

So pubs will have to sell up their ex-banks and new businesses will move in – specifically "retro-banks" where people can go and do their banking in person and meet other real people in the flesh. But soon this novelty will wear off because banks can be so frustrating what with all the queues and the leaflets and the window between you and the teller so you can't quite believe that they can really hear what you're saying and so you shout and everyone hears you begging for an overdraft. Consequently, everyone will go back to the internet again. But by that time "retro-pubs" will have arrived to buy up the old retro-banks and people will go and order drinks at a bar, not by email, and sit and chat with real people, not computer images of real people, and have real drunken bottle fights instead of safe virtual ones. And so it will go on. Forever.

Anyway, picture that scene I mentioned earlier. I arrive handily at the station at about ten to seven – ten minutes before the train is due to arrive. The ticket booth is closed because someone somewhere for some

---

[*] Having actually got off my arse and done a little bit of research (if you can call looking a word up in the dictionary 'research'), I'm pleased to be able to tell you that 'tun' means 'Large cask; measure of liquid'. My thanks to the Collins Gem English Dictionary of 1987 (pocket size).

reason decided that the times when the least customers are boarding trains are the times when it is most useful to have the booth open. So evenings and early mornings when people are travelling to and from work, it's closed. In the day, when only truant kids (who don't buy tickets anyway) and old people (who have yearly passes because they're so bloody organised) and night-shift workers (who are asleep) and other people who aren't at work (who amount to no more than three people a day at Wandsworth Town station) might need tickets, it's open – and a cushy shift it is too.

Fortunately, I have a decent amount of change, so I go back down the stairs and through a short tunnel until I arrive at the ticket machine unhelpfully and stupidly, placed about two minutes walk from the platforms. It's out of order, which I'd failed to notice on the way in. Probably because its out of order state is not particularly out of the ordinary. I return to the platform to find the Permit to Travel machine, where you can pay part or all of your fare if you have no other options available. On this machine I notice a small but cheerfully shining bright red light. Above the light there is some miniature writing which says, paradoxically:

"If this light is on, then the machine is out of order."

Why isn't it the other way around? I am left with no option other than to *not* buy a ticket. At this station there is a single small monitor high above the stairs that is supposed to give information about any train delays. It never gives any information as to which train will be arriving when and at which platform, yet on Platform 1 trains could be going on any of three different routes. On this windy and cold February night it is displaying the following message:

"Welcome to South West Trains. We are sorry but this screen is currently out of order. Please listen for announcements. SWT apologises for this inconvenience."

Again, how can it be out of order yet still be *in order enough* to explain that it's out of order? And, of course, there is no member of the apologetic SWT staff at the station to give the announcements we're listening for. They were there earlier when the trains were running fine and carrying only one person in each fucking carriage, though.

So I waited on an icy bench and, to my great surprise, a train arrived at only just after seven. I hopped on and soon my nose was buried in the newspaper. After about twenty minutes I looked up and realised that I was on the wrong train. We had just stopped at Chiswick, which is not on the route to Kingston. Just before the doors closed I managed to dash off the train. I legged it over the bridge, and waited for a train to take me back in the opposite direction. At about seven-thirty one appeared, and I rode it for ten minutes to Barnes where the split in the rail occurs and where my train had gone the wrong way; or had gone the right way but was the wrong train. Whatever. Barnes has little cover and by then the rain was lashing down heavily – it was the kind of cold rain that won't turn to sleet or snow or hail, it's just very, very cold water that makes your face hurt with the ferocity of its low temperature. All I had with me was a flimsy jacket that provided neither warmth nor protection, and water ran down my neck and under my clothes while simultaneously seeping through the crappy summer material of the jacket to dampen my jumper and shirt. Eventually the cold and the damp made it under my skin by osmosis and if the skies had cleared and a frost had developed I might have been in serious danger of turning into some kind of fantastic human icicle. Fortunately, though, it merely continued to piss down like a bastard.

To kill some time I tried to find a ticket machine. Barnes didn't seem to have a booth or any guards or even a crappy monitor to tell me that it couldn't help because it was out of order. This was annoying to say the least because there were three platforms, and I wasn't sure which one was the one where trains going to Kingston stop. Finally I found a ticket machine, but it didn't have a button for Kingston. I found another one. And, YES! It did have a Kingston button! At last! But, of course, this machine was broken. I returned to the platform and waited for over forty minutes in vain for a Kingston train. Well, perhaps one of the three trains that did stop on my platform was going to Kingston, but who knows? No-one was there to tell me and they all had the same final destination on the front as the one I had wrongly boarded earlier, and I wasn't willing to take the risk of returning to Chiswick again.

At eight-fifteen I started to lose it and, in a tantrum, threw my bag on the floor. It landed, rather predictably, in a puddle. As I was repeatedly and violently kicking it up against a wall, as if in some way it was to blame, I heard a nasty cracking sound and I remembered with dismay that my walkman was inside. I was about to irresponsibly boot the whole thing onto the tracks and perhaps follow after it myself, when a train going back to Clapham Junction pulled up. In utter desperation, I got on, knowing that at Clapham Junction there are all sorts of signs, monitors, machines, overhead coverings, on-site coffee shops that are actually open, and moderately helpful staff who can tell me where to go. At eight-thirty I arrived at Clapham Junction, having passed back through Wandsworth Town. I bought a ticket from a pleasant teller. I found with ease the platform from which to catch my train. At eight forty-five I boarded a train bound for Kingston. At eight forty-eight we stopped at Wandsworth Town. At eight fifty-eight we stopped at Barnes. At nine fifteen I arrived at Kingston and made my way to the pub, tired, stressed, angry and in a state of panic that I might miss the deadline of nine-thirty for the pound-a-pint offer. I just made it.

Now, this detour I've made from our main path – or rail track, if you will – does have a point other than allowing me to indulge in a nice long whinge. Although that would be reason enough. The great thing about whinging within a book is that no-one can interrupt. You might turn the page, but that's it. The point is that I wanted to emphasise the difference between train journeys in Britain and the Trans-Siberian railway journey. The stress, the anger, the smell, the delays, the odd obnoxious passenger and any of the other hundreds of things I could sit here, right now, and complain about – none of them apply to the Trans-Siberian.

One of the main reasons for this is the cabin facility. If you're lucky enough to have enough cash to luxuriate yourself, you can even get a cabin just for yourself. Simply load up with noodles, biscuits, chocolate and other nutritious goodies, and you barely need set foot outside your cabin for the entire six days. You could probably just emerge during the night to collect hot water from the samovar and succeed in achieving complete solitude for an entire six days. Imagine what you could accomplish in those 144 hours or so of solitary confinement! Go on! Just imagine. Even if you were not so hermitically (yeah, like 'hermetically' but different) inclined, any irritatingly drunken passenger or other objectionable can easily be avoided by simply retiring to your cabin. You could argue that if you were caught in a carriage in Britain with an annoying fellow traveller you could always get up and move away. But who would risk that? It's like leaving to go to the toilet in the middle of a stand-up performance by a particularly vitriolic comic. Walk out, make yourself known, and he'll crucify you for no better reason than you're in his line of vision and you broke his flow.

On the Trans-Siberian the mentality is different. Not that there's any shortage of alcoholic beverages (at least not at first, and depending on how many Russian lorry drivers or European boys bent on playing juvenile drinking games there are on board), but there's a certain protocol that is observed. If you want to stay on after dinner and drink, you're more than welcome to – if you're not into that kind of thing or your head still feels like it's being sawn open by a rusty hacksaw from the night before, then you can simply retire to your cabin. Or if you want a quieter drink then you can simply purchase a few bevvies and retire to your room. The only people who *really* suffer are the staff, but at least they're getting paid.

On the very afternoon in our story the train stopped for well over two hours at a station. It may have been the case that this was always going to happen, but the timetables helpfully provided in each carriage were almost impossible for dumb Westerners to decipher. Even if someone had managed to make sense of them, the continuing doubt as to exactly what time it was meant that any comprehension would immediately be rendered obsolete. Cast your mind back to my own impotent frustration, fury and incredulity at the lack of trains at Barnes. Now contrast that with Edson and Louis and the rest of the temporary inhabitants of the Trans-Siberian. There they all are, sleeping, reading, writing diaries, discussing the world. Stress barely exists there. What's more, for the train to be noticeably late it would have to be so by about a day. There has probably never been a paying passenger on board the train who ever knew exactly what time of day the train was supposed to arrive in Moscow. If it was due at noon but didn't arrive until six, who would notice? Taken over the course of six days these six hours would barely mean a thing. Proportionally speaking, it would be the equivalent of, hang on, let me get a pen and paper . . . a train trip lasting an hour being just *two and a half minutes* late.

Using the Trans-Siberian, even a fool can get from one end of Asia to another via a single journey – no stops to miss, no detours to be made, no underground to negotiate, no substitute slow buses from the 1930s swaying precariously around tightly curling country lanes. It's more like a cruise than a train journey. Only without dancing girls. Or a casino. Or amazing restaurants and shops. And it's not on water. And you don't get to go ashore to take in the sights . . . but it *does* last a few days in which you're virtually always travelling and it gives you time to relax and legitimately do absolutely bugger all.

III

Edson was reading *Garp* voraciously, devouring pages like a velociraptor eating an irritating child in Jurassic Park. But he had also drunk a couple of cups of jasmine tea, and was becoming desperate for the toilet. At the next paragraph, he placed the book face down on the bunk and told Louis he would be back in a few minutes. There was no answer. Louis was asleep – failing once more in his resolve to 'get off the pot.'

Edson walked quickly, but not so quickly as to lose dignity, to the end of the carriage and the bathroom. It was locked. He pushed his ear to the door and heard rustling noises resembling a newspaper being carefully refolded. If this hypothesis was correct the chances of gaining quick access seemed slim. A few seconds later he moved on to the next bathroom – each carriage had one at each of its ends so it wasn't far to go. Engaged again! So he walked a little faster to the next one. Engaged. And the next. Occupied. Was everyone still suffering from Lulia Kebab? Finally, the toilet at the end of this carriage was vacant and, with much relief, he stepped inside.

He strolled back towards his cabin in an altogether more refined fashion. Idly, he glanced out of the window at a derelict-looking factory from which fleecy grey smoke was emanating. It hung around in the still air, bored and menacing like a group of under-age teenagers on a street corner. "Hey Edson!" Lotte? He went back a pace and looked through an open door into a cabin.

"Oh. Hiya. How's it going?" She was sitting with her feet on the bunk and her back resting against the wall at the far end. Although Dorte wasn't there it was evident that they were sharing, and they had gone a class above himself and Louis as there were only two bunks. Today Lotte was wearing a rounded, small, smooth silver stud just below her bottom lip. It seemed a lot safer than that pointy one from the other day. She wore some oldish light blue jeans and an immaculate plain white t-shirt. All Edson's white t-shirts had turned a shade darker, more of a light grey, since he had started travelling. He stood uncertainly at the doorway.

"Yeah. I'm fine. What are you doing?"

"Er, I thought I might have . . . left my jumper . . . in the, er, dining car." Somehow 'I was desperate for a piss,' didn't seem appropriate.

"Oh. Where is it then?"

"Oh it's er . . . it's not there. Must be in my bag somewhere. I can't be bothered looking any more."

"I love that English phrase, "I can't be bothered!" So funny," she laughed, " . . .You *can* come in. It's okay." Edson stepped inside and sat at the end of her bunk, next to her feet, but right on the edge so he didn't appear too comfortable. He smiled at her and then looked at his feet.

"Thanks," he found his gaze kept travelling to her stud and so to her mouth. All the amateur psychology he'd ever accidentally read or seen on television started whirring through his head, and he started panicking about whether he looked relaxed enough, or if looking at her mouth was going to make her think he was thinking about something other than their stilted conversation. Even if he was, which he was, he didn't want her to know that. "So . . ." he struggled, "What're you reading?" and he gestured at a book lying on her stomach.

"It's by a Danish author, Chris Skov, in English it's called, er, Walking With the Giants maybe . . . it's about travelling in the mountains in Nepal – is that how you say it?"

"Neh-paul, yes," said Edson, "Is it good?"

"It's okay. I'd rather be there . . . Reading about it isn't enough. I have to, er, *experience* it."

"Do you like being on the train?" Edson sat back a bit, relaxing his shoulders, and then worried that doing that might make him look all hunched like Mr Burns out of *The Simpsons*, and he straightened his back up again.

"Yeah. It's pretty good. I don't like the food much, though," and she smiled. Edson wondered whether smiling made the stud wobble around in the flesh of her lip.

"Yeah. It's pretty bad!" She produced some tobacco and some cigarette paper. Edson watched as she carefully tapped some tobacco into the paper and then delicately rolled it up, "Have you been smoking for long?"

"About a year. Last summer I was working at a chicken factory. It was very bad, so I started smoking. Everyone was smoking there. People who smoked seemed to get more breaks, so I started."

"What's a chicken factory?"

"We had to make dead chickens ready for the company to sell. So we took, er," she made a kind of grabbing and pulling motion with her hand.

"You took the guts out of the chicken?" Edson screwed his face up.

"Yes. What is 'guts'?"

"Like the inside of the chicken – blood and stuff," his face was still screwed up and Lotte was visibly enjoying his reaction.

"Yes."

"Why did you do it?"

"They pay good money because no-one wants do it, and I needed the money," she shrugged, "It's okay." She looked around and about her. "Aaah! Where is?" and said something in Danish while mimicking the action of a lighter with her thumb and forefinger. "I think Dorte has it."

"Where is Dorte?" Lotte bent her head to look on the floor.

"Er, she's, oh! Look, over there in the . . ." and Lotte pointed at Dorte's bunk, "In her . . ." Edson got up and moved towards where she was pointing.

"Where?"

"The, er, the string," Edson shrugged. "On the wall." He looked on the wall and there was a kind of pouch made of squared elasticised material, that you could leave a book or a magazine in, and there, on top of a book, was the lighter. Edson retrieved it and attempted to light Lotte's cigarette like a good gentleman should. Unfortunately she wasn't expecting that and as he bent towards her with the flame burning she reached out to take it from him. The flame and her fingers seemed to converge for a second and suddenly she withdrew her hand very quickly.

"Oh God! Sorry! Are you okay?"

"Yeah, it didn't touch me," and she took the lighter from him and lit up.

"Are you sure?"

"Of course." She lit up, took a puff, and blew smoke through a smile towards Edson, who was still standing close to her. Edson, feeling distinctly gawky, returned to his seat.

"So . . . where is Dorte then? I haven't seen her recently. Is she was looking for Neil or something?"

"I don't think so."

"Don't you like Neil?"

"Do you?"

"Well . . . Louis says that if you start talking badly about someone behind their back it just eats you up inside and does no good to yourself. You know, bad karma."

"He *is* a fuckhead, though, isn't he?" Edson looked shocked, and then realised she meant Neil and not Louis.

"Er, that's a bit harsh, I suppose, but well . . ." he scratched an imaginary itch on his nose.

"Come on," and she sat up, warming to the task.

"Okay. He can be a bit annoying . . . I thought you really liked him . . . you're always hanging out with him whenever I see you . . . apart from now."

"No. He hangs around with *us*."

"Mmm. I see . . . I, er, I thought it was, er, me you didn't like."

"Why did you think that?" and she looked at him through the smoke. Her half-smile seemed a little superior, as if she was studying him, or challenging him.

"I don't know . . . you never said a word when we asked you take that photo when we got on the train."

"I didn't know you."

"Yeah, but you could have been a little more friendly," Edson smiled and he felt a bit of confidence as he sensed he might push her onto the back foot a little.

"We're friends now."

"Fair enough. Do you know that other guy, Damon?"

"The one with the . . ." and she stroked her chin in a manner that reminded Edson of David Baddiel talking about Jimmy Hill.

"Yeah – he doesn't, er, he doesn't speak much," he ventured.

"No, I haven't spoken with him, but, er, Dorte said he told her that he worked in Moscow for six months."

"Really?"

"Yeah . . . in a bar, I think." There was a moment of silence.

"Ah, dear . . ." Edson made a show of glancing all around the room, and then at his own feet. Smoke was drifting between them and Edson was suddenly reminded of being inside the tent of a fortune-teller at a country fair. "A-n-y-way, I, er, better get back to my cabin . . . Louis' probably wondering where I am. See you later," and he got up to leave, "See you at dinner, maybe?"

"Okay. See you later."

IV

"Guess who's just had a nice little chat with the gorgeous Lotte, then?" said Edson as casually and modestly as he could (i.e. – not very) on his return to his cabin. There was no answer. "Lou?" But Louis was still asleep. "Arse."

Edson lay on his bunk analysing the encounter. It was great news that Lotte invited him in – he hadn't seen her and she could easily have pretended that she hadn't seen him. But maybe she had caught him staring at her before, or noticed his increasing interest in her lip-piercing, and had decided to have a bit of fun – make him a bit nervous while simultaneously giving her ego a boost as he squirmed uncomfortably in her alluring presence. But he'd held his end up in the conversation, even if their chat was a bit stilted, and he'd done the gentlemanly thing in retrieving her lighter. And it was great to emerge victorious in a comparison with Neil . . . although there'd be something very wrong if he hadn't, surely. Bit embarrassing about almost burning her finger though. Then again, maybe she really did like him, and invited him inside in the hope he might make a move. He'd hardly ever made a move or *put the moves on*, as they say in America, in his life, unless the girl was practically erecting a large billboard with the words "KISS ME NOW!" written in ten foot high red lettering.

He'd picked up *Garp* in the middle of these thoughts and had managed to read about four pages without taking in a sentence of it. How is it possible to read and yet think about something completely different at the same time, he wondered? It isn't like watching television: reading isn't a passive thing – you have to make an effort to do it, yet despite definitely reading every word of four pages, as he read it back only a few lines seemed faintly familiar. He tried to convince himself that it didn't matter; that she didn't fancy him; that this was all adolescent, childish thinking and in a few days he'd never see her again anyway. It was like Louis always said in situations like this: "It's not even worth thinking about." Which said it all really. Except whether it's worth thinking about or not doesn't actually stop you from thinking about something – indeed, the very act of trying to not think about something means you are thinking about it. We're all just hostages to our minds will, aren't we? Or are we? I mean, that implies that we are simply a body without control over the mind, but surely we are our own mind, and the body is just a vessel carrying it. Is that right? Ah, amateurish philosophy.

An hour or so later, during which time Edson had drifted in and out of his book, dozed off, listened to Squeeze singing about someone called Daphne on his walkman, and thought more about things he was trying not to, Louis awoke. "Uuhh," he went. It was a noise he often made when waking up as a way of announcing his recovery of consciousness, like a cat meowing as it enters a room so everyone will look at him.

"Alrt," said Edson, deftly picking up his book again in a quick-thinking effort to look productive.

"Alrt . . . What time is it?"

"I dunno . . . have we passed any time zones today?"

"I dunno."

"Must be getting on for dinner time, though. Had a nice sleep?"

"Mmm. Waste of blahdy time, though."

"I've, er, I've been reading and stuff," go on Louis – ask *what* stuff. There was silence for a few seconds, "Yeah, went for a . . . for a walk, you know?"

"Yeah?"

"Yeah." Silence again. Oh, for God's sake, "Yeah, I, er, bumped into Lotte actually . . . Had a bit of a chat."

"What, in the dining car?"

"No, in her room actually – just me and her, you know?"

"What happened?"

"Not much. Just had a chat . . . lit her cigarette . . . talked about Neil a bit and she mentioned that *Dame-o* told Dorte that he's worked in *Mockba* before – I don't know whether that's true or not – sounds like he's done everything,"

"No. *Neil's* done everything, and better than Damon."

"Yeah, you're probably right there."

"So nothing happened then?"

"No."

"Not even a cup of tea?"

"No."

"Well done."

"Thanks . . . I er, I think she fancies me, though," he said in a nonchalant way. Louis knew he didn't mean it.

"So, what's the plan then?"

"I don't know, I'll probably never see her again in a couple of days, and I don't really think she's interested, so I'll probably just leave it."

"I meant about dinner."

"Oh . . . sorry. I thought John was going to knock for us . . . or were we going to meet him there?"

"So you don't actually know, then?"

"No."

"Good plan about Lotte, though. It's not even worth thinking about."

V

To dinner, then, and the part of the day where no-one could feel guilty for idly sitting around eating, drinking and dissecting the world's problems because doing so was a just reward for surviving another hard day at their Trans-Siberian office. And a veritable party had gathered, too. On one table sat John Thornley, regally beaming at his company. Edson was next to him, trying not to worry about the menu or look at Lotte too much, Louis was opposite John and was scanning the menu closely. James was next to him graphically explaining to John just how horrible the Lulia Kebab had been. The words 'putrid' and 'decomposed' featured heavily, but to gain a clearer picture of his description, just do what I did and consult a thesaurus. On a table across the gangway, Neil sat opposite Lotte and Dorte, switching his comments between their conversation and James's, desperate not to miss anything. Lotte was smoking and she smiled at Edson as he accidentally caught her eye. Dorte stared at Neil, looking bored and blowing great whirling gusts of smoke in his direction.

"Excuse me," said John, his great voice rising without effort or fuss above the general hubbub, "We'd, er, we'd like seven vodkas, and seven beers, please. Thank you. These are all on me, by the way."

"No, you don't have to do that John," said Edson. Characteristically screwing his eyes, John waved away the protest.

"No, it's a thank you for making me feel welcome here, me being the new boy and all that."

"Well, that's very kind, thanks," relented Edson.

"Any of you skunks worked out what's on the menu, then?" asked Neil.

"As long as it's not Lulia Kebab, I don't care," said James and he picked up the cardboard sheet to find out. He immediately put it down again, though, and said, "You know what, though? I'd love a pizza . . . yeah, a really big one, a Fiorentina, with a huge egg and extra spinach, ahh," and he closed his eyes to think about it.

"You're right there, Jimmy-boy. A McDonalds wouldn't go down too badly either, extra large fries and a double bacon Big Mac," Neil's eyes widened and he stared at the girls with a great lip-smacking smile on his face, almost as if he were imagining Lotte as the fries and Dorte as the Big Mac. Perhaps James was the ketchup . . . *any*way . . .

"Yeah, well, the pizza sounds good, but I eat pretty much anything," said Louis, with superiority and without looking up.

"Including dried noodles," commented Edson and James screwed his face up in apparent nausea.

"Oh, yeah, dried noodles are the dog's nads!" laughed Louis.

"Hey-oop, 'ere come thy drinks," Neil informed everyone in a strange approximation of a Yorkshire accent.

"Okay! started John, lifting his small vodka glass into the air, "Everyone ready?" the waiter hovered, perhaps expecting an imminent food order, but as everyone raised a glass he made the decision to dart past and speak to some other customers further down the carriage. "I suppose we should toast this beautiful train. Cheers!"

"Cheers!" echoed everyone, and they all began chinking glasses.

"Don't miss anyone!" said John, and he leant over to clink with Neil and then Lotte. Dorte was a different proposition, however, as they both couldn't quite reach far enough. In the end, Edson took John's glass from him and performed the chinking himself before passing it back. "Okay, after three, and don't forget to put out the fire . . . one . . . two . . . three!" and they all threw the liquid with unnecessary violence into their mouths, and then grabbed their beers for a long inelegant slurp.

"Aaahhh!" exaggerated Neil. Everyone else grinned through the adrenalin.

"Right, what about another?" croaked James, and then he cleared his throat to add, "I'll get them in."

Twenty minutes later and Edson had followed James's round with one of his own, although his lack of rubles meant he'd had to borrow the money from Louis, and finally Lotte also pitched in with a round. At this point it was decided that they should probably lay off the *wodkas*. At least until the end of the meal anyway. Once again just one of the meals had a price written in faint pencil next to it, and tonight they were to be treated to pork chops with potatoes and carrots.

"If I have any more *wodkas* I won't be able to taste anything anyway," remarked James.

"That's what I was hoping for," remarked Lotte.

"So, what's everyone got planned once they leave Moscow? – I'm flying home after a few days, myself," said John.

"Me too," replied James.

"Yeah, I'm a bit upset about that Jamie. We could have carried our little odyssey on a bit further couldn't we? Perhaps headed down to *München*, eh? Or," and he nodded at Lotte and Dorte, sporting a smile dangerously approaching a leer, "Maybe even Copenhagen." Lotte laughed dutifully.

"Yeah, shame," replied Jamie.

"So where are you going, Neil?" asked Edson, hoping for plans dissimilar to his and Louis'.

"Kiev, probably. Then I'll probably see what the best way to get to Germany is from there. Don't mention the war though! Hya, Hya! *Fawlty Towers* was fantastic wasn't it? Probably a bit before your time, though, Eddie. Making plans is a bit boring though, I reckon – you never know what's going to happen at any time when you're travelling," Edson expected another leery smile here, but surprisingly it never came and instead Neil nipped off on a tangent. "I got really stoned in Thailand for about six days in a row once. I hooked up with this Scottish chick, and when I finally came out of my trip, because we were constantly on the shit for days, I realised I was in Taiwan! I don't even remember how I got there, or why I went apart from blindly following this Scottish girl. Leslie her name was. Lovely voice." He leant forward on his forearms, his monobrow as joined and black as ever, and looked round with a devilish smile, waiting for some reaction.

"How did you get a visa for Taiwan in such a state, though, Neil? Or did the Thai one cover it?" asked James without looking up from the close examination he was performing on his fingernails.

"That's just it! I don't remember . . . Maybe we sneaked in, who knows?" and his nasty grin flickered for a moment.

"What about you, Edson?" asked John Thornley.

"No, I've, er I've never . . . take-oh! . . ." and the penny dropped, "St Petersburg, Prague and home, all by train, probably, if we can. Something like that, isn't it Lou?"

"Definitely Prague, yeah. We might have to go via Warsaw or something.'

"Prague? I hadn't thought of that . . . That's not a bad plan, dudes!" And suddenly Louis and Edson were seriously entertaining the notion that the Neil Experience might last longer than the next two days. Neil shifted to the end of his bench so he was almost facing Edson.

"Yeah, but you want to go to Kiev, don't you?" ventured Edson.

"Well . . . aha! The rations! Tuck in girls!" and he shoved the two plates of dull looking food that had been placed on their table towards them. The blond waiter turned and took two more plates from Side-Parting, who then returned to the kitchen. Very quickly the two waiters returned with three more plates. John waited for everyone to start and then began eating himself. Louis attacked the food heartily. James poked at the chop with his fork and watched it bounce off as if it were some amazing dead pig trampoline.

"So . . . you've, er, you've *got* to go to Kiev, then?" but Edson's second attempt at clearing up this confusion was rudely cut off.

"Mm-Mm! That's a pretty fucking good pork chop!" he said in an American accent, modifying a quotation by John Travolta's character in *Pulp Fiction.**

"Yeah, it's pretty nice," said Lotte, who certainly seemed keener on this than the stroganoff she had picked at a couple of days earlier. All this left Edson in a something of a difficult situation. If he were to ask his Kiev question for a third time he would seem a little over-anxious to know the answer. A far more sensible plan would surely be to divert for a moment and ask Lotte and Dorte where they might be going.

"But you're definitely going to Kiev, though, Neil?"

"I wouldn't say definitely. I'd never say definitely. As I said, Eddie, never make concrete plans, know what I mean?" his words were muffled as his head was bent low as he chewed on the cud-like well-done pig flesh.

"What about you girls over there?" asked John.

"I think we'll probably go back to Scandinavia by train, maybe go to St Petersburg as well," replied the hitherto quiet Dorte.

"Were you not tempted to do a bit of travelling in Russia, John?" asked Edson. John paused a moment while he patiently chewed on a piece of meat.

"Well, I'd have loved to of course, but, er, commitments at home, you see?"

"Family?" ventured Louis.

"Well, no, actually. Although I've been retired for a couple of years now I'm still pretty busy with other projects – there's an almshouse in Norwich that we're looking after, and I also do a bit for St John Ambulance. That's really why I've got to get back."

"Oh? What do you do with St John Ambulance?" asked Louis.

"Well in particular I support a special eye hospital that St John established in Jerusalem over a century years ago. We're always sending people out to lend a bit of moral support. It's been a real achievement

---

* *Pulp Fiction* is a film made in 1994 by Quentin . . . oh, you knew? Fair enough.

because facilities out there are so limited and the kind of treatment we can offer just isn't readily available there like it is in Britain."

Throughout the evening small subset-like conversations had constantly taken place, as is usual amongst a group larger than about three or four, yet John seemed to be able to sustain the attention of the whole group without obviously demanding it. But for a few seconds no-one said anything. Perhaps they were in fear of dragging the conversation down from the plateau at which John had just effortlessly placed it. John piled some vegetables onto the back of his fork and bent forward to devour them.

"I honestly don't know much about what St John Ambulance do, actually," admitted Edson.

"Yeah, it's one of those things you've always been aware of, but never known much about," concurred Louis.

"Like girls?" quipped Edson, smiling.

"Yeah, *good* one," replied Louis.

"Well, it's *mainly* first aid, of course," put in John.

"I was just going to say first aid," said Neil.

"I could see you were about to open your mouth," murmured James, and took a sip of his beer.

"What?" asked Neil.

"Nothing," said James, a little too quickly.

"But this hospital's achievements are quite astounding," John leant his fork on the side of his plate, "The staff work in the most incredibly difficult conditions you could imagine because of the political climate. The hospital is in Jerusalem, but the kind of facilities they provide are extremely rare, so the area they cover is massive, you know, it spans Jerusalem, Gaza *and* the West Bank."

"So people have to travel a long way to get treatment?" asked Louis.

"Well," started John, chewing doggedly like a herbivore on a particularly fatty piece of pork (which isn't very herbivorous, but I'm sure you get the point), " . . . more to the point are the problems that people encounter while *making* the journey, rather than it's actual length. There are road blocks along the way and they need all sorts of special passes and permissions and . . . and . . . well, it's just a forest of red tape, you know."

Edson tucked in, keeping his gaze as much as possible on John, but he could hear the other table already drifting onto another subject. "I read one terrible story about a girl who was six months old the first time she visited the hospital," continued John, "The doctor said she had a slight squint and surgery would be required in the future. But because her family lived in Gaza they were unable to get a permit to take her for the operation for three years – a year late for her appointment. By this time there was no travel either into or out of Israel from and to Gaza, so her Mother had to apply for a Palestinian passport to get to Jordan. She was forced to leave her other two small children alone in Gaza.

"She went to Amman and then Hebron before finally arriving in Jerusalem where luckily the hospital was able to operate on her eye and keep her in for a few days. But they still had this awful journey back to Gaza to face, and the orthoptists weren't able to examine her again for another few months, although fortunately the operation had been a success. But just think about that: something that would be routinely corrected back in Britain, a simple operation, you see a doctor, make an appointment, go to it and under decent conditions have your eye seen to. Yet the same thing there took years to resolve partly because the facilities weren't readily available, but partly because the whole operation was hindered to an unacceptable extent by the political climate."

Edson, sitting next to the gangway, had become increasingly aware of a different strand of conversation taking place behind him. Because he found John fascinating, he couldn't help wondering what else Neil could be talking about. He kept feeling his ears prick back, cat-like, as he periodically heard an odd word or phrase and it was becoming increasingly distracting. "Prague" he heard. This set him off wondering and worrying if Neil was debating whether to accompany Louis and Edson to the Czech Republic. Then, "Kiev". Against his will his ears strained for more information. Louis was asking John how the hospital was funded and Edson tried hard to focus.

" . . . fortunate enough to collect a great deal of money from legacies, although we can never rely solely upon them of course, and from any good form from our endowment fund and obviously from more general donations."

"That's amazing that you collect enough to keep an entire hospital running," observed James. There was a loud hyaena laugh behind them, and Neil screeched, "Oh, yeah, plenty of ac-*eed*!"

"Mmm, it's an astounding achievement. We've even started sponsoring nurse training as well which costs something like nine thousand a year." Edson heard both Dorte and Lotte laugh, at what he didn't know – Neil had apparently lowered his voice. He wanted to flick his head round, but was afraid of insulting John. It was excruciating, and he was furious with himself for even caring what they were talking about. He tried to block it out . . . but what was that? Did he say 'prostitute'? " . . . We're already starting to do many more of the smaller operations in Gaza which is *absolutely vital*, purely because access to Jerusalem can be so difficult."

"And is the sponsorship working . . . well?" asked Edson, trying to involve himself in the conversation.

"Even better than we could have hoped," and he popped a piece of carrot into his mouth to finish his meal. "Our last nurse came top of her class at Bethlehem University." Edson nodded and leant back in his chair, tired of chewing pork. As John finished his sentence Edson thought he heard Lotte say "lighter" (was she relating the embarrassing story from earlier?) he panicked and turned his head, but almost immediately John said, "Edson?" *Damn.* He turned back.

"Sorry?"

"You *haven't* been on a first aid course, have you?" said Louis, clearly repeating himself.

"Er . . ." Edson looked at Louis and in swift succession swung his head back to Neil's table then back to John, and back to Neil's table and then back to Louis again as he tried not to lose the thread of either conversation. This only succeeded in confusing himself further. "Er . . . n-no . . . my brother has, though."

"Oh really? He's not here, though, *is* he, Edson?" said Louis with a snile (that's a half smile and half snarl – it's a bit like the word 'Chunnel' which people use as a shortened version of 'Channel Tunnel.' I invented the word 'Chunnel' back in the 80s when the idea was first being seriously mooted. I only invented the word 'Snile' a minute ago, though). Edson replied via the medium of a sardonic smile, and then continued.

"Actually, doing a first aid course is something I've always meant to do. I remember seeing a man keel over in the street a few years ago. There weren't that many people around and I ran up to him, and he'd obviously had some kind of mild heart attack or something – he wasn't unconscious – but I got someone in the shop he was lying outside to phone for an ambulance, which was fine. But I didn't know what else to do, and suddenly all these people were appearing out of nowhere and crowding round and blustering about, until one guy with his chest all puffed up started going "'Scuse me, I'm a first aider . . ."

(Sorry, I just want to break in here to say that I find the words "first aider" weird. Why do people say it? "Aider" isn't even a word. Why don't they just say, "I know first aid"? It's almost like they're claiming to be a member of some mysterious new healing religion:

"I'm a Christian."

"Oh, really? I'm a First Aider myself – you know, my hands have healing powers."

"Oh, I learnt first aid, as well, I was qui-"
(rude interruption)

"Ah, but you're not a *first aider* though, are you? You're a Christian who knows *first aid*. That's different"
I'm sure you see my point.)

". . . let me through.' And the crowd parted and he had it well under control, and I just thought, 'What's the point?' and went to have my hair cut. I wished I could have done a bit more though." He heard a great cackling laugh and gleeful applause from Neil. At first Edson thought he was the butt of the mirth, but interspersed with the laughter Neil giggled,

"On the *cur*tain?! Classic!"

"?" thought Edson.

Neil was wiping an imaginary tear from his eye with the hem of his greying T-shirt with unnecessary exaggeration. Dorte was also, uncharacteristically, laughing – so much so that she was having trouble rolling a new cigarette. Edson turned his head back towards John as he heard a glass lightly thud on the table. "Well, I could do with another – is everyone joining me?"

"Oh, come on John," protested Edson, "You've already got a round, I'll get these . . . er, Lou, you couldn't lend me a few more *Rubes*, could you? I'll have to get some when we get to *Mockba*."

"I'll get 'em, don't worry," said Louis in mock-weary fashion, "Is everyone having one then?" Louis called out to the party-table.

"Ayyy," replied Neil in a reasonable attempt at impersonating *The Fonz*, and then added, "Does a bear shit in the woods?" Edson had always hated this particular turn of phrase that was probably quite funny the first time someone made it up, but had become redundant and irritating because of it's frequency and because people like Neil still thought it was original and funny.

"So . . . have you actually visited the hospital before, John?"

asked James.

"Well, as a matter of fact I have – it's quite an experience," he replied with a broad smile.

"Quite impressive, then?" put in Louis.

"Well, of course, the hospital is a real triumph with some incredibly dedicated staff, but the whole experience of actually *getting to* the hospital was pretty unforgettable. I mean, whenever anyone from St John goes out there they always take some supplies for the hospital because they're so hard to come by out there, and we save money on postage as well. So in my bag I had various bits and pieces of equipment, and amongst them were a few knives for some of the surgical equipment. At Heathrow I declared them as not being my own, and that caused no end of problems. I was immediately subjected to an intense interrogation by three officers, and I wished I had just lied a little and said they *were* my own. I did know what was in the package, so I was perhaps being a little too specific. At one point I thought they weren't even going to let me on the plane – they probably thought I was some old duffer who'd been fooled into carrying the thing – it's not like I look like a terrorist, is it?"

"Oh, I dunno, John, you have got a shifty look about you," joked Louis, his hand holding the tip of his chin and his eyes squinting at John as if studying his features closely.

"Yes, yes, I suppose so," laughed John, waving away the views with a flip of his hand. "But fortunately, their methods weren't very sophisticated, or, at least, they didn't seem particularly so to me. I tried to explain that I was just a respectable old gentleman and told them that I was a retired senior executive of a major worldwide bank. But immediately they asked why I wasn't travelling first class! Which I hardly thought had very much to do with whether I was a terrorist or not! I explained I was from Norwich, but they saw this as suspicious too, and one of them who clearly had little grasp of basic English geography said that Norwich was in the North, so why wasn't I travelling from Manchester? Still, eventually I was allowed to continue my journey."

"That's quite frightening," said Edson.

"I know my Mum was really paranoid about me being persuaded to carry some package to China for someone, or someone slipping it in my bag or something, so I'd get arrested in China for drug trafficking or something," added Louis.

"I'm always panicking that someone will slip something into my pack when I'm not watching or something . . . I mean, you hear about these people . . . they're not always teenagers either . . . and loads of them that get arrested say they had no idea that the stuff was there, and . . ." stumbled James.

"Well, they would say that, though, wouldn't they?" said Edson, cynically.

"Doesn't mean it's not true, though," argued Louis.

"N-no, but you do wonder."

"Oh, you can *wonder*," said Louis, a gobbet of sarcasm dripping from his canines. He took a great gulp of beer and smiled through the glass.

"So how was Jerusalem once you finally got there?"

"Pretty hairy, actually. I was prepared for the airport security to have guns and the like, and there were plenty of soldiers patrolling the airport, but the first real shock I had was on board a local bus. I was on my way to visit *Yad Veshem*, the Holocaust memorial exhibition. As I tried to get off the bus I tripped, stumbled forward and tried to grab onto something, but there was nothing to grab onto. Luckily, I stumbled forward rather than flat on my face, and this quite lovely young woman steadied me. I looked behind to see what I had tripped on and it was the butt of a rifle! The guy wasn't a soldier, but I remembered that off duty soldiers carry their rifles with them at all times," John leaned forward, "And I'd been told about it, and I'd expected it. But just the very fact of seeing someone carrying a rifle, well, not even carrying it, just having it leaning casually up against his leg, just like how most people would lean an umbrella against themselves, was shocking. The *casualness*, the sheer *nonchalance* . . . but the context as well, because he was dressed as a civilian. And that was what disturbed me the most, that was what really made me *think*, that was what made me *realise* how dreadful the situation is out there. I knew all the background of course, but I suppose there's nothing that can actually prepare you for the reality of it."

"I bet you apologised pretty quickly!" said Edson, then wished he hadn't, but John was quick to agree.

"You, er, you could say that!"

"Was he all right about it?" asked James.

"He was fine, as a matter of fact, he smiled and looked a bit embarrassed, really. He brought his gun in closer to him, out of the gangway, as well. But there were other incidents as well – more frightening than that one," John took three man-size gulps of his beer, reducing it to a half measure in a few seconds.

"Like what?" asked Edson, sipping at his own drink as if it were hot chocolate.

"Well, the hospital runs clinics in various occupied territories along the West Bank, and I went with a doctor, an orthoptist, two nurses and a driver in the hospital's van to visit some of these clinics. This in itself was dangerous, just travelling in the van, because of the Jerusalem number plates. Travelling in a Palestinian part of the country with these plates meant we were pretty likely to be taken for Israelis and ran the risk of being stoned by Palestinians. So on the front of the van we flew the flag of St John to try and discourage any violence. But we had to take it down when we approached roadblocks because they were guarded by Israeli soldiers. By this time I was more used to seeing guns and armoury everywhere, but it was still shocking and particularly at these road blocks because some of the men holding those automatic weapons . . . well, you couldn't call them *men* exactly. They were *boys*, you know, school age. They might have been very good soldiers but seeing them fingering their weapons was pretty unnerving."

"When I hear stuff like that I always feel like I've had the most sheltered up-bringing imaginable," interrupted Edson.

"I know what you mean," John agreed, "It took us a couple of hours to get close to the refugee camp anyway. Once there we were going to operate the clinic in a local school. But as we were arriving our driver spotted some youngsters eyeing us and they all had rocks in their hands, ready for some sport. The West Bank can be extremely stony and pretty barren, and there are simply hundreds of good-sized rocks and stones, you know, handy cricket ball sizes, to throw at enemies. It's like an endless supply of ammunition. The driver took a risk and stopped the van and shouted to them something along the lines that we were friends and we were going to the refugee camp. They told us to follow them and they ran around the corner. They'd set up some kind of crude barrier with old planks of wood and some rocks, so that any vehicles would have to slow down just long enough for them and some other boys from the local school to get a few decent shots in with their rocks!

"I was expecting the refugee camp to be full of tents like a kind of shanty town, but people had been living there for about forty years, and it was pretty much just like a normal town with around twenty-odd thousand people living there. The Mosque broadcast our arrival over loudspeakers and the doctors and nurses started dealing with literally *dozens* of cases. It was really very humbling to see them working so hard under such difficult conditions and under such tight budgetary constraints. The driver took me out for a walk around the camp and I spoke to a few people, and they told stories about the troubles and showed me the conditions that the refugees live in there. The driver showed me some plastic bullets that he'd found following some rioting in the area." John held his thumb and forefinger up in the air about half an inch* apart, showing the rough size of the bullets. "They were supposed to be plastic, but they had a nasty metal core, so I'm not sure if they were much better than real bullets. We came across an Israeli military prison, and there were some more boys there who were taunting the soldiers who were guarding the gates. They were pretty relentless and didn't stop until the soldiers suddenly fired their weapons over the boys' heads and they scattered. I never really got used to the huge amount of guns I saw everywhere."

"I know what you mean," agreed Edson, and then, at pace, burning off the fuel of beer in his stomach, "I went to Egypt a couple of years back and saw the tourist police with these bloody great rifles, and at first your eyes just kind of pass over them, but then something inside your head goes 'that's a *real* gun, and it's *really* big, and *really* heavy.' I've always thought of it as a kind of a *half* de-sensitisation. You see guns on TV all the time, on the news, on films and all the rest of it, and everyone says we're being dangerously de-sensitised to guns because they're on TV too much, but I really don't believe that. I mean, there's a fucki- . . . I mean . . . there's a *really massive* difference when you *actually see* some bloody great rifle slung casually over some soldier's arm, than from seeing it on the news or something. On the news it's a completely different world, but when you're actually there, just a few feet away from a real gun, from something that . . . that's got the power to kill you in a second, it's completely different. You do a kind of double-take: 'Oh, it's a gun . . . JESUS LOOK AT THE SIZE OF THAT EFFING GUN!' And I always think, 'I bet that's heavy.' I mean, I had loads of guns as toys when I was young, like a cowboy cap gun, and space guns that made different noises and stuff, but it's the weight I always think of."

Louis was smiling and finding all this quite funny. His glass was empty, though, and he was already looking round every now and again, searching for the waiter. John spotted him.

---

* That's about 1.25 centimetres if you're like me and went metric at a young age.

"Yes, quite. Where *is* the waiter?" and he drained his glass with another mammoth glug. "Ah, here we are," and the blond waiter appeared, as if by magic, at the convenient moment. Edson's glass was still a third full – he was trying, not very successfully, to pace himself. His plan was failing mainly because he was going to be given another beer whether he had finished or not, so being on go-slow wasn't really helping at all. In fact now he'd have to catch up with everyone else, which would probably make things worse. In previous similar situations – when he could feel his whole body bloating with gassy beer – he'd surreptitiously pour some of the liquid onto the floor whenever he thought no-one was looking. It was great because he looked like he was keeping pace, therefore saving face, (yes, well done, that does rhyme, I know) but it also stalled a nauseous discomfort. Unfortunately, this trick was out of the question here on the train.

"Okay, that's seven more beers, please." John spoke very deliberately, and the waiter nodded in his solemn way.

"Spaseeba," chipped in Edson. It was a strangely satisfying word to say. Try it. Go on. Say it aloud to your neighbour on the train. Feel your mouth revel in the odd pleasure of saying this word. See if you can tell from your neighbour's smile whether they've read this book (there must be a good chance they have), or whether they know a bit of Russian, or whether they *are* Russian, or whether they are just being sympathetic.

"Anyway," said John, intent on finishing his story, "I returned to the camp where the locals had cooked an enormous meal by way of a thank you. Chicken and rice it was. I was pretty famished by that point and it was absolutely delicious. Very simple, but delicious." Edson slipped the last dregs of beer down his throat. At the end of the corridor Edson could hazily see the waiter returning with some drinks.

Chapter Five

Certificate: 18

That's equivalent to about an 'X' (or is it an 'R'? Well, who cares?) in America. Anyway, there's nothing that would upset the kiddies here, it even gets quite exciting at one point, actually. However, for all the times the under 18s have ruined great movies at the cinema by throwing popcorn, shouting smart comments and getting up every fifteen minutes to go to the toilet, this is revenge. They must skip the following chapter. I just wish there was some sex and violence in it so they were really missing something.

I

It turned into one of those nights when, having discarded clothes in a quickfire and disorderly manner, you fall asleep so quickly upon climbing into bed that you wake up marvelling at how your consciousness was retained so expertly right up to the exact moment when it suddenly became unnecessary anyway. One of those mornings where you confidently reminisce to yourself about how charming and witty you'd been the night before . . . until you remember that you need to check nothing embarrassing occurred. You're sure nothing did, but you try and remember. Just in case. The memory, you see, is still struggling to tread water in the gushes of alcohol that swamped it and attempted to submerge it the night before. The part of your brain that informs you whether or not you are suffering from an acute hangover is in a similar state to the memory department and cannot yet properly process the signals. So you lie there for a few moments trying to decide whether it's safe to lift your head and make a slow dash for the bathroom or whether it's more prudent to rest the poor skull for a while longer.

Edson was lying quietly in just such a state that morning. I'd tell you the correct time if any of the passengers or I could hazard a guess at it, but by Day 5 on the Trans-Siberian time becomes an abstract concept. Edson's head felt absurdly clear. I don't mean clear as in the world suddenly made sense after a good drink and having absolutely no responsibilities for four days in a row, I mean clear as in *empty*. He was just staring, barely aware of consciousness, his whole body locked into the clickety-clack (as they used to say in some of the first books I ever read) of the train.

Louis announced his nicely coincided awakening (strange how often that happens when you travel with someone – is it to do with the moon? You know, like women's periods synchronising when they live together?) in his usual manner.

"Uuuhh." Edson didn't answer.

"Why . . . hasn't one of us moved to that bunk over there?" Edson was looking across at the spare set of bunks. There was a long pause that lasted probably ten seconds.

"Because . . . if one of us did, the first thing I'd see every morning would be your ugly face," replied Louis. Another long pause.

"That's where you're wrong . . . I was trying to keep this quiet, but each night I've been smuggling Lotte in here to play, so she'd probably be what you'd see first in the morning, and *then* you'd see my ugly, but *smug* face second in the morning . . . you only haven't seen her so far because she sneaks out when you wake up. I have to create a little diversion every day."

"I see. So where is she now – has she left yet?"

"Well, I admit that last night she didn't come back here as she'd had a couple too many *wodkas* and as you well know I'm too much of a gentleman to take advantage of a lady in that kind of state."

"Sorry. Didn't mean to cast any aspersions on your gall*ante* character."

"That's all right. And I'd appreciate it if you didn't go blabbing this around the train as some kind of cheap gossip as Lotte happens to be very sensitive, and she was brought up a good Catholic girl." Another long pause.

"I thought you were getting somewhere with Lotte last night, you know."

"I just told you I've been plenty of places with Lotte, I'd just rather not go into it," another pause, "I don't think so, though. I still think she's got some kind of weird thing for Neil."

"She said she didn't though, didn't she?"

"But she would say that. You know . . . he's got advantages. He's a bit older . . . wouldn't necessarily say more mature . . . but more worldly – bit more mysterious."

"Magnificent cock?"

"Well, possibly. I don't think I've got any chance, really."

"No, probably not."

"Oh cheers!"

"Well, you said it."

"I was fishing for a compliment."

"Look, you're not a girl, and I'm not your boyfriend, all right?"

Edson started running over the latter parts of the night in his head. The next beer had arrived and he remembered hitting a rhythm where his hand barely left the glass, and he sipped at the beer almost constantly. John suggested that they should all reconvene at some point once everyone was back home. Edson had readily agreed and had immediately asked Lotte and Dorte if they might be able to make it over for the party. They were in a pretty good mood – what with the vodka and all – and they promised to visit England very soon. Then Edson remembered he couldn't really recall speaking to John very much for the rest of the evening . . . in fact, he wasn't even sitting in his place for much longer. He remembered John going to the toilet, and then . . . oh yes, on his way back he started talking to a couple of Russian men at a nearby table. Soon after, the waiter brought vodkas for everyone – a gift, apparently, from the two Russians. John and his new friends were speaking very loudly in their different languages and gesticulating enthusiastically to add some pictures to the words that patently neither party understood. Whenever comprehension was achieved, though, loud laughter always seemed to follow. Edson couldn't hear what they were saying very clearly, but he had the impression that they were trying to talk about experiences in the armed forces. They must have shaken hands about fifty times. At the time Edson had invented a story in his head that John was some sort of spy, and his friendship and his stories were all an elaborate cover so that he could bump into these people on the train. He had no wife, no son in Hong Kong. The Trans-Siberian was the perfect place for a covert meeting after all. The gesticulating could even be some kind of clever code understood only be these three spies. Edson imagined they'd never hear from him again until his picture and real name would appear somewhere on the internet a few days after some MI5 agent got careless with his laptop.

He also remembered ending up sitting next to Lotte for the last part of the night . . . when they had started . . . oh dear . . . playing drinking games. It was Louis' idea – in fact whenever Edson had ever been involved in the regrettable pastime of drinking games it was always Louis' idea. At that point, though, everyone was well past the stage of thinking *anything* was a bad idea and everyone piled over to Neil's table. Even James seemed happy to join in. It was all very close and cosy. The full horror of Neil's eyebrows were inescapable at that distance. It was like a forest in there – wild animals roaming around, ivory-hunters stalking elephants, that sort of thing.

Edson, with most of his timid inhibitions momentarily banished from his psyche, had taken the plunge and sat down quickly next to Lotte before anyone else took the chance. From close-up and sideways on her lips looked very inviting, and the small sparkly star-like stud she had put in for the evening just under her lower lip added a *frisson*, an element of danger. I mean, what if your tongue got caught where the nut and bolt type thing is on the inside of her mouth? You might get stuck together until Moscow. Now there was an idea. Edson recalled her suddenly turning and catching him staring at her, and then she turned and said something in Danish to Dorte who leaned forward and glanced at him. Edson could remember seeing her, out the corner of his eye, but he had looked away and pretended to be concentrating really hard on something James was saying. That was the best thing to do – just act like nothing had happened – maybe they'll even think they were mistaken. In the cold, empty morning after, Edson cringed under his blanket.

Louis had tried to teach them a drinking game that had something to do with holding your fingers up to your head like rabbit's ears and then waggling them and pointing them and stuff. They started playing, but the two girls obviously hadn't understood a word of Louis' game instructions. James and Edson didn't have a clue either, so the problem obviously wasn't just the language barrier. People just seemed to be getting it wrong all the time and everyone was laughing, while Louis gamely, desperately re-explained and re-re-explained the rules. Of course, Neil knew the game, only he knew a different version. A better one. He said Louis' one was easier, and although he thought that was better for Lotte and Dorte he claimed it meant less drink would get drunk, which was the main point of a drinking game.

And then . . . oh no! Lotte had pointed the wrong way again, or wasn't making the right kind of ears with her fingers or something equally as bafflingly wrong, and she was required to down the rest of her beer. At this news, Edson had reached around her back and pulled her towards him in a commiseratory hug. And she sort of half-reciprocated, and did the kind of smile that Edson interpreted as alluring at the time, but he now realised that it could be more accurately described as either 'sympathetic', 'passive' or, perhaps, 'confused'. He remembered looking at Louis who winked at him in a deliberately overt manner, only just stopping short of giving him a laddish thumbs-up sign.

"Do you remember me hugging Lotte last night?"

"Vaguely."

"Did she seemed pleased?"

" . . . Non-plussed might be a more accurate term."

It was James, with a voice of something only approaching maturity, that suggested continuing the game indefinitely would end in substantial costs and inevitable vomiting. A new game was needed. Edson spoke up with the only drinking game he knew. Someone would start off by saying the name of someone famous. Then the next would have to say the name of another famous person, but the first letter of his or her first name must be the same letter as that which started the surname of the previously named person. For instance, if the first person said 'Clint Eastwood' a correct response might be 'Edward Woodward'. If someone pauses too long or can't think of an answer at all, they must drink two fingers-width of beer, and, to add excitement, if someone says a name and the first and surnames start with the same letter, the play switches direction. Examples might be, 'Bill Bryson' or 'Terry Toweling.' Everyone swiftly agreed and ordered fresh beers for the new game, and, Edson remembered, it went a little bit like this:

Edson: "Okay, I'll start . . . John Wayne."

James: "Oh God! My turn! Erm . . . Wi . . . We . . . W- . . . William . . . Windsor! Ha ha! William Windsor! Your turn again.!"

Edson: "Yeah. Cheers. Erm . . . W- . . . William Whitelaw! Your turn again!"

James: "Bugger . . . er . . . what's another name beginning with 'W'? Walter! Er . . . Walter Matthau!"

Louis: "Mmmichael Owen!"

Neil: "*O*? You bastard! Jesus. Oh, I know, Olivia Newton John! Hya hya! What a *fox*!"

James: "So will that be 'N' or 'J' for Dorte, then?"

Edson: "J, definitely. So a famous person whose first name starts with J, Dorte – should be easy."

Dorte: "Okay. Jack Nicholson."

Lotte: "N? How about . . . oh no, erm . . . Oh I don't know . . ."

"Oh Jesus," thought Edson. As he remembered this part he recalled squeezing Lotte's thigh for encouragement.

Lotte: (shooting a brief alarmed glance at Edson) "Nils Malmros!"
There was a brief silence as everyone looked around the table at each other.

Edson: "People you just *know* in Denmark don't count, Lotte."

Neil: "Yeah, come on *two fingers!*"

Edson looked hard at Neil, who was barely able to keep a leer from his face.

Lotte: "He is famous. He's a Danish film director."

Neil: "Ah, but we've only got your word for that, haven't we? . . . And maybe Dorte's. Come on, there should be punishment for trying to cheat – *four fi-*"

Edson: "Yes! Okay! I think we'll give her the benefit of the doubt on this one. Michael Jackson."

And so it went on, with the girls mining a rich seam of 'famous' Danish people. Edson strained to recall whether he made any further lame attempts to gain Lotte's attention, but fortunately he couldn't remember any.

II

It was hangovers all round as Louis, Edson, James and Neil gathered for a belated breakfast in the dining car. James was silently staring out of the window, brazenly refusing to acknowledge anything that Neil was saying. Neil wasn't getting the message. "Jimmy-lad, come on, coffee is no *damn good*" – he emphasised 'damn good' in a Mr T type fashion, for some reason, " . . . for hangovers. Y'see, the reason we get hangovers is because of the lack of liquids getting to the brain and the body's lack of energy from all that drinking shit. The brain swells and you get a headache. You feel sick because of the exotic mixture of Russian lager and Russian *wodka*. 'Course, I've got a cast iron stomach," and he leant back and patted his tummy like a fat man after a big, greasy fry-up, "'specially after all the weird stuff I've eaten in the Far East – chicken feet, fish eyes, cow guts,"

"*Cow guts?*" asked Louis, incredulous.

"Yeah, that's what it looked like," and, in a cockney accent, "*So, y'know, bit of wodka ain't gonna do me no 'arm, know what I mean?*". Louis opened his mouth, but Neil held a pudgy finger up to stall him, "BUT! I do admit to having a slight headache, so what I need to do is get energy and fluid to my brain as quickly as possible – and coffee just ain't gonna do that!" He said that last part with a patronising laugh in his voice and a condescending you're-so-naïve smile on his face. "So, Jamesie, come on, what do I drink?" Jamesie was still looking out the window, or maybe *at* the window – at the tiny specks of dirt on it – anything, in short, that wasn't Neil. He didn't answer. "Come on Jamesie! Have a guess – you're an intelligent lad!" James must have been a good five years older than Neil. "Come on. Have a guess. *Go on*," he whispered. With supreme effort James shrugged his shoulders without turning his head. His comprehensive indifference might have been heartbreaking to some people. "Coke!" he paused a moment for affect, and then, shaking his open hands about in front of him, said, "No, boys! I don't mean *cocaine*!".

"I didn't think you did," said Edson.

"I mean *cola*! It's brilliant – gets your blood sugar levels up quick and aids your recovery much faster than any pharmaceutical shmarmaceutical druggy drug you care to mention." He was leaning right forward, his elbows on the table, his eyebrows alternately rising and falling, and his hands flourishing around liberally like a flamboyant primary school music teacher. "Now, *not a lot of people know this*," very crap Michael Caine impersonation – oh you'd guessed? " . . . but, to every can of cola there are twelve teaspoons – heaped teaspoons, mind, of *sugar*," Neil paused again, revelling.

'Surely *everyone* knows that,' thought Edson.

'Surely *everyone* knows that,' thought Louis.

'Cabin fever,' thought James.

"So, come on then, whose having some cola?"

"I'm fine with coffee, thanks," replied James.

"What about you boys?"

"I'm a jasmine tea man, myself – think I'll go and fill my mug up and get some rolls or something," replied Louis. "The Chinese know what they're doing. Jasmine tea's the cure for just about everything, I reckon."

"Eddie?"

" . . . Yeah, go on then, might as well try it."

They ordered and Louis went to fill his mug. James sipped at a black coffee already in front of him. Edson wondered how long James had escaped to this sanctum of coffee and peace before Neil had searched him out with his heat-seeking radar eyes. A large plate of bread rolls arrived, but Edson's mouth was as dry as a pensioner's bank account and he didn't fancy tucking into some tough bread just yet. As soon as the two small plastic bottles of cola arrived, however, he immediately began to revolt against the idea of adding to the fur already flourishing on his teeth and tongue, like bracken on a Scottish hillside, with a drink consisting of twelve teaspoons of sugar mixed with some *brown*.

The bottles were similar to the kind you might have taken to school in your lunch-box as a young child, as opposed to a proper can, which might have contained a bit too much gas for your little tummy.

"*Orange Star Cola*?" said Edson as he poured and examined the label. Neil, meanwhile, was already necking it straight from the bottle. "Made in *Bury*?" said Edson aloud, "*Bury*?" The strange concept of never having seen *Orange Star Cola* in England, *ever*, and now suddenly encountering it in the middle of Siberia seemed fantastic to him. Neil threw his head back, gargled a gobful of cola, swallowed, and characteristically wiped his face dramatically with his cuff, "Aaah! Man, *now* I need a coffee!"

Louis returned from filling his mug and immediately tucked in to the bread.

"Look at this. It's made in *Bury*!"

"Ha! Really?" Louis took the bottle and examined it. "It's got a design from about 1977! Is there a sell-by date on it?" The label was indeed of a peculiarly 70s yellow hue and was fading slightly – the colour of vomited custard. There was a big dull-carrot-orange star in the middle, with 'Orange Star Cola' written across it in blue bubble writing – desperately trying to give itself something of a mad, zany image. "I'll stick to this," muttered Louis, gesturing at his tea. Edson wished he had had tea. He swigged at the dark liquid and felt his mouth fill with bubbly sugar. He winced. "What's it like?"

"All right, I s'pose. Different. I don't really like cola, to be honest."

"Why d'you order it then?" asked Neil.

"Because y- . . . because *I fancied something cold*."

"Is it like any cola you've ever tasted?" asked Louis.

"I guess so. Sweeter, maybe. I don't know, I'm not a connoisseur of the world of colas."

"Virgin's the best," Neil put in quickly. "Did you know, a year after launching *Virgin Cola*, they'd captured 18% of the market share in Britain! That's a sizeable share of what is a pretty lucrative market. Only to be expected, though, Branners is a genius."

"Didn't *Branners* make a guest appearance in *Friends*, though?" asked Edson.

"Yeah, lucky man getting to meet that Jenni Aniston. Don't see what that's got to do with it, though, *Friends* is superb!"

"Oh, it's got a lot to do with his credentials as a genius, I reckon," said Edson.

"Yeah, all right," Louis interjected, keen to return to the main point in hand, "What I'm trying to get at here is how many different types of cola are there? There's *Coca Cola*, *Pepsi Cola*, *Virgin*, and our new found friend *Orange Star*. What others?"

"Well, you've got the supermarket's own brands, I s'pose," said Edson.

"Although most of them are pretty inferior, in my opinion," added Neil.

"*Panda Pops* is another one. . . er . . . Oh, I used to try to make Coke. I used to get a glass of water, and then buy like ten of those penny sweets that were shaped like cola bottles . . . I think they were called cola bottles, actually. Some kinds were covered with sugar and some kinds weren't. I'd get the ones with sugar and try to get them to dissolve in the water because I thought then I'd get a drink of Coke," explained Edson, getting a little bit carried away with nostalgia. Dangerous ground of course. They were perilously close to a conversation about how much they loved *Mr. Ben* and *Bagpuss* and swapping urban myths about *Captain Pugwash*.

"Kind of a primitive, childlike version of alchemy? Did it work?" asked James, suddenly forsaking his abstinence.

"Yeah, Jimmy. He let it dissolve and what was left was this gorgeous drink that no-one had ever tasted and he named it Coca-Cola and he became the richest man in the galaxy! Hya hya! Come on Jamesie! Use yer noddle!" and Neil jabbed at his temple with his forefinger.

"Any others?" asked Louis.

"Hmm, oh! *Rola-Cola*!" said Edson.

"*Rola-Cola*! Fantastic!" said James, laughing.

"Okay, so we've got a few kinds. Now what I want to know is, are there a whole load of cola breweries up and down Britain, throughout the world even, like beer breweries or wineries? You know, does cola taste different in Somerset than it does in Sunderland? Does the water have different qualities, do they ferment them in different kinds of barrels and for varying lengths of time, do they do tours of the breweries, do they use special sugar, or common-or-garden *Silver Spoon*, or just raw sugar cane? Can you actually become a cola connoisseur? It's taking the Pepsi-Challenge to its logical conclusion. You could travel throughout Britain looking for a good vintage with it's beautiful hazel-brown colour, with a sickly sweetness that can be enough to make you want to swallow a slug to soak it all up – oh no, that's salt, isn't it? And the carbonation is just right so as not to fill your stomach with gas after two swills."

"Yeah! I can just imagine people saying stuff like, 'The E-numbers in this are just right to make it *eeeeezeeee* on the palate,'" said Edson excitedly.

"Yeah, or, 'The berry-like, fruity edge to these home-counties colas really tingles my tastebuds,'" said James.

"Unlikely, unfortunately," said Neil, and he downed the rest of his Bury cola with the slight Newky Brown twang to it, wiped his mouth with his cuff, and burped loudly before quickly blowing in James' face, "Get a whiff of that, Jimmy – that'll get yer senses woken up! Hya hya!" James turned his head away and issued a smile as weak as a pint of *Kaliber*.[*]

III

"Right, I need a dump," said Neil. Edson hated people who announced things like that. His mind immediately and helplessly conjured an image of Neil pulling down his cotton trousers and underpants. (The same pants, indeed, that had been removed for only brief moments over the last few days in order to perform operations such as the one mentioned and some that were even *more* repellent to imagine.) His mind continued to give brief pictures of Neil leaning back contentedly on the toilet seat, his hairy legs outstretched, holding Nick Hornby's *High Fidelity* out in front of him (he'd probably swapped it with another traveller for his copy of *The Beach* by that rich bloke.) Meanwhile James was almost audibly grimacing. His own mind's eye pictures were so much the clearer because,

---

[*] At the risk of spoiling any kind of humour I might have generated there, I should explain that *Kaliber* is an alcohol-free beer. Some of my younger readers may not even be aware of the drink at all because it hasn't really been advertised since the 1980s, when Billy Connolly endorsed it. Yes, a person from Glasgow advertising alcohol-free beer. Was the irony lost on the *Kaliber* makers, or did they revel in its richness? Anyway, the hook was that because it was alcohol-free you could 'drink as much as you like' and still drive home. At which point, Connolly was presented with a huge glass the size of his upper body filled with beer. What the advertisers failed to mention was that if you did drink that much you'd still be a menace on the road home because you'd be stopping for a piss every two minutes. Being young at the time I thought people only drank beer for the taste (no need to laugh, the *Kaliber* inventors *clearly* thought the same thing) and that alcohol was simply an unfortunate by-product of the beer-making process. I thought *Kaliber* was just about the most impressive invention since *Sodastream*.

unbeknownst to Edson, Neil insisted on providing follow-up reports regarding his bowel movements, delivered as casually as you might remark on the weather: 'Bit runny today'; 'Good firm texture – all out in one large *log*, hya hya!'; 'Greenish.' Just a comment, nothing more. Not even an explanation as to what he might be referring to – surely, he must have reasoned, it was *ob*vious.

Louis suggested that they should retire back to the cabin for a few tunes and he invited James, who willingly agreed, "I'll go and get a couple of tapes as well."

"What about Neil, though? I mean, he's, er, welcome, of course, but, er . . ." James was quick to dismiss his pussy-footing.

"No, he'll be half an hour in the bog. Bit of luck and he'll go to sleep afterwards as well."

"Okay, well we'll meet you back at our pad, then," said Louis.

In a few minutes they reconvened in Edson and Louis' berth which was jiving to the considerable talents of *Incognito*. James came in with three cassettes in his hand – all recorded, not original, with the artists and album titles written with a neat hand in dark red ink. "What did you bring, Jim?" Edson was lying full length on his bunk, but he sat up as James perched on the opposite bunk and placed his tapes on the table under the window. "Let's see . . . oh, not bad! Louis – he's brought a bit of Chet Baker – you old *smooth*ster James! What else . . . *Jamiroquai*, very nice, and *Acoustic Alchemy*! I love *Acoustic Alchemy*!"

"Really? I hardly know anyone who likes them."

"No I love them! They're cool. Have you seen them live?"

"No, I've always wanted to though."

"I saw them in the Pizza Express Jazz Club on *London's fashionable Dean Street, in the very heart of London's trendy SoHo.*"

"Really? I bet they were amazing."

"They were pretty damn good, actually. They had this amazing horn player guesting on the night we were there as well. First of all he came on to play the saxophone and he was amazing. I mean, I've seen one or two really good horn players – like Alan Skidmore, you know. He's just so . . . *serene* and he plays almost effortlessly, without movement . . . just total concentration. But *this* guy, I mean, it's a different kind of music of course, but he was *loving* it! His whole body was just *jiving* and *swaying* to the sounds he was making. It was fantastic. And at the end of the number, they introduced him as 'Snake Davis'. Now the guy's already got a head start with a jazz surname like that, but 'Snake' was it. You know, whoever thought up that name is a genius.

"I was watching him do his stuff and I couldn't put my finger on it, and 'snake' was *it*, absolutely perfect, and in so many ways. The way his body was like, *coiling*, and so thin and the way he was dancing with his sax made him really look like a cobra swerving and swaying to the sound of a snake-charmer, it was fantastic. His left shoulder was jutting right out as well which somehow made him look even more snakey, and he was so *thin* . . . oh, it really was the perfect nickname. He even made his sax snake-like because it swerved and danced with him. Honestly, if I had invented that nickname I'd be the bloody poet laureate or something, or at least very proud, anyway. Come on, let's have a bit of that on."

"Snake Davis," affirmed Louis, to himself, enjoying the sound of the words. And '*snake*' is a great word.

"I haven't seen Damon for a while," said Edson in an off-hand way.

"We saw him last night, Ed," replied James.

"Did we?" he replied, a smile on his face, "Must've been when I was in Lotte's room."

"What?" asked James, "What's going on there then?"

"Oh, nothing, Louis was just winding me up earlier because I've got a few blanks from last night."

"Oh," said James.

"Don't you remember seeing him, Ed?"

"No."

"He came down the dining car to have some food or something, it was quite late," started James.

"But Neil kept asking him to come over and join us, except he *obviously* didn't want to. He was chatting to some Russian woman and some bloke she was with, and he had a book with him and everything. Neil must have gone over there about four times to try and get him to play that stupid drinking game you got us playing."

"Wasn't stupid – at least everyone understood mine."

"Well, whatever, but no-one could blame him for not coming over, especially with you leching over Lotte the whole time!" countered Louis.

"Yeah, yeah."

"But in the end he just told Neil to go away," added James.

"Really? Was Neil upset?"

"No, of course not, he thought he was mucking about. He's got no idea," said James.

"Mmm." It all went silent for a moment as they considered this. *Acoustic Alchemy* melodically accompanied their thoughts in the background.

"Have you ever actually spoken to *Dame-o*, James?" asked Edson, after a bit.

"Not really. A few words here and there. I think he thinks I'm like Neil, or at least that I'm deliberately travelling with him, so I can't blame him for not being enthusiastically friendly towards me. I wouldn't be. Why?"

"I'm just interested. It's like, everyone else on the train is pretty open and we've spoken to Russians, and John, and you and Lotte and Dorte, but not really *Dame-o*. I just wondered why no-one has really spoken to him."

"Maybe he's just trying to be mysterious. He was probably a Goth when he was younger."

"D'you reckon?" replied Edson.

"Yeah, I think so. He'd have had that bored look down perfectly in those days. And he'd be used to being a lonely bastard, well, when he wasn't at a concert full of other people wearing black cloaks and DMs. Or perhaps he just thinks we're a bunch of uncultured drunken knobs . . . I dunno."

"I can't believe that, it's so patently not true," asserted Edson, not without irony.

"He did tell me that he had a degree in English and Drama – I don't know if that's a particularly Gothic thing to do."

"Hmm, that does sound a bit too extrovert," conceded Louis, "Although I can't remember ever meeting any Drama students so I wouldn't know."

"Is that because you're at Oxford and they don't do subjects like that because they're not worthwhile enough? And because all your friends do Chemistry and all you talk about is Bunsen burners and the periodic table?" asked Edson.

"Exactly. Drama is an extra curricular subject for people to do in their spare time *after* they've finished learning the skills that they need to help the people that do Film Studies as a degree or Media Studies as an A-Level to struggle through life."

"Nothing wrong with Film Studies. *Anyway*, James said that he did English as well, so the drama might have just been a minor and he might be some expert on Chaucer or something."

"*Chaucer* didn't invent *penicillin*, though did he? He didn't invent the *aeroplane*, he didn't invent the *telephone* and he couldn't perform *heart surgery*. No, *he* did . . ." and Louis repeated his best pretentious voice, all high and sardonic, while sarcastically making the quotation sign with his fingers, ". . . *Social Commentary*. *Mar*vellous."

"Anything else, James?" asked Edson, ignoring Louis completely.

"Not a lot."

"Oh come on Jim. He must have said something else. When were you talking to him?"

"I bumped into him when he was out in a corridor near the dining car staring at the silver birches. We chatted for a bit, you know . . . well, I did most of the talking, to be honest."

"Makes a change, Jimmy-boy!" said Edson, and James shuddered, "So, how old is he?"

"Well, he didn't say. He said he'd been travelling for ages, though, and if he went to Uni, and then did a couple of jobs and then travelled for ages, it must make him in his late 20s, I s'pose."

"He's one of those people who could be any age, isn't he?" said Louis.

"Well, not *any* age, Lou. For example, I'd wager he's not *twelve*," said Edson in a deliberately lame attempt at one-upmanship.

"No, I mean I wouldn't be surprised if he was mid-30s, or mid-20s. I mean, the hamster-beard's not grey or anything is it?"

"Did you hear that he's been travelling for four years?" asked Edson.

"No. I can't believe *that*."

"It's possible, I guess," reasoned Louis, "If you've got a bit of bar experience you can usually get work anywhere. He might have stopped every now and again for a few months to get a bit more cash, but never actually gone home for it."

"Yeah, I s'pose it's *possible*," agreed James.

"I *bet* he's running away from something," said Edson, a little mysteriously.

"What are you basing *that* on?" asked Louis.

"Oh, I dunno. Why would you leave home for *four* years? And . . ."

"Yeah, but we don't *know* that," interrupted Louis.

"But assuming he's travelled for a fair amount of time, which I think we can take as read because no-one would grow a beard like that around people they actually *knew*, maybe there's a reason why he doesn't want to go back."

"What, he doesn't want to go and do a nine to five job in the City, own a *Mondeo*, have a huge mortgage on a dull semi-detached in Billericay, have two kids – a girl and a boy, and play golf at weekends?" said Louis, "You mean he'd rather do whatever he wants? Just occasionally being forced into doing some bar work on a beach in blahdy Bali with women in grass skirts dancing around all day tanning their midriffs, but spending most of the time living cheaply, carrying his stuff around in a smallish bag and just travelling from one beautiful place to the next only occasionally being plagued by Neils and Edsons? Nightmare. Look, I've got all I need in *that* rucksack," and he thrust a finger out to point below the bunk James was sitting on, "Why bother with the material world, if you're happy with this one? He doesn't *have* to be running away from something."

"Yeah. I was just saying, you know. Just *spec*ulating . . ." Edson made an irritated listen-to-him face at James, who did his weak smile.

IV

Neil stalked into his cabin, and with calculated carelessness threw his book – Richard Branson's autobiography, *Virgin* – onto his bunk. Without looking around he said, "Nice n' chunky . . ."

"What was that?" John was lying full length on his bottom bunk reading a Moscow guidebook with a picture of St Basil's Cathedral on the front.

"D- oh, nothing, John, I, er, I thought you were Jim. Sorry."

"That's all right," said John. He was balancing the book on his chest as he read. As he spoke he lowered it so Neil could see his face, and when he had finished he resumed reading. Neil sat on the edge of his bunk opposite John, (he had made James go on the top bunk, "Because, Jimmy-boy, I like a late night with a few vodkas, and I don't wanna wake you up every night by climbing all over you when I get back absolutely steaming, know what I mean?"), "Did Jim say where he went, John? Did he come back from the dining car?"

"Briefly, yes. But he was only here for a moment," John turned back to the guide book, "I wish I was going to stay in Moscow for a while. I've never been to Red Square, you know."

"Hmm . . . He's probably gone to see Eddie."

"Might he have gone to see those two girls?"

"Jamesie?! No chance Johnny – Jimmy doesn't have a great deal of sway with the ladies. Bit inexperienced, I think."

"Oh, I don't know. They seem to get along pretty well as far as I can see."

"Ex*a*ctly," Neil leaned forward, "Jimmy's fine in a crowd, isn't he? He's fine when we're all there and he can sit and *listen*, and make the odd quip – he's a great quipster, isn't he? I've noticed that. But try and get a one-to-one conversation out of him, BT-style, and he's lost for words. You might as well be talking to a brick wall, know what I mean?" John looked slightly confused.

"I haven't really had that problem, he's quiet I admit, but . . ." John laid his book down and sat up straight.

"Quiet? Listen Johnny, I know Jim better than anyone here, and he's just not a conversationalist. He's not like you and me, John, or Louis, or even Dorte. I'm not saying he's not a nice guy, I love him to bits . . ."

"You've been friends for a long time . . .?"

"'Bout 4 days. But I'm perceptive, you know. I used to be an astrologer and Jim's the classic shy Libra if ever I saw one, and my Mum was one of 'em. It's not a criticism, John, just a fact of life. He's a quiet guy, that's all."

It went quiet again for a moment, and both men drifted into reading their respective books. "John, do you know where Dame-o's cabin is, I might go and see him."

"I don't, I'm afraid. He . . . he seems like a nice chap, though . . .?"

"Dame-o? Oh, he's great. Likes to keep himself to himself, you know, no different to the rest of us really, in that respect."

"I hear he's done a lot of travelling,"

"Well, that all depends on what kind of criteria you're looking at John, and who you're comparing him to. I mean compared with Louis and Eddie back there," and he made a thumbing gesture in no particular direction, "he's a very seasoned traveller, yes. Because, and let's be frank, here, they're a couple of greenhorns."

"Are they?"

"Well, yeah. What are they? Eighteen? Nineteen?"

"I'm not sure."

"Greenhorns. It's not a criticism, Johnny, don't get me wrong. They're great boys. Just not very experienced, that's all. Like Jimbob – he's a bit older, but even this train is a bit of a jungle for him. Yeah, Damon's been around a fair bit, Russia, China, Fiji, India. But we've all done that to some extent. He's followed a path that's been nicely cleared for him. It's not like he's ever had to hack his own way through the bushes. Plus, he stays at a lot of these places to work, so he tells me, so you can't really count however long he's been out of Britain as one long trip as such."

"How long has he been away for, then?"

"Not too sure. Bit of consternation about that one. I've heard four years being mumbled, but I'm not so sure about that. But the important thing is that he might be well travelled compared to those guys, but to people like you and me, Johnny, he's not exactly Wally Raleigh – he hasn't discovered any countries and he hasn't invented the BMX, hya hya!" John did a passable impression of James' *Kaliber* smile. "You know, he probably eats in McDonalds once or twice a week if he can just like the rest of us . . . Man, I could do with a double Big Mac with bacon and extra cheese right now. I've had it with the borscht, John."

"Yes, doesn't always hit the spot, does it? I've got some chocolate here, though, do you want a piece?" John reached down to a plastic bag next to his suitcase and pulled out an enormous tablet of *Dove* chocolate, broke off a couple of generous pieces, and handed one to Neil.

"Jee-sus, John, that's some large slab o' choc you got 'dere!" said Neil in an absurd attempt at an American deep-south accent, "Thanks."

V

Dorte and Lotte sat on opposite bunks, passing a single cigarette between them for alternate drags. They had their heads either side of the door so that they could lie and look out of the window as the train rattled on towards *Mockba*. Dorte made Os in the air with the cigarette smoke. There was a knock at the door, and Neil poked his head round. "I'm not disturbing you am I? I'm looking for Dame-o. He's not here is he?" Dorte sat up and looked around their small cabin with exaggerated deliberation.

"No," she said. Lotte looked up at Neil and smiled.

"Ah, well, I'll try the dining car . . . you girls around for dinner tonight?'

"Yes. Unless there's some other place we can eat?" said Lotte, with a smirk.

"Well . . . I just meant . . . are we all going to have dinner together again tonight?"

"I guess so," said Lotte.

"Right. I'll, er, I'll go see if I can find Dame-o. Leave you girls to it." He shut the door again. Dorte and Lotte looked at each other, pleased[*].

"Why doesn't he just leave Damon alone? I mean, how many

hints does the guy need?' said Dorte.

"Doesn't Damon like him?"

"Hates him."

"Hates him?"

"Well, maybe not hate. But he can't stand talking to him."

"I didn't know you'd talked to him that much."

"Well, I haven't, really. Just a couple of times."

"You didn't tell me."

"I saw him in the corridor this morning and he just went off on one about how people couldn't leave him alone, and how he was fed up with people like Neil who were desperate to get 'inside his head'."

"I bet that made you feel welcome!"

"Exactly! And then he started saying that he'd been travelling for nearly four years and the whole time he'd been trying to get away from people, or, at least, other travellers, and wherever he went they were there."

"What does he expect, though? *He's* a traveller, isn't he?"

"I know. So he started saying that this is the second time he's been on the Trans-Siberian, only last time he was going the other way, and that was a couple of years ago. He said last time was a lot better because he spoke to more Russians and there weren't people in the dining car getting pissed at night. Well, I guess what he meant was that there weren't any *travellers* in the dining car getting pissed at night, because I know that we don't drink the majority of vodka in that place."

"What? He said that to your *face*?"

"I know! It's like," and Dorte switched to English and a Californian accent for a moment, "Jeez! Sorry for ruining your life dude!" Lotte laughed.

"Maybe he was talking more about the guys than you and me."

"Yeah, maybe. He just takes it all so seriously, though. And he thinks everyone is fascinated with him."

"So was he all right with you apart from being fed up with our

* Please note that the following conversation took place in Danish. However, for your convenience I have translated the aforesaid conversation, so you don't have to scurry away to your Danish-English translation books and waste countless hours deciphering their foreign tongue. Danish readers reading the English version of this book should contact the publishers for the original transcript of this part if they so wish. Note to editor – do not leave the English translation of this conversation in English when translating the entire book into Danish for the lucrative Copenhagen market.

drinking and people trying to be friends with him, then?"

"Well, I think he quite likes us because we're not English."

"Oh, right. Has he been to Denmark?"

"I asked him that, actually, and he said he wasn't really interested in Europe." Dorte lit the cigarette she had been patiently rolling and passed it to Lotte.

"Do you think James is gay?"

"Not sure. I caught him staring at my tits the other day."

"What about Neil?"

"Er, no. Unless his chauvinist attitude is some kind of amazing cover up for a raving homo underneath," Dorte suddenly swung her legs round and leant right forward towards Lotte, "Why?! Fancy him?"

"No," she said with admirable casualness, "You have to wonder about Damon, though, don't you?"

"Oh! So you like the mysterious type eh?"

"No, that's not what I meant."

"Ooh, he's so *experienced*, I bet he's been to Cambodia and Afghanistan and Iran!" Lotte remained extraordinarily casual, refusing to take Dorte's bait.

"No. I mean you just wonder if he's looking for something, don't you?"

"What and he's been wandering the Earth for *nearly four years* trying to decide whether he's gay or not?"

"You never know."

"I just think he's fed up with the rat race, you know. Work, social etiquette, pollution, personal hygiene . . ."

"Personal hygiene?"

"Well, it's a pain, isn't it? Washing."

"Mmm."

"He probably just wants to get out of all that. He doesn't have to talk to anyone, he can be as rude as he likes all the time, and there's no-one to tell him what to do."

"But a life without rules must be boring, I mean if he hasn't got any rules what's he got left to rebel against?"

"I don't think it's a rebellion," said Dorte, and she swung herself back into a lying position, "I just think it's an ongoing quest. Like that Scottish woman that walked round the whole world until she got home again."

VI

Damon Crabb was twenty-seven years old by the time he boarded the Trans-Siberian train for the second time in his life. The last time he had travelled in the opposite direction after leaving a bar job in Köln, Germany (that he had held for five months) to head east, specifically to China. Now he was returning to Russia, a country he had largely ignored two years previously. It had seemed grey, dull, and in his desperation to lose himself in China, he had registered very little about it.

Damon grew up in Twickenham, went to Bristol University to study English and Drama, and gained an upper second class degree. He spent his first summer out of education working for a telemarketing company. He sat in a large open plan office with a headset on and a computer in front of him that automatically and randomly dialled numbers of businesses around the country. Once the call was answered he would ask various tedious questions regarding the size, age, and type of the business, as well as other similar gems of stimulating conversation.

I don't know if you've ever been on a reception desk, but if you have, and it was a busy one, you'll know that it's these kind of calls that *really* get put on hold. If you phone your gas company or the local council you can guarantee a wait on hold, but that's nothing compared with how long market research people spend in the magical world of
Greenlseves every time they make a call. I worked on a busy switchboard in Wandsworth, South West London for a while at one time. The longer I worked there, the more frequent these telemarketing calls became – indeed, I heard recently that the telesales game alone now employs around 600,000 people in Britain! The receptionist's job isn't easy. With important business calls, wives phoning in to check on husbands, and people arriving at the offices for meetings or whatever, it's common sense that the one person you can safely afford to keep waiting is the market researcher. You can't help being rude when you're busy, either, because they're just *getting in the way*. It's especially irksome when they ask to speak to the Managing Director, and you just think, 'Why? Why is the Managing Director going to be interested in answering your dull questions when he's not going to get a thing out of it? What makes you think he's even got *time*?"

Anyway, Damon pressed on with this job by day, and then went back to his parents house at night and paid them a small amount of rent each week – about £30. It was the kind of job you would only do for the money, and money is just what you need when you come out of University. When he first started the job he'd flop out every night in front of the television. He just didn't have any inclination to do anything else. He even found himself switching over to make sure he watched *EastEnders,* when previously he had turned his nose up at all soap operas.

As the job dragged on for week after week he became more and more frustrated, more and more irritable, more and more *angry* in general. Short-tempered, easily bored, less interested in everything. It was like his brain was being numbed, shredded, even, by hours of monotonous and repetitive conversations with people who had no interest in speaking with him. Worse, he felt guilty for feeling this way. He knew this wasn't the worst job in the world – factory jobs could be even more repetitive and certainly more uncomfortable, and plenty of other jobs had more stress and virtually every other job in the world had more danger. But all that was of no consolation to him as he wallowed around in a mud-hole of self-pity and boredom.

Then late one Sunday night Sky TV screened *Apocalypse Now*. It was the first time he'd seen the film, the first time he'd witnessed that breathtaking performance from Marlon Brando. The conditions for watching it had been perfect. Damon's parents had gone to bad early and the house was silent and dark. He knew little about the film, possessed no expectations, and as a result was simply sucked in and then blown away by its power. It affected him to the extent that he felt ashamed about his own ignorance of a war that so affected much of the second half of the 20th Century.

So he began learning about the war in the evenings – no, don't roll your eyes, he didn't turn into some kind of war-obsessed nutcase – he was just fascinated by that part of history. After he had read a couple of books on the subject he decided to expand further, going more in depth and then reading books about icons of the 20th Century like Malcolm X, Mohammed Ali and Margaret Thatcher. It was amazing. Almost instantaneously his frustration subsided and, at work, his mind replaced thoughts about the lives of fictional cockney stereotypes with more intellectual musings. Unfortunately, though, this state didn't last long. The dullness of his job became progressively more overwhelming – perhaps the stimulation of the evenings and the weekends had actually ended up exacerbating the original problem even further.

The British playwright Dennis Potter, in an interview with Melvyn Bragg shortly before he died, admitted that for him writing was a vocation. He said that to have a vocation had become old-fashioned – that it was almost reserved for dusty musty schoolteachers. Yet a vocation is what most of us aspire to . . . at least, everyone wants a job they *like*, while others also want a job they believe in – one in which they are of some use to other people. Damon, like many graduates – and arts graduates in particular – knew that he wanted a job he would both believe in and enjoy. But, also like many arts graduates, he had no idea what that job was.

Despite his drama training at University, acting wasn't a profession he was interested in – out of work actors always seemed rather pathetic to him. It was a profession with far too many people for the jobs available. It meant street performing; competing for space and an audience in Covent Garden; persuading people to part with their change so you could eat; it meant taking temporary (or so you told yourself) jobs in TGI Fridays and Chicago Rock Cafes and other American-themed chains so you could "meet people" and "perform". It meant having an ego big enough to believe that your talent would eventually be spotted: *some*one would be impressed by your brief appearance in *The Bill* [*] as the nasty husband that gets nicked for making his kid collect packages from a dealer. Before you knew it you'd have a medium-sized part in the latest British cockney gangster flick. You know, the ones that like to inform us how exciting and loveable those murderous organised crimesters are. Then you'd be hired to play an English baddie in a propagandist Hollywood film. And then perhaps a nice steady role in *EastEnders* – and from there a singing career would surely blossom, because, by that time, people will encourage you do whatever the hell you like no matter how much you suck because you're a star and no-one has the guts to tell you when you look like a fool anymore. Get the cash while you can and help your agent pay for his loft conversion. But Damon knew he didn't have that kind of ego, no matter what his distant workmates thought.

He had to leave though. He couldn't go on living at home paying

[*] Most low-key jobbing actors seem to have had roles in it for the odd episode. Some have even had more than one part! For hard evidence go along to any London West End musical and buy the the matchday programme. In the vaguely diverting biogs that accompany the names of the leading players, virtually all of them list a performance in *The Bill*. Even children's presenter/radio presenter/radio producer/teacher/journalist/all round good egg Tommy Boyd had a part in it once.

cheap rent and eating his Mother's cooking. He couldn't continue to go out of his mind every day at work, asking the same questions again and again, feeling as if he should apologise for wasting the receptionist's time even before he started on the usual spiel.

His guilt, however, was tempered by the knowledge that at least he was working and, like everyone else, was just trying to make a living. The open plan office was cruel – full of recent graduates and people who were earning money for their year out after A-Levels. Some were career-minded – those people that might end up one day calling themselves "Marketeers". Did they fancy themselves as a bit of an Athos, a D'artagnan, or something? This group was always heavily competitive: who was the quickest, the most accurate, the most charming, the most successful? Who, moreover, would be the first to secure a date with one of the hundreds of receptionists they spoke to each week?

If he had been allowed to deviate from the strict script he might have said:

> "Hi. Please listen for just a second. I know this is boring, but I'm just doing a job – a pointless one that I hate, but it *is* a job. Please, I know it's a pain, but we can get this done really quickly if you give me a hand with it."

And then fire off the questions quickly and leave them to get on with their work. But you weren't allowed to do that – as with most jobs, he reasoned, there was a set 'way of doing things,' and only if you were excellent, or lucky, or both, might you ever escape from the strait-jacket of the 'way of doing things.' For two months he trod water. He applied for a job here as an advertising trainee, a job there as an editorial assistant (whatever that is). He was unsuccessful on each occasion but he barely cared because he didn't want them anyway – they'd all been little more than token efforts of getting out. He heard rumours that another market research firm in Kingston were paying better wages and were looking for new recruits. For a while he pondered the merits of moving sideways for the sake of a few extra quid, but soon decided he couldn't be arsed.

He eventually landed a job at the National Film Theatre (NFT) on the South Bank, London, as a booker and cashier. It was a great atmosphere there, relaxed, yet upbeat, quiet yet buzzing. He stayed there for about six months or so, but despite the good atmosphere, the reasonable pay (well, compared to the market research place, anyway), and the wealth of films he was privileged to enjoy, it was still a job that didn't require a lot of actual thought. Neither did it require him to utilise any of his knowledge or skills – another problem that many arts graduates encounter.

However, his experience at the NFT persuaded him to pursue a career in the world of moving pictures – film certainly, and possibly in television. He joined a temping company. Not the most obvious thing to do, but his theory was that if he was doing a series of crap jobs with no prospects and no security he would be compelled to put all his spare effort into applying for jobs in the TV and film industry, as well as to send out a series of speculative letters. He'd heard about one person who was so desperate for a break in TV that he waited for Michael Grade at Channel 4 every day (this was, obviously, when Mr Grade was still the controller of C4), bugging him for a job, until finally Grade gave in and offered him a position. And that person turned out to be, well, I forget, but fortunately that's not really the point. Wherever he sought advice, whether from *Guardian* articles written for young media graduates, or from first or second hand accounts, what you needed was luck, a toe in the door, and a willingness to be persistent.

Persistence, just about everyone seemed to agree, was the key. Yet in reality there can be very few things more irritating to a busy TV company than an annoyingly confident, starry-eyed, inexperienced, helplessly and naïvely enthusiastic graduate ringing up every few days to "See if a position has come up yet?" Damon was quick to recognise this, and it was pretty depressing – the one solid piece of advice he'd been consistently given was actually complete codswallop. While doing his first temp job – data inputting (vague term for a vague job) at a High Street bank – he applied for a job as a Runner for a TV production company. He saw the ad in *The Guardian*'s Media section, and sent off his CV and a quick covering letter the same day. A couple of days later, acting on The Modern Theory of Persistence, and following guidelines laid down by a careers adviser at University[*] - "It's never a bad idea to give the employer a follow-up call to check if they received your application. It might just push your CV to the top of the pile" – he called the company.

"Er, yeah, hi, erm, I saw your ad, and . . ." Damon could virtually hear the bastard gesticulating with impatience and barely suppressing a sigh as he stammered and stuttered his way to the reason for calling, " . . .

[*] As with most careers advisers, she looked like she should have been a librarian.

well, I applied for the job . . ."

"Hmm-mm . . .?"

"So . . . I just thought I'd call to check you got my CV."

"Hold on." There was a pause of maybe five seconds. "What's your name?" It was a blustering male voice: gruff, impatient, confident, and condescending all at once.

"Damon, er, Crabb - C-R-" he was cut off in mid-spell.

"Listen Damon, I don't wanna be rude, but we're in the middle of tryin' to sort out a guest for Sarah for tomorrow's show, ok? We've been let down at the last bloody minute, and we've all had a rocket up our arses because of it. Do you know how many people have applied to that job you're talking about?" but before Damon could answer, the man continued, "I assume you mean the Runner's job?"

"Yes, but it –"

"Right, well, in the three days since that bloody advert went in we've had nearly a thousand – probably more, I dunno, letters, and about another twenty phone calls – even though it said "No phone calls" on the ad – being able to read is something that whoever gets this job is going to need to be able to do, by the way – from people all wanting this job. Now we're all bloody busy here, and I really haven't got time to wade through fifteen-hundred begging letters just to give you the peace of mind that your letter got here safely . . . Listen mate, it wasn't a terrible idea to call, you've got to be persistent in this game, but the fact is we won't start opening any of them for a couple of weeks, and even then it's going to take a few more days until we've looked at all of them, so don't hold your breath. So, yeah, it's probably arrived, but I couldn't say for sure."

"Right. Sorry to bother you."

"That's all right, I don't mean to be rude, but this is the media . . . know what I mean?"

"Right. Good luck with the er, the er, the guest."

"Yeah. The guest. Cheers."

He fared little better with the speculative letters to people who weren't advertising positions. Bracing himself, he followed one letter up and asked to speak to Personnel. A woman with an excellent telephone voice – she sounded like she should be reading the travel news for BBC Radio 4 – answered.

"We don't really have a personnel department, as such . . . May I ask what it's regarding?"

"Er, yes, I sent my CV and a letter in a few days ago . . . I was hoping you might have a vacancy or something coming up in the near future, or, or, at any time, really."

"And may I take your name, Sir?"

"Yes, it's Damon. Damon Crabb, C-R-"

"One moment." He was put on hold listening to Baddiel and Skinner's "Three Lions" for nearly two minutes, although every twenty seconds or so, Miss BBC came back on the line to say, "Sorry to keep you." But she was on and off the line so quickly his answer of "That's okay" was drowned by Frank Skinner's singing. Finally, she returned and said, "Thank you, Mr Cram. We received your CV and it's on our file, so if anything comes up we'll be in touch. Okay?"

"Right. Thanks. Bye then."

"Bub-eye." This last word made him wince, made him feel weak. It was a kind of sympathetic word, yet it's sympathy wounded him. He felt patronised by this person, snug and smug in her job while he dabbed away quietly and repetitively on his keyboard all day. It made him think of out of work actors.

His futile job-hunting continued for six months, while his temping agency found him more data-inputting work, then some customer service employment for a mail order gift agency, and then, after a couple of weeks without work, he was forced into doing some telesales – offering personalised free designs of new kitchens. Free, of course, until the design was completed, and then you would have the real professional hard-sell sales geniuses round your house to convince you to make the design a reality. But there was no way, in today's savvy society, that anyone is going to agree to something like this as a result of your persuasion. They know you're selling something, and unless they're very stupid that's all they need to know. Most will say they're not interested – it doesn't matter what the deal is – even if it's a good one: they watch consumer programmes[*], and they're minds are not for changing. Jean Baudrillard claimed in the sixties that we were living in an 'ecstasy of communication' – that information is omnipresent and has become pornographic. Everywhere you look there is advertising, information, commercials, or worse: *infomercials*. And people

[*]Don't take this lightly. What I'm about to tell you is true – it's not knocking the programme makers, but I try to avoid all consumer programmes as I find them unnecessarily alarmist and dull of stupid and gullible people who will readily complain about anything and everything. As an example of their often ludicrous and desperate attempts to bring some company or other to book,

there was recently a segment in one show where they were dealing with the size of a loaf of sliced bread. The bread makers claimed that it was great bread for toast. But the programme discovered that this bread was too large for most toasters. They actually bothered to show this on prime time TV – they had a whole row of toasters, and they tried the bread for size in each one. And on most the bread, sure enough, poked out the top so the whole slice wasn't toasted. Imagine that! People were actually complaining that the bread was too *large*. A myriad of questions popped into my head: Just how were people getting ripped off here? What stops them from turning the bread over half way through to get the whole thing toasted? Since when did *any* bread fit exactly into a toaster? How desperate for ideas was this programme? The poor bread manufacturers immediately, powerlessly, meekly conceded defeat to the power-hungry and mighty consumer programme. They issued a grovelling statement (I find statements are often 'grovelling', don't you?) admitting that maybe their bread was more suited to being toasted under the grill rather than in the electric toaster. Another famous victory for the consumers! Hurrah! I really felt for the manufacturers then – there they are with their lovely bread product – no qualms about taste here, you understand – a couple of people complain that it's *too large* and next thing you know a national TV programme is embarrassing them in front of all their unhappy – and happy – customers. It wasn't even like they'd made any false statements like "Fits perfectly and fully into all toasters on today's toaster market," and no-one had been forced to buy the stuff under such a misapprehension. I wanted them to issue a more retaliatory statement like: "We acknowledge the problems that some of our customers have been experiencing regarding the size of our loaf and it's ability to fit fully and perfectly into every toaster on the market. However, we feel that this complaint is, quite frankly, extremely petty and we have resolved to issue no apology for it. The bread is of a consistently high quality, and, despite the fact that we have found that many people like to have a "bready" part to their morning toast, we suggest that anyone who likes our product and is such a pernickety toast connoisseur as to have complained about such a minor factor as this should try grilling the bread instead – it's the best way to make toast anyway, or, alternatively, complain to the manufacturers of toasters who plainly have no concept of the size of sliced loaves nowadays and are making toasters blatantly too small for the modern loaf. Furthermore, shouldn't a reputable consumer programme such as this one be more concerned with chasing up all those naughty pharmaceutical firms who always manufacture their poisonous pills to look like 'Smarties', so children might eat them and die? As far as we are aware, no-one has ever died or even had a serious injury or illness as a result of having a small portion of their bread untoasted – indeed it is actually safer as it gives a conveniently cool part of the toast to pick it up by when removing this tasty carbohydrate product from the toaster, thus avoiding any chance of a burn. Many thanks for your points but, frankly, you can Fuck Off." And then the presenter could have done a really moralistic bit to camera about how the big companies don't care. Not like they used to. Honestly – there should be a consumer programme warning people about watching consumer programmes . . . if such a thing wouldn't spontaneously combust as a result of it's own excessive self-reflexivity.

have developed a defence mechanism against it. Throughout the last century people were duped by all kinds of rogue advertising – cigarettes being healthy, stout is good for you, every single washing powder/liquid/tablet gets your clothes whiter than the next one. People have realised it's simply safer to say no, even if they are missing out on a truly good deal. The odds just aren't worth it.

No, the 'salesperson' only has three chances here. The first is if someone has said that very day to their 'partner', "Oh, Colin, we do need a new kitchen, if only someone would just phone up over the next few days before we do the sensible thing and go to a kitchen superstore place like most people would do, and offer us a free design of some sort." Which, frankly, is unlikely, but with twenty people phoning a hundred people a night during their dinner and/or in the middle of *Coronation Street*, it did happen a few times each night. The second is the stupid person that agrees because it's 'something free.' But then when the hardcore salesman arrives he quickly realises they've got no money and can't afford anything and everyone's time has been wasted. The third is if the person is excessively lonely and likes the company of hardcore salesman.

And the stupidity of his bosses made him angry: how they were too lazy to set anything up apart from complete cold-calling so the success rate was depressingly low and their phone bill needlessly high; and how they considered motivation to be paramount. Of course, motivation *is* important. They just had no idea how to do it properly. Shouting at the top of their voices "COME ON THAT'S ONLY THREE SALES TONIGHT, I WANT FIFTEEN ON THE BOARD BY THE TIME YOU GO HOME, COME ON! *SELL*!" while everyone was trying to convince people on the phone that they weren't actually *selling* anything, was the limit at which their feeble ideas at 'motivation' became exhausted. Brilliant.

But just as he felt he had reached the absolute bottom, he had a phone call. It was from a television company he had written to a couple of months previously. They were looking for a runner for their latest comedy production and asked if he'd like to come to an interview. Salvation. At the beginning of the week leading to the interview his present work bothered him less, but as the week progressed he experienced an acute fear that ate from the same bowl as his excitement: if he didn't get this job, how would he feel, and how would he deal with coming back to this job after being so close to a getaway? He tried not to think about it –

he had rarely failed in any interviews, although in most of them all he had to do was appear confident, enthusiastic and vaguely bright. This one was different, they'd probably ask that bloody question: "So, what would you say your *faults* are, your *negatives*?" Who hasn't longed to say, "I'm not telling you – I'm trying to convince you why I *should* get the job, not why I *shouldn't*. I doubt you're being completely honest with me – that pay review after three months, for example, I bet that doesn't ever happen." But of course you can't.

The interview actually went peculiarly well. The producer was a smallish man with an enormous head that made him look like a caricature of himself, and he had a Desperate Dan chin. He seemed okay, but there was a firmness there, a sense that he was totally in control and wanted to make sure everyone knew it. When Damon paused for too long over a question about what kind of guests might be good for this particular show, he hurried him, shooed him on: "Come on, come on! Two names, quick!" It rattled Damon, but not as much as he thought it might have done, and he came up with a couple of names to pacify the man, who then leant back in his swivel chair and smiled – not saying anything for a moment. When the Producer (Peter) made him a cup of tea, Damon felt uncomfortable: Peter had the faintest of smirks on his face, as if he was willing Damon to recognise the irony that if he was to get this job[*] their current roles of tea-maker and tea-taker would be reversed forever.

He landed the job, though, and took it without needing to consider it for a moment. The fact that he would be earning less money than at any time since graduation simply didn't matter, as long as he was shot of temp work and kitchen sales. Although the contract was only for four months, he finally felt that it was reasonably safe to move out of home. He was increasingly suffocating there, and now he had found something approaching a proper job and he had proved to himself that he could survive living purely on temp work if he had to, he started looking for a

[*] I believe that 'position' is now the correct terminology in many spheres of work. When I was first applying for jobs a few years back, I made the mistake of using the word 'job' instead of 'position' and was reprimanded by some pompous PR company whose job it is to invent new words to replace perfectly serviceable old ones. It's all to do with connotations, as my old English teacher, the glorious Mr Mar, would have said. 'Job' connotes a 9-5 workaday work day, an old-fashioned, boring thing you do because you have to five days a week; 'Position' is something that you have chosen to do, and are dedicated to – you don't degrade your work by giving it the ungainly title of 'job' – especially in PR.

flat. His parents also seemed increasingly impatient to start the next phase of their lives.

Flat shares are bastards. It's as simple as that. You go round various houses visiting people and presenting, not your skills, or your academic record, but your personality, which is surely much worse. If they turn you down, it wasn't because there was someone better qualified than you, it was because they didn't like you. It can be pretty morale-sapping looking for a flat-share. The offices of the company that he was to start work for were in the Notting Hill area of London. Full of trendy sandwich shops, celebrity chefs and bookshop owners with floppy hair. Obviously, he had no chance of affording anything there.

Eventually he found a very small bedsit on Ladbroke Grove. Anywhere on Ladbroke Grove is usually horrendously expensive, but this place was basically a room and nothing else, which seemed to justify the relatively cheap rent of £60 per week. He used the intercom on the outside of the house when he arrived to scope it out (as the Aussies say). It was a tall building with maybe four floors including the basement – perhaps five if they were using the loft. A posh-sounding woman buzzed him up with a, "Second floor, number three, chick." He knocked on the door, and she called out, "It's open, chick, come in," she was sitting right on the edge of the single chair in the room – a molting burgundy armchair – as if she was keen to ensure that as little of her body as possible came into contact with the old fabric in case she caught something. As he entered she got up quickly, almost stumbling on her heels, "Damien, isn't it? I'm Emma," and she held her hand out to be shaken. He shook her hand, but she intimidated him a bit. She was a city-type, and wore an expensive black suit with a jacket that almost met her short skirt at the hem. Her blonde hair was slapped back and tied behind her head in a ponytail. This made her face seem quite large and made Damon briefly think about Queen Elizabeth I. She could have been 25 or 34.

While showing him round the pokey little place she explained that the flat belonged to her mother but that she was living in the countryside now. She sounded a touch bitter about it. There was a tiny bathroom with a shower, but when she turned it on for Damon to see it was more of a dribble than a spray. The toilet looked like it belonged in a rich girl's wendyhouse. In the corner of the main room was a plug-in stove with two hobs ("Bring a toaster and you can have your usual beans on toast, chick," she said), and next to it was a kind of dual-purpose sink that was deep enough to hand-wash your clothes in. The carpet was old and dark blue. It looked like it had been installed by a child – stuck down, perhaps, with blu-tack or that white glue from primary school that you'd slap on with baby spatulas.

Damon had his doubts, but it looked like the best he was going to get for what he could afford. He said he'd like to think about it overnight.

"Ok, chick, let me know tomorrow, but I think it'll go pretty quick."

"Yeah . . . sixty a week, wasn't it?"

"Ah . . . I thought I might have forgotten to tell you that on the phone!" she stamped her heel, and Damon feared for the floor, "It's *one*-sixty a week, chick. That bloody paper's shit. I've told them about three times, now. You can still do one-sixty, though can't you? You said you were in TV?" There was a faint tinge of desperation to her voice. Damon thought there was a lick of Australian in her accent somewhere, or maybe South African.

"Er, probably not, I'm afraid."

"Well, you're not gonna get much for sixty quid, chick!"

"Mmm. I'll, er, I'll let you get back to work. Thanks for showing me around." He gave up looking after that, reasoning that he could do better when he had a higher paid job, hopefully in a few months. His parents didn't seem to mind either way anyway; they just shrugged and told him he knew he could stay as long as he wanted, stopping short of saying they were pleased he was staying, though.

The first couple of weeks of work were pretty good, despite the time it took him to get there each day from Twickenham. It was all pre-production work: quite a lot of admin, a lot of shifting of boxes and much getting the office shipshape. There were only four of them for these couple of weeks, and it was all very relaxed. It was just what Damon needed after weeks of hard sell on the telephone. There wasn't quite enough for him to do in these early days, though, and this made him uncomfortable – it felt like the calm before the storm, and he sometimes thought he preferred the storm to the *anticipation* of the storm. At least you knew how violent the storm was once you were in it. Peter the Producer though, was a stickler for time-keeping. Even if Damon had finished all his day's work by six he had to wait until half past before he could go, and keep looking busy in the meantime. He hated that, too. He found few things more difficult than trying to look busy when he had nothing to do.

One day, towards the end of the second week, when the other

three in the office had gone into a meeting (he was never allowed into these – he had to 'man the phones' – like they were ringing off the hook), and he literally had nothing to do. A few times that week he had been compelled to ask for stuff to do because he was so bored. But now there was no-one to ask, so he took out his film magazine and started reading it. About half an hour later, Peter came back in. The other two (Katy, the production co-ordinator, and Lisa, the production manager) walked past talking about Chris Evans (it wasn't complimentary, so I won't go into it here), but Peter stopped behind Damon, whose desk was right next to the door but positioned facing away from it. Damon could feel him there, looking over his shoulder at his magazine. His first instinct when they came in had been to fold it up quickly and concentrate on something else, but he realised that this might have made things worse, so he kind of left it open and studied his book of notes. Written neatly at the top of a clean page were the details of the single phone message he'd taken in the previous hour. Peter was still behind him. Damon turned his head round, a smile on his face. Peter's great face was looking perplexed, his round jaw looked larger than usual and his eyes squinting at the magazine. Without looking away from the open article he said, "Nothing to do?"

"Well . . ."

"Come and ask me if you've run out of stuff, there's plenty you could be doing . . . I'd put that away if I were you." There was just a hint of menace in his voice – what he actually said was fair enough, but there was an edge to it that made Damon positive that this guy wasn't going to tolerate anything. He held back the protestations that welled up inside him, about how there was no-one there to ask, about how if he had things to do, then he would certainly be doing them. He hated "If I were you". There was never, he thought, as his ears began to burn red, a more condescending term invented. It said "I'm wiser than you, and I know better than you, and you should know that I'd be angry about it if I was still me." And it even said, "Even if I *was* you, I'd still have the sense to realise that this was the wrong thing to do, so why didn't *you* realise that?" Damon folded up the magazine and put it in his bag as Peter walked off. The room was almost silent. Peter strode around to his desk where he plonked down with great force into a black leather chair not too dissimilar from the sort made famous by *Mastermind*. "Damon."

"Yes?"

"You can make us all a tea. I'll have one of those fruit ones – not the rosehip, though. Girls?"

    "No thanks," said Katy.

    "Hmmm . . . I'll have an Earl Grey if there's one going. Ta."

    "Earl *Gay* more like," said Peter.

    The rest of the crew arrived over the next week or two, and 'crew' is the perfect word because Peter welcomed everyone with a friendly, "Welcome aboard!" Eventually Damon's job became more involved and he started to enjoy it more. It was a topical show, so he got to do a few bits of back-up research that supplemented his largely menial duties, and it helped that he was allowed to exercise his brain properly on a few occasions. Despite the fact that he spent most of the day ordering courier bikes (people in London, mostly those in television, are often obsessed with 'biking' things everywhere. Everything's far too urgent to use the Royal Mail like everyone else); making countless cups of tea and coffee; making sure the star of the show had everything he needed; acting as an all round dogsbody to just about all the other ten people in the room; hours of photocopying and so forth. It did actually require a decent amount of intelligence and organisation to ensure that all these tiny tasks – ridiculously small in themselves, but vital to the running of a TV show as a whole – were successfully completed.

    The first couple of shows were tremendously exhilarating, and after the filming had been completed for each he forgot his countless gripes and how he felt like little more than a slave at times. They'd all go to the Green Room and knock back the free drink, and there was a fantastic camaraderie between the workers on the show. But once again Damon slowly became more and more disheartened with his lot. After the third week of watching the team, the director, the stars, and the unrecognisable hangers-on (who seemed to be congratulating themselves on a good job well done as if they'd had a single damn thing to do with it), chugging Becks after vodka after white wine, he became angry. He worked up to 60 hours a week, more sometimes, often coming in to help with research at weekends because the *actual* researchers were too tired, for just two hundred quid a week before tax – a pitiful £3.60 an hour – barely the minimum wage of the time. Yet they'd gone some way to make sure they had the best candidate only to pay him peanuts simply because he should feel lucky to have the opportunity. As Damon's friend Warren explained to him: "It's supply and demand, mate." Damon was beginning to wonder why on earth there was any demand at all. These people must have drunk a good £400 worth of drink plus eaten a hundred pounds worth of food supplied by a trendy catering firm (they did, admittedly, make superb chocolate covered pieces of fruit on cocktail sticks), while he was barely able to survive on his mean salary. Sure, the financial rewards could eventually be great – even the researchers earned double his money and that was the next step up – but why was the remuneration so poor now? It wasn't as if runners don't work hard – good ones kill themselves to get noticed and get on that next rung.

His relations with Peter were souring by the day. He came to dread the sound of his voice raising above the rest of a humming room that only really sprung to life when someone would put a Britney Spears CD on to cheer everyone up. Although, in truth, her music only served to depress Damon even further. Peter's voice would raise above it all: "Damon! Tea!" Nothing else. It didn't matter how busy he was: how many tapes he had to send away to people, how many bikes he needed to book, how much research he was doing, he had to drop everything so the man could have his tea. And of course he'd have to ask everyone else in the room if they wanted one, so it was rarely a short job.

His attitude was worsening and he knew it. For the first couple of weeks he'd jump up and say yes, and give a shout to the rest of the room to let them know that a brew was coming up, but his enthusiasm for dipping eight PG Tips bags into eight polystyrene cups and then adding just the right amount of milk and sugar for everyone quickly waned. Soon he didn't even answer, he just got up and did it, barely even looking at Peter. He knew Peter wasn't impressed, but he didn't care. In the evenings he was reading voraciously with red eyes about World War II: the Battle of Arnhem, the Normandy landings. He read about the John F. Kennedy conspiracy theories. He read about Nelson Mandela.

His reading gave him a confidence, perhaps even an arrogance: he looked around the studio and felt superior. While these people made programmes dubiously described as entertainment, Damon was learning about life. Sometimes he just wanted to shout at them that forgetting to tape the Soap Opera Awards[*] was hardly going to cause some massive natural disaster, let alone make much of a difference to the success of their own

[*]Yes, it is a very *specialised* awards ceremony, isn't it? If I didn't know better I'd say the whole thing was just a nice annual publicity stunt where everyone gets pissed for free – maybe even get the chance to do some cross-breeding with some soap stars from another channel. Actually, that did happen, and the result was *Family Affairs*.

show. He started hating how people in the media are captivated by what other people in the media are doing. They obsessively study newspapers and magazines and adverts and TV programmes and films and the internet and they really do care about Calista Flockhart's weight problems.

He found the once-a-week media sections in certain newspapers quite dizzying in their self-reflexivity – like two mirrors facing each other. Here were newspapers discussing and gossiping about other newspapers, making stars out of correspondents and editors and literally writing about their own everyday office gossip and calling it 'news'. Yet the infighting and power battles and boss-hating happens in car-dealerships, supermarkets, condom factories, and bookstores every day. It's just that, while 'normal' businesses will always have egos, few, if any, have the sheer size and number of egos to compete with the journalists, correspondents and editors working on national newspapers. What some papers became particularly adept at doing was quite astounding when broken down: Firstly they would report a news story. Secondly they would use their comment pages to (obviously) comment on the story. Thirdly and fourthly they would use the media section to comment on that comment and comment on the different comments made by other newspapers. And fifthly they would use the media section the following week to comment on the comment from other newspapers that were commenting on the comments made by their paper the previous week about the comments they were making on the original news story. But by that time few people could quite remember what the original news story was, or its relevance, which was a shame because it was a probably a damn sight more interesting than the counter-counter-counter (counter? I've lost track) comments that were being expressed by the end of this horrible spiral of self-reflexivity and self-indulgence. It was amazing that some newspapers didn't eat themselves.

Damon, as you may have noticed, was a little more than mildly disheartened. Yet he was upset with himself, worrying that he was being too high-minded, a snob, even. The show he was working on regularly brought in over three million viewers, so it must have been doing something fairly right, even if the magnetism of it's writer/presenter was probably more responsible for it's success than any kind of originality. It wasn't that he didn't like TV, more that he felt its huge potential was continually wasted. Artists like Alfred Hitchcock and Dennis Potter admired the immediacy and intimacy of TV that could never be obtained on the cinema screen, yet true, original, individual, sparkling talent such as they possessed seemed to Damon to be in remarkably short supply. Or, more pertinently, that it existed but was never going to be allowed anywhere near a TV studio because all channels are too obsessed by ratings to take any real risks. Even satellite and cable channels, which weren't expected to bring in large audiences, rarely took a real gamble because of pressure from advertisers.

These worries about his own possible snobbishness bothered him and he could not shake it off. And then one day at the studios he overheard an Executive Producer discussing a very low budget programme that was being made for a major satellite channel. The Exec was talking to someone fairly important from another programme in production at the studios, and was unashamedly singing the praises of their programme. It was a clips show of the cheapest and lamest variety.[*] It had no originality, but, importantly to the broadcaster, it was incredibly cheap yet would still garner reasonable ratings simply because it was easy to watch, it might very occasionally be able to raise the tiniest corner of a lip of a viewer, and because there was probably not a lot else on. Well, there might be, but it was easier to watch this than flick through forty channels looking for something else.

The clips were generally the typical ones taken from foreign shows: Japanese people torturing themselves for fun, Italian women exposing their tits, and baffling Mexican game shows. As Damon was queuing up at the café to buy Peter a banana, (Oh yeah, it could be a demeaning job sometimes, especially as Peter fished around in his deep pockets only to find he hadn't a penny on him (or nothing smaller than a fifty pound note, anyway). Would Damon mind, awfully? Well, he was only earning about an eighth of this guy's weighty weekly payments, but what the hell.) So, as Damon queued like a downtrodden Russian serf before emancipation he overheard the Exec say, (I've changed the names to protect the personalities involved): "You see, Rob gave us so much with his wit and appeal to different ages, but Julie just gives us something different we didn't have before, she really is fantastic, you know, so talented. I loved Rob, but Julie has really added a new *definition* to the

[*] Far be it from me to shamelessly quote from adult American cartoons, but Fry, the lead idiot in Matt Groening's *Futurama*, once quite brilliantly described this type of show when discussing his taste in television. He said, "I prefer programmes of the genre, 'World's *Blankiest Blank*'".

show." Yeah, bigger tits, nicer legs. Damon was stunned at this brio on the behalf of the Executive – he couldn't quite believe that they were discussing this piece of dreck as if it were some kind of work of art. That she could speak of these two people as talented human beings was shocking. The show required the presenter to do nothing more than read some extremely predictable and lame gags directly off autocue in between lamentable clips of performing kangaroos, ('They looked hopping mad there!') and people eating live cockroaches ('Tasty! They followed that course with a dessert of *lice* pudding!').

Increasingly Damon was struggling with the mind-numbing rigours of the job and becoming more aware of the complete lack of any kind of acknowledgement of reality that many TV people had. Whilst on set if, say, a table needed moving the only people who were permitted to do it were the stage hands, no matter where they were or how busy they might be elsewhere. The idea that someone else could shift it a couple of centimetres did not seem to cross anyone's mind. It was astounding. Everything you are taught as you grow up, be kind, share, help others – all the *Sesame Street* basics – seemed to go out the window. The rule of shout was the only law in this town, and the only person allowed to pitch-in wherever it was needed was the Runner. No-one else could risk a splinter – Damon was the only expendable person. He also happened to be the one desperate for a break in the game and would do anything to move upwards. There was a frighteningly military-like chain of command which should have ended somewhere between the Director and the Producer but all too often rested with the star of the show because, as good as they were at shouting at underlings, neither of them were willing to cross 'The Talent'.

One of Damon's disproportionately important jobs on the day of each shoot was to be waiting in the foyer of the studio complex for the star of the show to arrive. He would then escort him, like a distinctly un-menacing bodyguard, to his dressing room and then down to the make-up room, furnishing him with a paper cup of white tea, no sugar, on the way. This was despite the fact that the personality knew the way very well, and had indeed managed to arrive at the studios having travelled from the other side of London perfectly well by himself. Damon even had the impression that the poor guy was a little surprised that he was doggedly waiting for him every week for the regulation stroll to the dressing and make-up rooms.

On one particular day Steve arrived a good fifteen minutes early and found his way very easily to the production room, next to make-up, without Damon's help. Peter looked incredulously at Damon as Steve walked in and collapsed into a comfy armchair.

"Where were you?" Peter demanded, then looked at Steve and said, "Morning, Steve."

"Mornin'."

"I-I, er . . . he was quite early."

"You should've been ready. Anticipate, things, yeah? Tackle problems before they happen, yeah?" Damon hated those 'yeah?'s.

"But he's never, I mean . . ."

"Sorry, Damon – I was a bit early, Pete."

"Yeah, okay." Peter looked again at Damon for a moment before turning to Steve and starting to discuss the latest David Beckham story in the newspapers. They talked for about five minutes or so, until Peter finally said, "Can we get you into make-up? We need to get a shift-on, yeah?" There was a brief pause, and then,

"I'm, er, I'm waiting for someone to offer me some toast." Peter glared at Damon for a brief second, then pointed at him with an outstretched arm and said, with as much restrained anger and pure authority that he could muster,

"You're fired." It was a joke, of course, but no-one laughed. It was humiliating and it certainly felt to Damon like a threat, however veiled. He walked out the room in mock-shame with his head bowed, trying to make light of the warning, pretending he hadn't noticed the underlying seriousness. As he queued at the small café in the next room for the buttered toast, Peter came out to visit him, eager to reinforce his point. "That's two strikes," he said holding out two potato-croquette fingers. He widened his eyes and lifted an eyebrow questioningly until Damon nodded his comprehension.

Two weeks later they were back at the studio. As usual it was hectic, and Damon found himself running all over the place taking tapes up and down stairs, setting up TVs and videos for various clip viewings, sorting out Peter's special lunch, and keeping a constant eye on Steve to make sure he had everything he needed. Steve wasn't in a great mood. Damon was also knackered – he had been up until very late the night before. He hadn't been able to sleep, and had found himself reading Cornelius Ryan's *A Bridge Too Far* until nearly 2am. He finally drifted off, only to be haunted by dreams of being part of the 1st Airborne, stranded for days in dire conditions with little rations or weaponry, desperately trying to hold on to the bridge at Arnhem until the back-up arrived.

Midway through the afternoon everyone who was involved in the show gathered in the studio to undertake a rehearsal of the evening's show. Damon was about to join everyone in the studio when Lisa, who was on the phone, waved at him to wait a moment. He hung back and Peter said, "I want you back in the studio as soon as possible, yeah?" Damon nodded and smiled. Peter went to the studio.

"Damon, there's a package come for me – can you go and bring it back for us, love?"

"No probs." Damon waited a moment until Lisa turned her back, then quickly grabbed his small backpack that contained his paper, his sandwiches and his *A Bridge Too Far*, and slipped out of the room.

When packages arrived at this studio they were delivered to an office on the exterior of the main building, a kind of annex where about three people worked, collecting packages, signing for them and informing people when they had arrived. To get there, Damon always walked through the back of the studios where all the sets for various shows were stored, out of the building, and around to the front where the annex was situated. He was not in a hurry, but he didn't dawdle. Often he would take his time a little on these errands to give himself a quick breather. Not today. He walked outside, past the barrier stopping any traffic from stealing in, and towards despatch, as it was known. He walked up to it . . . and then walked straight past. He carried on up the road, crossed over, walked under a bridge and turned into Waterloo station. He went down the escalators, up some more escalators and out into the main station. He scanned the imposing train timetable board that you have to stand about fifty metres back from to read, and then boarded a train to Twickenham from Platform 16.

Forty minutes later he was in his bedroom. He walked in, picked up a few books and chucked them into his small backpack, and then heaved a much larger and heavier rucksack onto his back. He walked downstairs, the smaller bag dangling from his right hand. He left the house and caught a train back the way he had came, only this time he alighted at Clapham Junction, nipped over to Platform 12 and in five minutes boarded a train to Victoria. Once there he walked to the coach station, and boarded a coach bound for Dover. From there it would ride the ferry across The Channel, and a few hours later it would eventually terminate in Prague.

VII

Mindful of the problems that his plan could cause, Damon had prepared well. The evening after the "two strikes" warning he had bought his ticket to Prague and told his parents that he had resigned from his job, had saved up some money and was going to go travelling for a while. After the initial shock, neither seemed that bothered, or even particularly surprised. His Mother worried about the money aspect, but he assured her that he wouldn't be gone for long. He even told her that he had a friend in Prague, his mate Matt who his Mother had met about five years previously and liked very much. The truth was that he knew his Mother didn't know Matt's home number, and he hadn't seen or spoken to Matt for at least three years. He had heard that he was abroad, though, and it provided his Mother with the kind of reassurance she needed.

He sent a delayed email that would arrive at five o' clock in Lisa's inbox at the studios simply explaining that he had gone to Europe, wasn't coming back. He apologised for the inconvenience. As for money, although he was paid poorly he had saved enough thanks to living at home to at least buy him a month on the road – about a thousand pounds since he had graduated. All he had to do was to ensure that at all times he had enough money to go home if he needed to.

Four years later and by now he was accustomed to making full use of all the money that he took from various jobs – usually bar work, but occasionally something different. For two months he sold cleaning products door-to-door in Melbourne, Australia. It was great. Not only did he get abuse for being an irritating salesman, but also for being a Pom. It was all pretty lighthearted, though. In Germany he had sold hamburgers at carnivals up and down the country one summer after meeting a German in Italy whose mate made his whole living doing exactly that. He had been home just once since he left. Nothing had changed, so he left again.

VIII

"I was kind of marooned in a jungle once," said Edson. Everyone, who was James, John, Louis, Dorte, Lotte, and Neil, stopped their loud conversations and looked round. They were all sitting in varying poses in a rapidly emptying dining car, each of them clasping glasses of vodka and coke. Edson, Lotte, Dorte and James sat around one table while John sat at the one next to it across the gangway. Neil was on the same table, but on the other side – his back against the carriage 'wall' and his legs straight along the seat. Louis was lying down in an uncomfortable-looking position in a third booth with his elbow on the seat and his hand supporting his head which poked out near the gangway so he could see what was going on. John was passing round plenty of chocolate – well, he was trying to – Dorte and Edson both refused. "You're not great chocolate eaters, are you?" John observed. There were no beers because the train had been drunk dry of that particular beverage. At dinner they'd all ordered (despite still feeling the effects of the previous night) their usual *wodkas* and beers. But there was no beer. It was like Homer Simpson's worst nightmare, because, as you may have guessed, they didn't have doughnuts or TV either. There was still vodka, of course, but no-one fancied drinking many pints of that – so a couple (James and Lotte) ordered water while the others went for the Orange Star Cola and made vodka and cokes.

Chicken was on the menu and they all received one chicken leg and some vegetables. In fact, everyone on the train had chicken *legs* and our friends (for that is how I hope you think of them by this time) began to wonder aloud where the rest of the chicken had gone. Was Olga keeping the breast for herself, or had someone ingenuously cross-bred a centipede with a chicken and made a killing in the lucrative Russian barbecue market? It was their last night on the train and it seemed a pity there were no beers to celebrate with, although John made a point of purchasing a whole bottle of vodka (of the Black Death variety, Edson noticed) and plenty of Orange Star Cola, which he dealt out liberally once dinner was finished. Edson's apparently random comment (yes, you might want to return to the top of the page to check that again, sorry) was a reaction to a conversation that James and Louis had been having. Louis was explaining to James how panthers and leopards are one and the same creature, that black panthers are in fact just black leopards and that cheetahs were a different species altogether.

"Where?" asked James.

"In Kenya," said Louis and Edson simultaneously.

"Were you there too, Lou?" asked James.

"No. I just know this story. He tells it enough times." Louis shifted his body a little on the seat as if he was getting ready to quietly doze off.

"Is it a dull story, mate?" asked Neil – his eyes were incredibly wide, like he'd been doing speed.

"No – it's quite good actually." Edson smiled at Louis' grudging praise.

"Tell it then . . . what happened?" asked Lotte.

"Well, okay, but seeing as Louis' heard it before I won't do the epic version. The epic version probably is a bit too long."

IX

"I was in Nairobi and there were around 25 of us on a big trip this company makes very vague arrangements for you and then you go out there and stay with locals, maybe teach some local kids, or maybe run some kind of holiday activity thing for them or something. That's what we'd been doing and as a kind of reward we were off on Safari for about three days before going home. The place we were staying in was a house which had been converted into a kind of base for local young kids. The house was known as the Depot – spelt D-E-P-O-T and pronounced *dee-pott* because it's an acronym – the 'Dan Eldon Place of Tomorrow'. Dan Eldon was this fantastic young photographer and artist who was killed in Somalia when he was taking pictures of the conflict there, and his parents converted this whole house so his name would live on and young Kenyans could be inspired by him. I think they had financial support and stuff from the local Rotary Club as well.

"Anyway, the day of this jungle marooning we were off to the Great Rift Valley during the day, and then to the jungle to camp for the evening and then a proper safari the following day. The whole day was bizarre because we were just bombarded with signs and omens that the whole thing was a bad idea. It was like someone was trying to warn us, to tell us to go back."

"What kind of signs?" asked James

"Okay, almost as soon as I got up and went for a shower I slipped on the floor, and I mean really slipped, like in a cartoon, and my whole body just flew in the air and I crashed down right on, like, the upper part of my back. Knocked the wind right out of me."

"Painful," observed John.

"Yeah, but that's not all. We were expecting a couple of jeeps or something to take us on this trip, but our guide hadn't organised anything. So this guy, his name was Hasan, he went into town on the morning of our trip to try and get some transport. It took him ages, and when he finally came back he brought back this thing that was about two-thirds the size of a single-decker bus. It was metallic purple – perfect for blending in with the bush, of course, and it had kind of designer graffiti on various parts of it – on the front it said 'Detroit' for some reason, on the back it said 'Bad Boyz' – with a 'z' – and then underneath the number plate it had a skull and crossbones. And the bloody number plate had '666' in it! You know, unless someone had got some silver spray paint and written 'DO NOT GET ON THIS BUS' on it, the signs couldn't have been clearer. It blatantly wasn't the kind of bus that would be ideal for the jungle – you know, the reason there aren't many bright purple animals living in the bush is because purple isn't the best colour for camouflage.

"When we finally made it to the Great Rift Valley, we took this stupid short cut and got lost and got even further behind schedule. We had a good walk, though, up to the rim of this huge crater – there were amazing views – but on the way down someone fainted because we hadn't taken enough water with us up there and she was dehydrating. Anyway, we all got down and packed into this bus that couldn't fit us all in and carried on with the journey.

"Up to this point it had been pretty sunny and pretty hot, and the bus had this small sunroof. But when we first got in it had been kind of clipped down, so no-one could poke their heads out and it wasn't letting a lot of air in either, so we kind of accidentally dismantled it so there was basically a hole in the roof of the bus. Which was great . . . until we were nearing the main road we were heading for, when in the space of about ten minutes the sun disappeared behind some black clouds and it pissed it down monsoon-style. The dusty track we were following got really muddy and these big dips and pits filled up with water in about ten seconds and were even more dangerous than they were before. And of course the rain came pouring through the hole in the roof. Most people were okay, but I was at the front with my mate Jim and the rain started pelting down on us, on Hasan, on the driver and his girlfriend and brother who had come along too.

"So three of us were struggling with this blahdy sunroof while people in the back were pissing themselves laughing. Eventually we found some old tarpaulin lying in the bus somewhere – I don't know where it came from, maybe someone ripped it off part of a tent, I dunno, and we tried fixing that somehow, but still water was pouring in. I mean, it was raining so hard that there just didn't seem to be anything that could stem it. The bus was still peaking and troughing like a fucking fishing boat in a Pacific storm so even when it looked like we might be getting somewhere someone would invariably fall over as the bus rocked and the whole operation would be ruined. At one point we had the tarpaulin all fixed up somehow, but the water pressure pushed the tarpaulin down and a whole gush of water just dropped down and splashed us all. Finally we managed to rig up the tarpaulin and the sunroof somehow so that just a few drops were sneaking in, and at about the same time we got back onto a proper road again, although it was only marginally better than the track. But, honestly, it was like the Gods themselves just authorised the downpour, as if to say 'TURN BACK NOW! HOW MANY SIGNS DO YOU NEED?'

"Anyway, we survived all that and made it to the reserve really late – about six in the evening and we'd been aiming for three at the absolute latest. Over the last hour or so of the journey Hasan had been giving us a bit of information about the wildlife we were likely to see and not likely to see. He said we probably wouldn't see any big cats or any elephant, but then again we might get lucky. I personally doubted that any animal worth it's salt would come anywhere near our bright purple van unless it wanted to a) mate with it, or b) attack it. He said we would definitely see giraffe and buffalo, which, he said, are actually the biggest killers of humans in the jungle. I knew that hippo were a lot more dangerous than people think and they kill a fair amount of humans each year, but," he was interrupted by James.

"Really?"

"Yeah, they get very defensive if you go anywhere near their young, apparently. Anyway, I didn't know that buffalo were so dangerous. After about fifteen minutes or so of driving in the park it was getting dark really quickly and we passed a camping area on our left. I couldn't see it very well because it was so dusky, but there were some buildings there and a few tents and a whole expanse of grass that was obviously set aside for campers like us. Hasan stopped the bus and stood up at the front. It was weird sitting at the front because we could hear Hasan discussing what to do and where to go. He stood up and said we had a choice: either stop there and camp for the night and run late for most of the following day, meaning we might have to rush our safari a bit; or push on to the next camping area which was about an hour or so away, and put up with the discomfort of doing everything in real darkness and not being able to eat until probably about three hours later."

"*This* was the real crossroads of the whole day. Without realising it or without recognising it we'd had all these signs throughout the day that said things simply weren't going our way, and now finally we were being asked to make a decision for ourselves. We didn't know what the consequences could be. I definitely had a sense of something in my stomach, you know, just butterflies that you could mistake for excitement, or hunger, even, but it was one of those deep down feelings that means you're worrying about something, only I had no idea what it was. There didn't even seem to be any reason to worry because we all trusted Hasan completely – well apart from when it came to securing proper transport for safaris, anyway.

"We were all starving, so there was a bit of a split in the bus. The loudest initial reaction came from a couple of the blokes at the back who wanted to press on and couldn't see why we shouldn't, apart from the minor food issue. It looked like we'd definitely go on, but then a couple of people started saying maybe we should stop and play it safe. This encouraged a couple more to agree and suddenly there were little individual debates and arguments going on all over the bus. Then a guy at the back asked Hasan what he thought we should do. It all went quiet again, and Hasan paused for a moment and said that he was keen to catch up with his timetable but it might be better to leave it until morning. So we were on the verge of all agreeing to stay, when another guy spoke up and asked what we'd really gain from staying. He said we'd all get a meal, feel better and then probably immediately wish we'd carried on.

"It was bizarre – the events for the rest of the night were resting on this one decision without us realising how important the decision was. Someone asked Hasan if he thought we would make it to the other camp without too much of a problem. Hasan suddenly became a bit more positive and said we could and he'd been there a few times so he knew it fairly well. And someone shouted, 'Let's do it.' And after a couple more bits of dissention we finally decided to go on. As we moved off Hasan said that under no circumstances were any of us to get out of the bus until we reached the campsite. He said that night-time was the most dangerous time in the jungle and we should stay on the bus at all times."

By this time only Edson's voice and the murmurings of other assorted last night drinkers broke the silence in the carriage. Despite Louis' scepticism and the fact that he'd heard the story before, despite Neil's overpowering personality, and despite Lotte and Dorte surely not being able to fully keep track of the story, especially as the speed of Edson's speech really increased at certain points, everyone seemed to be paying their full attention to the story. Edson took another large glug of his vodka and coke to finish his glass. "Is there any more of this?" he asked, as if he wanted payment for his story.

"Of course!" said John, and he took his glass and poured a generous shot and a bit of coke into it, and then busily began to refill everyone else as well. James seemed about to refuse the offer when he caught a glance of Neil readying himself for a comment, so he relented. Neil smiled as if he were a step closer to James' soul.

"OK. We drove on for about forty minutes. The lights on the bus were really shit, so even though me and Jim were right near the front we couldn't see much, and a lot of the time trees either side of the track were arching right over so it was really dark. It was definitely quieter in the bus, but the mood was still pretty good, despite a few people complaining they were hungry. The problem was that we had no idea how far away this other campsite was – Hasan had reckoned about an hour or so. The track was pretty good and we seemed to be making good time. Jim asked me how much money it would take for me to jump out of the bus and run a hundred metres into the plain and back again. After a short discussion I said no money and he said the same. It would probably have been safe, I mean, the chances of meeting a dangerous wild animal in that space was low, but after that warning from Hasan neither of us fancied it.

"Then the bus suddenly slowed down and stopped. I looked through the front window and could just make out that a tree had fallen on the track in front of us. It wasn't a massive tree or anything, but it still completely blocked the track. For a minute Hasan talked quietly to the driver, and then, and I couldn't believe this after his earlier warning, he *got out of the bus* with the driver and the driver's brother and went, I guessed, to see if there was any way round. Now, in retrospect, this was the biggest clue we could ever have, the biggest omen, the most blatant warning. For the first time there was something *physically stopping us from going any further*," Edson pounded his left palm with the back of his right hand to emphasise his point, "All that was missing was a sign hanging on the tree saying 'TURN BACK' in big red capitals, you know. When they went outside my stomach really tightened up. That was really the first time that I started to consciously believe that, I dunno, that we were in trouble or something.

"Now, to our left was a kind of bank going upwards because we were on the side of a slope. The tree had fallen *uphill* across the road, from right to left but Hasan reckoned we *could* go round the tree by coming off the road on the right, going around the base of the tree where it had snapped, and then come back onto the road the other side. There was the problem of coming back up the slope on that side, but the driver reckoned it was do-able. So we all had to make a decision again. It was easier to make this time because either way we had to drive for an hour or so, so we might as well continue going forward."

"The driver backed up a bit, then went forward, then he veered right. There was a kind of step as we came off the road, quite small but pretty steep, and the whole bus rolled, and I mean really rolled and for a moment it felt like the whole bus was going to topple over onto its side, but the driver, rather than slowing up, did what I later realised was the right thing, and actually speeded up! That scared the life out of me at the time – for such a difficult drive, it seemed to me that we should be taking it very slowly. We went round the tree stump and then he rammed the wheel to the left to start the climb. But almost as soon as the bus tried to move up the slope, we stopped. The embankment was just too steep for us. He tried rolling back and really gunning it but we just didn't get anywhere.

"Hasan and the driver got out to look at our mess, and we were off the road now so it was somehow more worrying than last time. Hasan came back and told us we couldn't turn round because there was no room to move with all the trees and bushes, so the only way we *could* go was forward. He said that if it hadn't rained that day there probably wouldn't have been a problem. But it had. He said that he needed some of the guys to get off the bus and help push it back onto the road. So about eight of us got out. It was pretty silent now on the bus, and there was a real tension about the place. It was pretty slippery back there behind the bus as we got ready to push. All I could think about was Hasan telling us never to get out of the bus. We started pushing and the bus went forward, and almost made it. Then it rolled down again and we quickly had to run backwards so it didn't knock us over. We tried again. It didn't work. Someone said 'Third time lucky!' And we started pushing again but it still wouldn't go. The bus rolled back and we all kind of stood safely away with our hands on our hips and I remember feeling something in my stomach approaching panic.

"Hasan suggested we should get a few more people out of the bus. But before we could do anything one of the guys started shouting at us all to COME ON!" and Edson started punching the air in front of him in imitation of a footballer-style encouragement. "We all started shouting as well and we pushed as the bus started to go again and this time we were definitely pushing for a couple of seconds longer and the bus definitely moved a little further. We all paused like we were catching our breath, and it rolled back an inch, but it felt like we kind of caught it and then just drove it back up the slope and soon we were pushing something that didn't need pushing anymore and it was back on the road. We all started cheering and going a bit over the top about it, but Hasan quickly told us to get back in the bus." and Edson shrugged his shoulders before polishing off his vodka and coke.

"Another one of them, Edson?" enquired John.

"Yeah, that'd be great, thanks. The whole bus was quite quiet all round after that. All day it had been really noisy with music and people laughing and flirting and complaining and stuff, and now everyone was just really quiet. We carried on driving and by about eight-thirty I think a lot of us had begun to realise that Hasan may have misjudged exactly where this camping area was. He was looking at the map a lot and talking very quietly with the driver. It wasn't a nice feeling, being lost in the jungle in the night. Then, a few minutes later we came to a part of the road that was very muddy. The driver could see before we got to it that it was really bad, so he slowed down and tried to navigate through it. Hasan stood up and told us all this was a difficult part to pass, but he was sure that we couldn't be far away from the camp. Just the way he phrased it worried me because he wasn't one hundred per cent sure anymore.

"We got through the first bit and it looked like we'd be okay, but then the engine stalled and when we tried to move again, we couldn't. This time we were pretty much right out in the open – there was just grassland on both sides of us and a few trees. The driver kept trying to get us out, but he couldn't. Hasan got out, but came back very quickly and said that this time we were really stuck, and he was sorry but *everyone* had to get out. Some would have to push, some would have to just wait by the bus, but we needed as much weight as possible out of the bus to help stop it from sinking any further. Most of us just had trainers on, and when we jumped off the bus our feet sank into the mud, right up to around the laces. In some places it was all sticky, but in others it was really slippery – it was so dangerous.

"All I could think about was lions. I've read quite a lot of books by this guy called Kenneth Anderson who was a British expat living in India and he wrote books on his experiences in the Indian jungles and lots of the stories were about man-eating tigers. He was an expert on man-eaters and how and why big cats become man-eaters. I was thinking about all that now, and I was thinking about the way Anderson described the attacks. I knew that there weren't tigers in this park, but there were lions and I also remembered all the stories about the workers that were killed by lions when they were building the railways in Kenya. I thought about the huge weight of a lion on your back, its claws in your shoulder and the split second between the moment when you realise what's happening and the moment when you're neck is shattered by its jaws. I know it was irrational. A lion was unlikely to be in the area, especially with all the commotion, but I just kept thinking about how a lion could just pick one of us off if he wanted to.

"I was standing at the front of the bus for some reason – I can't remember why, I think we were just waiting for everyone to get off and there was more light at the front so we kind of instinctively gathered there. I was feeling sick. I think it was worse for me and Jim sitting at the front because we could see how worried Hasan was. We'd seen him mumbling and looking at maps and saying we should have stayed at the first camp and stuff like that. The others were a bit ignorant I think. I said to this girl, I can't even remember her name now, but I remember saying, and it was a stupid thing to say – it would sound stupid in a Hollywood movie, but I said, 'Do you realise we're probably in more danger now than we've ever been in our lives?' And she looked at me for a moment, looked down at me, because she was quite tall and I was kind of speaking to the ground anyway, and she said, 'You must have had a pretty boring life, then.' I felt like smacking her in the face. The last thing I wanted was someone with no experience of the jungle telling me that if the most frightening experience I had ever had was being stranded in darkness in the middle of a jungle in Kenya with a purple bus that was built for roads not mud and a guide who was clearly out of his depth, then I had had a boring life. What was I supposed to do? Apologise for not having been a survivor of a plane crash?"

"She was just trying to keep spirits up, though, surely?" said James.

"Yeah . . . I know, that was just how I felt at the time. Anyway, Some of us moved round to the back of the bus, and the rest kind of stood at the side. We all started pushing and we got it moving fairly quickly this time, but then it got stuck again. Someone's shoe got stuck in the mud and his foot came out of it and the shoe was left stuck in the mud by itself. We tried again, and we managed to move it a bit further, and the whole process went on for about twenty minutes or so I guess, and there was mud *everywhere*. I actually got off pretty lightly, to be honest, but the last time we pushed the bus it kind of shot out of the mud onto some firmer ground – some of us had felt it moving and had let go. Others had started to put less weight behind it, but one guy, I think his name was Bill, was still pushing like a fucking prop in a scrum and as the bus shot forward he felt flat down in the mud. I'm not joking, he was covered from head to foot in really sticky, wet, black mud. All over his face and in his hair, oh God, it was disgusting – I really felt for the bloke. We all clambered back in, but we got mud everywhere – it was going over our clothes, our tents, over some of the food, the seats, everything. It was grim. And the atmosphere was getting even worse. A couple of arguments started at the back of the bus and there was some shouting, and although it calmed down it didn't feel like it had gone away totally." Edson took another drink and looked at everyone for a moment.

"As we went deeper into the jungle the bus got progressively quieter – like we were just waiting for the next thing to happen. At about nine o'clock we still hadn't found the campsite and I could see that Hasan was . . . well, he wasn't exactly *fran*tic, but he was certainly very concerned. He started saying to the driver and to us that he hadn't been to this place for a while, and he'd never been there at night. His map didn't look very good either. Finally we slowed right down and then stopped. We were in a very dark area and I couldn't see why we had stopped, but Hasan and the driver got out again with a couple of torches and wandered around in front of the bus for a few minutes.

"They came back and explained that in front of us was a big dip in the track, and then a waterfall. He said that he was pretty sure that if we went down this dip, over the bridge where the waterfall met the river, then the campsite was pretty close by, as he could remember seeing this waterfall before. That didn't sound very convincing to me, to be honest. I mean, he was only *pretty* sure that he'd seen this waterfall before, and I started to believe that if we weren't lost yet we weren't far from it. The problem, Hasan said, was that the dip right in front of us was a very steep one – it was more of a step or a drop rather than a dip and it was very risky to take the bus down there. He thought about it for a minute and said we didn't really have much choice because there weren't any other tracks to follow. Unfortunately, the drop was so dangerous that we all had to get out of the bus again. A couple of us went forward and had a look at the drop, and it really was bad – it was almost vertical and at the very least a foot deep – it would have been a struggle for a jeep let alone a blatant blahdy street vehicle.

"The driver edged forward and slowly went over the drop, and the whole bus literally just swayed crazily to the left so it looked for all the world like it was about to topple over and I remember thinking, 'That's it! It's gone!' and some people just shouted 'Nooo!' and covered their eyes and some just had their mouths wide open – I mean it wasn't far away from being on two wheels – but somehow the bus righted itself again and then stopped. Then he tried to move but he was stuck in more mud. We all went down to the bus and the situation was the grimmest it had been the whole day. The bus was stuck. The bridge looked incredibly flimsy and to get across the bus would have to back-up and change direction slightly, which it couldn't do. Also, on the other side of the bridge was a very steep and muddy slope, so even if we could get the bus over it didn't look like we would make it up the slope anyway. Don't ask me why they didn't check that first – I suppose they didn't want to wander too far from the bus, and I don't blame them. So we were well and truly stuck there for the night. The waterfall was absolutely deafening, and that just seemed so much worse than having silence, it was like it could provide plenty of cover for anything to creep up on us.

"Hasan asked us all to get back on the bus. We had all realised that this time there was no way we were going to be able to shift the bus and even if we could, there was nowhere to shift it *to* – we were stuck between a river and that ledge that we had just come down. Hasan said that we had to camp over the bridge on a piece of grass next to the pool that the waterfall fell into. He said he'd camped there before we'd be perfectly safe once we'd set up a big fire. The plan was for most of us to set up the minimum amount of tents possible, with as many as possible squeezing into them, and any left over would sleep in the bus. Whoever wasn't setting tents up would build the fire and cook some stew and make some hot drinks.

"I was one of the ones setting the tents up. And then I needed a piss. This was terrible because obviously I had to move away from everyone else into the darkness and away from the fire, and, basically, I was cacking it. I walked over to near this bush, undid my flies, and took a step forward. All I could think about at the time was lions and snakes and crocodiles that might live near the waterfall, and as I took a step forward I swear the ground moved under my foot and I almost shat myself – I was so scared and for a brief second I thought I'd trodden on a snake. It must have just been a bit of stony ground, but because I was thinking of snakes I was convinced I'd trodden on some kind of animal – my stomach was jumping all over the place and I just wanted to finish the piss and get back to the group, but it seemed to take ages.

"Anyway, I survived. At about eleven there was some kind of vegetable stew, but there was a big shortage of cutlery and plates – there was just a pile of them and you had to help yourself. And it got a bit ugly. We were all starving hungry and everyone started scrabbling and jostling around in the darkness for some kind of vessel to put a bit of shitty stew in. I just got a massive mug and kind of drank the stew out of that.

"Hasan said he'd be staying up all night with the fire to keep it burning high because he was concerned that the tents were quite close to it, which could be dangerous, and also that the tents would block the light of the fire if it died down, so it wouldn't act as much of a deterrent to any over-curious wildlife. It was weird because on one hand I was grateful that Hasan had recognised that and was staying up, but on the other hand I was worried that he was worried *enough* to stay awake all night.

"Our tent was yer standard two-man tent, but due to the small camping area and lack of time we only put three tents up – two two-man and one large one that held about five or six, I guess. So we all had to make sacrifices and the big tent had, I think, eight people in, and we stuffed four people into each of the smaller ones and everyone else went to sleep in the uncomfortable bus. But this two-man was a nightmare. I've said about the horrible feeling I had in my stomach all night, well now it was getting worse. We wanted to keep the tent flap open because it was hot in there and because we needed air, but we wanted it closed to keep out any arachnids or slithering reptiles. So we left it open a tiny bit and all slept with our heads at the front of the tent.

"There was me, Jim, a girl called Alice and some guy called Craig. We were packed in really tightly, so tight that we literally couldn't turn over or move, we were just dead straight, arms by our sides, like we were in a coffin. I was right on one end and, um, the diagonal line of the tent went right in front of my face, so there was virtually no space between my face and the canvas, and it was incredibly claustrophobic. I started trying to breathe deep breaths, which helped but when I tried to move I found I couldn't and my arms were just pinned by my sides, and I could feel myself panicking a bit – it's never nice when you feel trapped, is it? But after a while I dropped off.

"Then, I guess about twenty minutes or half an hour later, I woke up suddenly, like I had been having a nightmare and there was a kind of jolt inside me and I felt sick with panic. I couldn't breathe and I was sure something was going on outside, I felt really unsafe and insecure. I needed some air, but I could hardly move, and I could feel the panic rising a bit more as I realised I couldn't breathe properly, but I struggled and I wriggled and managed to poke my head out of the tent and gulp some air in.

"I could see Hasan, this guy Paul and another slightly older bloke called John Walsh who seemed very worldly and at times during the trip had kind of acted as a leader, by the fire. John was a nice guy, actually – wanted to be a writer or something, I think, and he was always trying to get us to sing old Irish folk songs in the evenings when we got pissed. The big tent was to the right of the fire and in front of me. And although I was getting the air I needed, I still felt a worry in my stomach, and now I started to realise that there was something going on. The three guys were talking quite quickly, and then Hasan poured some kind of liquid over the fire so it reared up a good ten feet in the air and then they carefully built up the fire with more wood.

"Maybe it was the shadow because of the fire, but Hasan in particular looked very worried. I waved at Paul and he came over and told me that there was a rogue buffalo that was upset with us being there and had come to investigate. As I said, buffalo are the biggest killers in the jungle, and a rogue buffalo meant real trouble. I don't know if you know much about rogue elephants, but it's basically when a bull elephant goes a bit crazy and leaves the herd and goes off by itself in a bad temper. Obviously it's a bit more complicated than that, but anyway, it just goes around causing destruction. Well, buffaloes do the same thing. Really they're just like a drunk bloke in a pub who's looking for a fight, except the rogue elephant or buffalo is a hundred per cent likely to win. Fortunately, Paul said that the fire had put him off and he'd ambled away.

"I edged back into bed and fell asleep again. But about half an hour later I woke up again with exactly the same feeling, perhaps even worse this time. It really was the worst feeling I've ever had, just utter panic and fear in my stomach, it was so bizarre, it was almost like . . . I don't know, I don't know how to describe it, but it was a horrible feeling. I struggled out and got air again – it may just have been a lack of oxygen that was doing it I suppose, but it was strange that both times I woke up just as they were having trouble with this buffalo. As soon as I poked my head out I knew the buffalo was back. They were pouring more stuff on the fire and it kept leaping high, then a couple of minutes later it would shrink a bit and they'd have to do it again. The buffalo just wasn't going away.

"I'm not a great one for the supernatural, but that whole day really felt unreal, really . . . *uncanny* with omens and feelings and stuff. I couldn't see the buffalo because it was approaching from the track and the big tent was blocking my view. The problem was that the tent was blocking the fire to some extent, so the buffalo was being braver than perhaps it might normally have been. Every time it got close they poured stuff on the fire and scared it off, but then it would come back again a few minutes later. This went on for about another half an hour. Finally, Paul came round to all the tents and told everyone to get their clothes and shoes on, and said that when he gave the signal, we should run down the hill, over the small bridge and onto the bus. Hasan clearly thought that the buffalo was considering charging the camp.

"Strangely, once he'd finally said that, I kind of felt slightly better, like at least I knew why I felt so worried and at least we were doing something and not just waiting. So we all got dressed, which wasn't easy in our limited space. None of us said much, and then Jim went, 'What a shambolic operation this is' for about the twentieth time that day and everyone laughed and it helped ease the tension a bit. About five minutes later Paul came round again and said the fire had scared it off up the hill for a moment, so we should all make a run for it back to the bus. The members of the big tent followed us. I was petrified we were going to get charged on our way down. It was so dark and slippery and you could barely see a thing.

"The people who were sleeping on the bus were a bit surprised to find us coming back in. We explained what was going on, but they didn't seem too impressed. That made me quite angry actually – it was similar to when that episode with that girl earlier. I mean, there was real danger out there, Hasan might have got us lost but he was really experienced and even he was plainly bricking it! Getting charged and trampled by a bloody buffalo isn't exactly a thing you take lightly, know what I mean? I didn't sleep all night.

"A couple of hours or so later Paul came down to see us. He said they had to stay out there until it got light. He told us that about fifteen minutes earlier John had tried to come down to check on us as they thought the buffalo had gone on walkabout again. But as he turned the corner to come down the slope to the bridge the buffalo was about to come *up* the slope. Apparently, John froze for a moment and then backed-up and slowly went back to the fire. When Paul had gone again I asked the driver and the driver's wife why it hadn't charged and they said they didn't know. Basically the guy was just very, very lucky – maybe the buffalo was off-guard or something, although I would have thought that would have been worse, and on top of that he did amazingly well to keep calm and not panic.

"About an hour or so later someone at the back of the bus shouted 'There it is!' The buffalo was standing no more than ten metres away at the back end of the bus on the left-hand side. I was sitting on the left and when I turned round I could see it. By now dawn wasn't too far away, and you could just make out this very large black cow-shaped blob on the grass outside just staring at us. The driver told us all it was important to be quiet. So we all shut up. I asked him if the buffalo might charge the bus and he said he didn't know. It just stood there, staring at our stupid fish-out-of-water metallic purple bus for about half an hour. It didn't move, just stared. Someone asked what would happen if someone got off the bus now and the driver and his wife and his brother all said they would be killed. Then we all started to worry about the other three. What if they thought the buffalo had gone and came down to see us, only to meet it on the way down like John had done earlier? From their position above the slope behind some trees there was no way they would be able to see the buffalo. There was nothing we could do, though. No-one could go up and tell them, and we couldn't shout firstly because the waterfall was far too loud and secondly because it could upset the buffalo even further, so we had to sit there and just wait it out and hope.

"Luckily, though, no-one came down, and then the buffalo ambled off and then a few minutes later appeared right in front of the bus, like it was circling us, like all he needed was a can opener to get at us. He was also very close to the bridge so anyone coming down from the camp now would be in serious trouble. It must have been close to dawn now as it was getting much lighter and I could see it reasonably well. It was huge. I mean, *cows* are pretty big, when you think about it, but this thing was massive – there can't be many land animals in the world that are much bigger than a buffalo. We just waited – that was all we could do. Finally it turned and ambled up towards the camp. We couldn't warn them, and it looked like it was going right into the camp, but we couldn't tell. There seemed to be a gap of silence while we wondered what was going to happen, and then suddenly the fire rose up really high again, and we saw the buffalo retreat and it wandered on up the hill and away.

"Obviously it had done this a few times during the night, but now it was light, so we were hoping that this was the end of it all. The three guys waited about an hour, and then came down, satisfied that it had finally gone away." Edson took a deep breath and polished off his vodka. His mouth was very dry and he was suddenly aware that he had been dominating the conversation for a very long time.

"So, did it come back?" asked John, after a moment.

"No, it stayed away, but obviously we still had to get out of there and the stupid bus was stuck."

"You must have been *knackered*," said James.

"Yeah, we were, just really drained, you know."

"How did you get the bus out?" asked Lotte

"Well, the first thing we did once we'd packed up was to help move the bus out of where it was stuck and turn it round to try and get it back up that drop we'd gone down. That wasn't too hard, as it happened. We didn't need to go across the bridge anymore because we were just going looking for wildlife now – from a safe distance of course, and it was lucky because seeing that titchy bridge in the daylight made me wonder whether the bus would even fit on it, let alone whether it could actually support us. Getting the bus back up that step was the real problem.

"First of all we tried having all of us pushing it and the driver just revving as hard as he could to try and get it up there, but that was never going to happen – we didn't even get close. So we tried building a ramp out of rocks and wood, and people were chopping away with an axe at this huge tree root which was really in the way too. Then about twenty of us started pushing – all round the back and all along the sides. We were knackered and you couldn't grip on the wet ground and it was so packed at the back with pushers that you couldn't put your back into it because there wasn't enough room, which was really frustrating. But there was this one guy who decided he'd be like the cox on a rowing boat – he may even have been a cox, he was pretty small, and he was urging us on at the side, shouting at us to push harder. And I got a bit pissed off with him. There we were, all sweating trying to get us out of that hole, and he was there . . . just . . . *shouting*. Thanks for your help, mate! Anyway, it worked in a way because it made us angry and after a lot of effort and some more work on our makeshift ramp we finally pushed the thing back onto the track. So we all got in, and went and looked at giraffes and a couple of rhino and some more buffalo and warthogs and plenty of monkeys and stuff. It was great. I really think the most amazing things were the giraffe. We saw a few of them and a few crossed our path, but we turned one corner and suddenly there must have been twenty or thirty of them, and it felt like Jurassic Park, they just looked so surreal, it was bizarre to see them like that."

"Blimey," said James.

"Astounding," said John.

"Are you finished?" said Neil.

"Er . . . yes, I guess so."

"Good, 'cause I've needed to go to the Russian Trog for about the last twenty minutes – I didn't know when you were gonna stop! Hya hya!" and he hopped out of the room. There was a silence for a moment while everyone looked at their feet.

"Great story," said Dorte.

"Yeah, fantastic!" said Lotte, and Edson was sure he saw her eyes sparkle and he felt his back tingle.

"Well . . . oh, wait! You won't believe this! I forgot about this, but I promise you it's the truth. When I had left Uni at the end of that first year I'd left some of my stuff in the house I was moving into when I got back. Well, when I got home Dad told me that the house had been burgled and everything I'd left there had been nicked – right down to my blahdy duvet! Loads of CDs, my TV, everything. But then I found out which night they'd done it, and realised that, because there's only a three hour difference between Kenya and England, I'd actually been burgled at the *same time* as the whole buffalo episode!"

"No way!" exclaimed James.

"I promise you it's true! I couldn't believe it either at first. Not only was I in danger of being trampled to death by a large mad mammal, a load of my worldly possessions were being pilfered a few hundred miles away. Yeah, thanks!"

"Astounding," murmured John, "Did that bus run over any black cats as well?"

Chapter 6

Certificate PG

Not a lot of swearing, a fair bit of drama, and, let's face it, this was never the place to come if you were looking for copious helpings of sex and violence. Just make your own judgement. If you think it's mostly okay, just substitute the swear words with more palatable ones – that can be quite fun, too . . . well, it'd pass a rainy afternoon, anyway.

I

James had grown tired and far too drunk. He rose from his seat, and tried to push his way past Neil. Neil, however, was too drunk to move and protested that 'Jimsy-boy' shouldn't be going anywhere anyway. Not a man to be beaten so easily, especially when in drunk-and-stubborn mode, James sat back down and then slipped his body under the table, bumping the bridge of his nose lightly on the way. There followed a complicated procedure lasting at least a minute in which he flailed around on the floor, crawling in bewildering directions and trying to worm his way past various kinds of legs. He emerged on the other side and wandered towards the exit of the dining car. "Where you off to James?" called Edson. James waved his arm behind him like a swinging elephant's trunk.

"Bed," he managed to emit.

"Come on Jimsy! Come back to Unky Neil!" called Neil, but James was already out the door.

"Do you think he'll find his way back?" asked Dorte.

"Yeah, homing iiiinnnstinct," powered Neil, beating his chest with the palm of his hand as he said 'instinct'. "Never fails when you're pissed – you can always get home much easier when sober than when pissed . . . I mean pissed . . . than when . . . sober," he spat the last few words out with great concentration on his face and his eyes screwed tightly closed.

After another half hour of the kind of inanity that always occurs when the booze is cheap and the bar only closes when you want it to, John announced his intention to also head off for a bit of shut-eye. "Don't know how you lot can keep going for so long," he said with a mischievous grin.

"Like you can't hold your own, Johnny!" cried Neil. "You could drink us all under the table if you wanted to, hya, hya!"

"Hmm . . . not sure about those girls," whispered John, nodding his head towards Lotte and Dorte, "Those Scandinavians know how to drink."

"That's just one of the many things they know how to do Johnny!" Louis and Edson were pretty blathered by this point, but not so blathered that they couldn't roll their eyes at that attempt at a wisecrack.

"Well, 'night all."

"'Night!" everyone else chorused.

As John made his way out of the carriage the conversation ceased for a moment. Everyone looked at their watches or looked out the window or tried, nearly in vain, to cram more beer into their bloated stomachs. Edson and Louis were sitting with their backs to the door that John had just exited. Louis was looking thoughtfully into his beer, his face a picture of mild perplexity – it was the look, Edson knew, that directly precluded Louis asking some vague philosophical question that he fancied having an argument about. Edson looked up and away from his facial analysis of Louis and noticed that there was only one other person in the dining car apart from their group. They'd driven everyone else out, no doubt, with their witty humour. And then, just as Louis was raising his hand into the air in front of him, ready to begin his onslaught, Edson said, "Ha! What just happened to that guy?"

Everyone looked around and laughed playfully. "Poor guy!" said Lotte, "What happened?"

"I dunno . . . he kind of suddenly sat up really straight, and then just slumped forward onto the table!"

"Must've passed out," said Louis, who was evidently still intent on redirecting the conversation towards his philosophical topic.

"Maybe we should see if he's ok," said Dorte. Both women looked a bit concerned. Neil had only turned round for a second. But Louis suddenly got up.

"Yeah, maybe we should." He walked over to the table, which was about ten paces further down the train. He squatted down so he could see the guy's face. Edson recognised the man's beige shirt and his crop-cut greying hair. "It's that Chinese guy we saw doing Tai Chi, Ed." It was very quiet. The waiters weren't there; they were probably in the kitchen cleaning up. Lotte and Dorte had turned right round in their seats and had hauled their bodies up a bit so they were half-kneeling to get a better view. Even Neil was looking now.

"He'll be all right," murmured Neil. Louis had his hand on the man's shoulder and was whispering something to him that the rest couldn't hear. Then he started shaking the man's shoulder slightly, then a bit more violently, but there was still no reaction. Edson suddenly felt a bit sick and he could feel his head swimming, his eyes clouding. Without looking up from the man's face, and with firmness and authority Louis said,

"Someone get John. Quickly."

Neil got to his feet, but Edson was already down the carriage, as if anticipating Louis' command. Although his head was already beginning to clear, he felt unsteady as he skated along the floor. He could barely feel his feet touching the deck – they seemed so far away, almost detached from his body. He wondered how far John had got. John was no slouch, even with a few beers and vodkas and a large dinner nestling in his comfortable stomach. Edson realised that if anyone was coming the other way he was going to clatter them; he wouldn't have time to stop and dodge. There wasn't room anyway. He almost felt like he did when he was on those Chinese buses whose drivers overtook on blind corners. They didn't waste time not taking chances. Through two carriages he flew until, at the end of the third car he saw John's frame at the far end. He suddenly felt like a child. "John!" he didn't care if he woke everyone on the carriage up, this was important. He carried on running, and although John had already turned round, he shouted "John!" again.

"What's the matter?" asked John, who looked slightly concerned but also amused at the sight of this skinny young man unsteadily sprinting towards him.

"Come back," said Edson breathlessly, "Come back, this guy, that Chinese guy, he's collapsed."

"Collapsed?" said John, but he was already striding behind Edson's excited skips that led the way back to the dining car. Despite himself, Edson experienced a real exhilaration at his importance in this operation. He was the one who went to get John and bring him back to help this guy – he was the quickest to react. Even as he began to consider the gravity of the situation, he couldn't keep the thrill that coursed through him at bay. Was it still the alcohol, he wondered, or would he have felt like this anyway?

As soon as Edson had left, Lotte, Dorte and Neil had crowded up to Louis and the Chinese man. "Maybe you guys should get back a bit, make sure he's got plenty of air."

"Is he breathing?" asked Neil as he stepped back awkwardly.

"Not sure . . . what do we do? Sit him back up?"

"Or put him in the recovery position?" suggested Neil.

"Christ knows. I don't even know what's wrong with him." There was silence for a minute and Louis decided to push the man back up so he was resting his back on the seat again. He pinned him there with his hand on his shoulder. "Where is fucking Edson?"

"I'll go," said Neil.

"Jesus," said Louis. Lotte and Dorte sat down awkwardly on the seats on the other side of the gangway, their view of the Chinese man obscured by Louis' body. Louis was bending over slightly, perhaps wondering whether to slap the man lightly around the chops like they do in films and cartoons. "Think I might take his pulse," he said quietly, more to himself than anything. He took the man's wrist. A moment later he laid it back on the table. "Think I can feel something." The truth was he couldn't be sure what exactly he could feel because his senses were so dulled by alcohol, besides which the scene had encouraged his whole body to feel as if it was beating and pulsing like a single giant heart – how could he possibly distinguish the difference? It felt like being in a nightmare – the situation had the same surreal atmosphere, and the alcohol made him feel dizzy and helpless, and without any control over events at all.

Neil was marching back through the dining car with a wobbly Edson and a determined John Thornley in tow. As they neared the scene, Edson stepped aside to allow John to overtake him and tend to the man. Edson already felt a bit calmer. He'd completed his job successfully. With John there he felt safe. He reminded him of his dead Granddad: immeasurable experience, a lifetime of knowledge, reassuringly large hands.

"Let's have a look," said John as Louis moved aside for him.

"I don't think it was drink," said Louis, vaguely. John took a pulse from the man's neck, his tongue licking his own lower-lip in concentration.

"Very faint. Heart attack," John stood up straight and looked around. "We need to lie him down somewhere."

"Cabin?" suggested Edson quickly.

"No time," and then he mumbled to himself, "No room on this floor either." Indeed, the gangway between the tables was incredibly narrow – almost as narrow as that of the aisle on a 'plane. "We'll have to get him up on this table," said John. "Give us a hand, Louis." It was a struggle, because this wasn't a small man.

Even once he was on the table, it was still awkward. For John to reach the man's mouth and begin CPR he had to kneel on the bench-like seat, which was hardly ideal and certainly pretty ungainly. To add to the problems, the man was obviously too long to fit onto the table, so his legs were hanging off the end. "Ok, let's shift him down a bit, and then balance him across the two tables," said John. "Quickly now." Now the man formed a kind of barrier across the width of the carriage.

He felt ashamed of himself, and blamed it on the drink, but seeing the man like that made Edson think about the day he went to Tianenmen Square and was part of a great queue of people who were rushed in and out of a room containing the embalmed Chairman Mao. This man in front of him didn't even pass much of a resemblance to the deceased leader – and he certainly didn't have the same plasticky look about him that Mao had had in his chamber. "Right, someone go and get one of those waiters or the chef or someone, just let them know what's going on, if we can we need to get an ambulance or something waiting at the next stop."

With that John turned his attention solely onto the prone Chinese man. All this had happened extraordinarily quickly, probably in less than two minutes, but everything seemed to be moving in slow motion. With every passing second everyone knew that this man's life was in further danger, and by the time John began to administer CPR it felt like about ten minutes had elapsed since the time Edson had spotted the man slump forwards. All of which made John's incredible composure even more impressive. "I'll go," said Neil. Edson felt a pang of resentment – he wanted to be the messenger.

John had already tilted the man's head back and was just about finished checking that there was nothing in the man's mouth that was blocking the airway. He leant forward, pinching the man's nose tightly, turned his own face slightly so he was looking down the length of the man's body, and then covered the man's mouth with his own and breathed hard twice. Edson watched the Chinese man's chest inflate with the breath – it seemed so unnatural. Louis was standing awkwardly on the other side of the man's legs, trapped at the far end of the train. Lotte and Dorte were sitting on the benches either side of his legs, holding them down so they couldn't suddenly slip off somehow. Edson sat hopelessly at the next table from them, wanting to say something intelligent or do something heroic, but feeling he was incapable of doing either.

John was now performing chest thrusts on the man. Louis

winced. He'd once heard that it was possible to break the breastbone or some ribs doing this – anyone inexperienced could easily kill someone while trying to save their life. He, too, felt completely helpless. He stood there, all ungainly, staring vacantly at the man and wishing he had known what to do while Edson was fetching John. Usually he was in complete control of any situation. At school he'd been masterful in exams – his intelligence was such that he didn't need to do a lot of revision. He could absorb so much more and understand ideas and theories so much quicker than most people. He'd been in China alone for a few months, overcome the language problems and embraced the culture almost as if he'd been living it all his life. In short, there had always been something he could do to positively affect a situation, even if it was offering advice, or confidently bluffing his way through a problem with a mixture of intelligence and charm. But now he felt almost useless.

To Edson, it seemed as if John had been performing these chest thrusts for a very long time, and it did look painful. John was not a small man, and he was pushing with some force. By the time he finished the round of thrusts he was breathing quite hard and Edson's drunken mind suddenly produced a darkly comical image of John calamitously collapsing on top of the Chinese man through sheer exhaustion. Again he felt guilty at the inappropriateness of his thoughts. He shook his head and told himself it was the drink producing these images and not a warped mind.

John was looking for a pulse in the neck. All that could be heard in the carriage was John's heavy breathing – his tongue was even hanging out slightly like a knackered dog. "Okay, we've got a pulse, we're lucky. Is Neil coming back yet?" John didn't look up from the prone body as he said this. Edson looked at Louis who looked hopelessly trapped behind the man's legs, so he said,

"I'll go find out what's keeping him." John nodded.

"Right. We can hopefully keep him alive by breathing for him, but I might need some help."

"Whatever you say we'll do, John," said Louis.

"Of course, whatever you need," said Lotte. John nodded again, then leaned forward to provide more artificial respiration. Everyone stared, as if hypnotised by the man's magically inflatable chest.

After a couple of breaths Edson and Neil returned with the moustachioed waiter and the blond waiter behind them. Wordlessly Neil pointed at the scene as they arrived. The two waiters looked remarkably calm, and immediately began speaking very quickly in Russian. The blond one then said, "Thank you for your help. I . . . phone," and he put an imaginary receiver to his ear to indicate his intentions.

"Okay, we're going to need some help here. Does anyone know how to administer mouth-to-mouth?" As soon as he asked the question he was back down to breathe more life into the man, but he was clearly tiring.

"I think I know, in school we . . . learned this," said Dorte uncertainly. Edson wasn't sure if this was Dorte struggling with English or worrying whether she could precisely remember the procedure.

"Okay," said John, come here quickly and do the next few breaths and while you do that, I'll talk the procedure through with everyone else while they watch. We'll have to get a production line going I think." John moved off the bench and Dorte very quickly moved onto the opposite seat and positioned herself ready to perform the procedure. "Louis, you'll need to duck under him and come round here so you can see properly." Louis did so with a little difficulty – he was a tall man, and the legs were only a couple of feet off the ground. "Now, you see what Dorte is doing here? She's pinching his nose – if she doesn't do that when she breathes a lot of the air will simply pour out of his nose, so this is vitally important. Then she covers his whole mouth with hers and creates a vacuum and breathes quite hard. See? She's watching his chest expand so she knows how much air she's getting into him. Right, then a rest for a couple of seconds and repeat. We'll have to take turns because we'll tire ourselves out otherwise."

"Right, can I ask your name?" John said, looking at the waiter with the moustache.

"I am Oleg," he said.

"Okay, can you help us too? Can you do that?" John spoke slowly and pointed at Dorte.

"Yes."

"Good. Okay there's plenty of us so this shouldn't be too hard. Who feels confident enough to go next?"

"I will," exclaimed Louis quickly.

"Right, take over from Dorte when she's out of puff. Don't overdo it, Dorte, there's plenty of us here to take over." Dorte nodded and then bent down once more. John looked around and said to anyone and everyone, "I'm assuming that the other chap has gone off to try and organise an ambulance or something at the next stop. Let's hope it's not too far away, I'm not sure exactly how long we can carry on doing this for.

I assume as long as we need to, but there are limits."

Once more there was silence, broken only by Dorte's breaths. John's own breathing eased also. Soon it was Louis' turn, and John guided him through it. The blond waiter returned and spoke quickly again to Oleg.

"Okay, two hours to the next station," he said, and held two fingers out in front of himself.

"*Two hours?*" exclaimed Edson, "Jesus, there isn't one before that?" Oleg looked at him and shrugged.

"Don't worry Eddie, we can do it," piped up Neil, but the colour had gone from his face and the bounce had disappeared from his voice.

"That's right, this isn't a problem, Ed, we've got plenty of man power," reassured John. "Will there be an ambulance?" John asked Oleg slowly. Oleg looked perplexed.

"Er, *woo-woo woo-woo!*" John tried to imitate an ambulance's siren, even though it was perfectly possible that ambulances in deepest Siberia might make a quite different sound, and he twisted his hand in the air above his head. For a moment Oleg smiled in acknowledgement, and then replied.

"Ah, yes. But two hours."

"Right. We can do this everyone, let's just try and keep going – use all those beers and vodkas as fuel," encouraged John.

Neil was the next person to administer mouth-to-mouth on the unfortunate man. As he acted under John's tutelage, Edson thought of something. "John, do you think the amount of alcohol fumes we're blowing into him could, erm, have some kind of, I don't know, adverse effect on him?"

"I don't think so, Edson," said John, without looking up. He was still concentrating hard on Neil's technique.

"Good," replied Edson, suddenly feeling a little embarrassed. Lotte smiled at him.

"Have you ever had to do anything like this before, John?" asked Louis.

"Well, I've administered CPR once before, but never nothing like this, no."

"What happened that time?"

"Erm . . . it was at our local Church back in Norfolk. It was odd, actually. Everyone was lining up to receive communion, and this elderly gentleman was kneeling down waiting his turn, and he suddenly just slumped forward onto his face, and cracked his head on the stone floor – it was a massive heart attack so he probably didn't even feel the fall. I was just walking back to my seat when I heard it. I went back, and it wasn't nice because there was a huge cut on his head and a fair amount of blood. We tried CPR and an ambulance was there within ten minutes, but unfortunately he, er, died." It went silent again. "I think this guy's got a great chance, though."

"I'm going to need a break," said Neil.

"Okay, good job Neil," said John.

"Well, we'd all be fucked if it weren't for you, John, but thanks."

"I'll go next," said Lotte, just as Edson was about to volunteer. He was a bit annoyed about this. He was now going to be the last person apart from Oleg to help save the man's life and he worried that it looked like he was either squeamish and didn't want to do it, or that he had some bizarre hang-up about putting his lips on another man's mouth or something like that.

"I'll go if you like, Lotte," he said. Lotte turned around for a moment, and was about to say something when Neil jumped in.

"Don't worry Eddie, everyone will get a chance!" Lotte smiled and hurried into position. Edson could feel his face glowing. John was now sitting on the bench at the table where the Chinese man's feet were resting, supervising the rescue operation. Dorte moved next to him and said a few words to Lotte in Danish to accompany John's own advice.

She leaned forward and covered the man's mouth before blowing. As she finished and straightened up again, Edson suddenly found himself saying, "Good job you're not wearing that pointy stud today, Lotte!" No-one laughed. In fact some tumbleweed silently rolled slowly down the length of the dining car. "Sorry," Edson said quietly.

After about five or six breaths, John stood up and said it was worth just quickly taking the man's pulse again. It was still there and John smiled. "I think we've got a great chance here," he said stirringly. "Edson, your turn I believe?"

"Okay," Edson bounced to his feet, eager to play his part. Despite his gaffes and his drunken state he'd made sure he had watched everyone's technique and listened to all John's directions. He knelt on the seat, bent his head down, pinched the man's nose and then covered his mouth with his own and blew. He watched as the chest rose, almost alarmingly high. If it had looked strange before it looked even stranger from this angle. He almost feared that his chest might burst – and that brought visions of the film *Alien* into his mind.

When Edson was tired, Oleg, who had been standing silently and completely still in the gangway, stepped forward gingerly and commenced his own contribution to the life-saving cause. John didn't need to say much, Oleg had clearly been watching carefully and he had no problems. After Edson had finished congratulating himself he began to consider the next steps of the operation. Presumably this 'production line' as John had named it rather clinically, would continue until they arrived at the next station, still almost two hours away. Once there he'd hopefully be taken away in an ambulance. Would someone go with him? Then he wondered whether the man was travelling with anyone – he couldn't remember ever seeing him with anyone . . . and what about his *stuff*? "I've just thought of something," said Edson, "What about this guy's *stuff*? We can't leave it on the train, can we? It'll have to go with him otherwise how the hell's he ever going to get back?"

"Good point," said Louis.

"Yes, I hadn't thought of that," admitted John, "We'll have to pack his stuff for him." Edson silently forgave himself for his earlier ill-advised comments.

"Where is his room?" asked Lotte.

"Oh God, do we even know where his room is to get his stuff?" cried Neil.

"I think it's on our corridor, isn't it Ed?" asked Louis.

"Yeah, because we were taking the piss out of his Tai Chi the other morning when he jogged past our cabin," answered Edson, "Starting to feel a bit guilty about that now."

"Mmm," replied Louis quietly.

"That doesn't matter," John pointed out, "If you hadn't have done that we wouldn't know where to look for his cabin now, so why don't you two go and find it now and start trying to pack his stuff while we carry on here."

"You'll be okay just with you guys?" said Louis a little reluctantly. Packing bags wasn't quite as heroic as resuscitating a heart-attack victim.

"We'll be fine, just be as quick as you can."

Louis was in the lead as usual as they raced at a fast walking pace back to their carriage, but for once Edson felt like he could keep up with him. "How we gonna do this, Lou?"

"I dunno. Just knock on every door I suppose, apologise, and see if it's his room."

"How are we even going to tell it's his room, though?"

"Well, I guess they'll be an empty bed somewhere."

"What if there's more than one empty bed?"

" . . . If we do find any empty beds, they'll probably be our beds, Ed – no-one else is still up, and we know which one's our cabin, don't we?"

"You say that, but what if, you know, what if someone's having a, you know, a *liaison*, with some other cat on the train, and we take their stuff, and it's the wrong person? Could happen."

" . . . What *is* the matter with you tonight?"

"Nothin'. Just asking. Just trying to be prepared."

They marched the rest of the short journey in silence until they arrived at the first cabin. "I hope it's this one," said Edson, "It'd save a lot of hassle."

"Yeah, well, if he *is* on this carriage, which I'm sure he is, it's a one in, what," Louis leaned back and silently counted along the corridor, "A one in seven I suppose, once you take our room out the equation." How like Louis to give a probability, thought Edson. He almost said something sarcastic, but before he could think of a line witty enough to be worthy of uttering Louis spoke again, "Right, I suppose we better knock, then."

"You do it," whispered Edson.

Suddenly, Edson had a flashback to his primary school, to standing outside the headmaster's office with his friend Toby. They hadn't done anything wrong, they were just there to ask something about football practice. But they both stood there whispering to each other to knock, becoming more intimidated by the second by the huge white door with the wooden panel saying 'HEADMASTER' on it – as if some of the pupils might not know who resided there. Louis knocked. There was no answer. He knocked again a bit louder. Still no answer. Edson felt his stomach tighten. "Should we go in?"

"Yeah, come on. There's not a lot else we can do is there? With a bit of luck this might be his and he might not even be sharing." Slowly, and with all the skill of a rookie housebreaker, Louis slid the door open. It was predictably very dark inside. Louis peered into the gloom.

"Anything in there?" whispered Edson, barely audible.

"No, it's blahdy empty."

"Jesus. I can't keep doing all these cabins, I'm scared we're gonna scare the shit out of someone. God, if a girl's in one by herself fuck knows what she's gonna think."

"Look," Louis turned to him with his trademark karate chop hand pointing right at him, "We haven't got any choice, we need to get that guy's stuff. It'll be fine."

"Okay, okay."

They moved silently, like cat burglars, which just made Edson even more nervous, to the next cabin. Louis knocked on the door. Again there was no answer. "Shall I knock a bit louder?" whispered Louis.

"I guess so." Edson leaned back and looked up and down the corridor. How dodgy does this look, he wondered? Their movements, calculated to not wake people up or disturb anyone, just seemed to make them appear suspicious. Louis knocked quite hard, and Edson expected someone to scream out from inside, and if they didn't he was sure someone else in the corridor might come out to see what the banging was all about. He could almost feel the curtains twitching. There was still no answer.

"Right, we better go in," murmured Louis. He paused for a moment and then slid the door open just a crack, and tried to peer in.

"What's in there?"

"Not sure . . ." Louis opened the door a bit more, "Right, this could be it," he whispered very quietly. So quietly, in fact, that Edson couldn't quite make out what he said – his words were directed into the cabin rather than at Edson.

"What? It *could* be it or *couldn't* be it?" he whispered back.

"No. I think this is it. There's no-one else in there, just a load of stuff."

"It's not our room is it?" Louis didn't dignify Edson's umpteenth badly timed gag of the evening with an answer. He stepped inside sideways, slipping his body through the thin opening he'd made, rather than more simply sliding the door open to its full extent. Without questioning Louis' mildly eccentric action, Edson sidled in after him. Louis flicked the light switch, and they were faced with the mildly surreal sight of a cabin that was identical to their own in every way, apart from the luggage.

They stood there in silence for a moment, perhaps feeling a little like you might do if you've just gone into a girls room and are about to start having a little look through her bra and pants drawer. You must know the feeling, surely? Erm, right, anyway, they were feeling somewhat uneasy, a little intrusive, as they stood there glancing around the cabin without wanting to look too hard at anything. Clearly, the Chinese man had been lucky enough to have landed a cabin all to himself. On both sides the upper bunks had been folded up against the wall. On the left was the Chinese man's bed. On the nearest end, there was a pile of very neatly and flatly folded blankets, topped with a pillow. Edson looked at it and thought to himself what a pain in the arse it would be to have to come back to your cabin late at night and make your bed again. His own cabin might be a little untidy, but at least he could drunkenly fall into bed each night without arranging sheets and blankets for ten minutes first.

Two short-sleeved cotton shirts, one light blue with little flecks of white, one dark brown, hung neatly on separate hangers from the right hand side of the curtain rail. On the right bunk there was a small pile of carefully folded clothes, looking as if they'd been ironed on the train. Underneath the bunk Edson could see a small beige suitcase with its dark brown handle just peeking into the room. Louis bent over the small table under the window, examining its wares. "What're you doing?" said Edson, still in a hushed voice.

"Thought we should probably look for some ID with a picture or something, just to make doubly sure we've got the right guy's stuff . . . Can you imagine if he wakes up in hospital tomorrow or later tonight, and he's got some other guy's stuff?"

"That would be bizarre . . . Ha! What if he lost his memory, right, and had the wrong guy's stuff, maybe with no ID, and he starts trying to remember using stuff he never had in the first place, and he starts living some other guy's life?"

"Just shut up. Try and have a look through some of this stuff."

"Let's look at the evidence," Edson giggled in his best Lloyd Grossman voice, which was pretty rubbish, even by his own poor impersonation standards.

"Yerrrsss. Let's see if we can find his passport or something."

"What about his suitcase?"

"Yeah, good place to start."

Louis yanked the case out and placed it on the bunk. It wasn't a huge case – it was one of those ones with two wheels and the handle running up the back of it, so when you want to wheel it you can slide the handle up along the runners and roll it along behind you. Altogether a better class of luggage than Edson's ruckscack with the fraying straps that was still clinging onto life following some difficult years in the Scouts. "Right," said Louis, "How about in here," and he unzipped a front pocket and reached inside.

"Anything there?" Louis pulled out a few papers and looked at them briefly, shuffling them rapidly in his hands.

"Not here," and he carefully replaced them. "God, I don't want this guy to think we've been rifling through his stuff, even if we have."

"It'd be even worse if it wasn't his stuff, wouldn't it? What would we say if some guy came in here now whose stuff it was and asked what we were doing?" Louis didn't answer. He proceeded to unzip the main body of the case, then flipped the top part open to lay bare the contents.

As with the rest of the artefacts in the room, it was impeccably neat. There was some clothing, a wash bag with blue and yellow swirls all over it and there was a small flattish leather purse-like item with a gold buckle on the front. It wasn't a ladies purse, but it wasn't particularly masculine either. Louis picked it up. It was a very soft leather and it had a small strap that Louis was at a loss to understand where it might hang from. It was far too small to hang from the shoulder, for example, but to hang it from the forearm or wrist would be somewhat, well, *effeminate*.

"Looks promising," encouraged Edson, as he craned his neck over Louis'.

"Mmm," replied Louis. He unclipped the buckle and looked inside. "Excellent," he said, and pulled out a dark green passport. "It's Chinese," he said.

"Look inside." Louis opened it and flicked through the pages until it rested on a picture of a sombre Chinese man with a good amount of black and grey hair.

"Is that him? Looks a bit young." Edson squinted at the picture as Louis held it up for him to view.

"Hmm . . . gotta be. It's just an old picture. Same nose."

"Same nose?"

"Yeah. Same nose."

"Okay, let's get this stuff packed away then. Pass us those two shirts and have a look around the cabin, make sure we don't miss anything."

"You better hang on to that passport – they might need that."

"Good point," and he tucked it carefully into the breast pocket of his cotton shirt. Edson crawled around on the floor searching for shoes or any dropped valuables or whatever. In a matter of minutes the room was cleared. "Right," said Louis, slightly louder and more confident than previously, "Let's get back." He grabbed up the suitcase by a small handle on the side and left Edson to follow him.

"Sorted," said Edson, "Respect due."

Back in the dining car Dorte was taking her shift on the mouth of the Chinese man, her straggly hair momentarily covering his face. Edson suddenly wondered what would have happened if they had all gone to bed ten minutes before the man collapsed. Would the waiters have found him in time? He shuddered. He was awoken from this muse by John, who was still sitting on the bench opposite the man's body, his elbow leaning on the table next to him just centimetres from the man's feet. "How did it go?"

"No probs," and Louis lifted the bag a little higher so everyone could see it.

"Is that it?" asked Neil.

"Yep," replied Edson.

"Very carefully packed," observed Louis.

"Is it definitely the right bag?" asked Neil doubtfully.

"Yeah, we had a look at the passport first just to double check."

"Good thinking," said Neil.

"How's things going here?" enquired Edson.

"Seems to be going well," replied John, "The pulse is still there, and the production line is going strong," John gestured towards Dorte who smiled.

"How much longer?" wondered Lotte aloud.

"Did anyone look at their watch at the two hour mark?" asked Edson.

"Yeah, we've got about another hour and a half," rejoined Louis, "I don't know how accurate my watch is . . . in fact its probably way out, but I know we've only had half an hour."

"Blimey," murmured Edson.

Louis placed the suitcase on a nearby table and sat down. Pretty much everything was in place now, all that needed to happen was for the train to arrive at the next station, hopefully with the man's pulse still, well, pulsing. Edson sat down at the table opposite Louis. On the next berth up from him, Neil was perched on the table, his feet resting on the seat, his eyes fixed on Dorte and the patient. Opposite him Lotte sat on the edge of her seat, her legs and knees in the gangway, her elbows resting on her knees and her hands supporting her chin. She looked deadbeat. On the other side of the table Oleg sat quietly facing away from the Chinese man and towards Louis, but every few seconds he twisted round to see how things were going. He seemed to be following the conversation (what little there was of it) fairly well, but his moustache seemed bigger than normal – it appeared to totally cover his mouth, hiding his emotions. Edson watched John and, following up his previous thoughts, wondered what on earth they would have done if John hadn't been there. None of them, not one, would have known what to do. Would any of the staff? Were they trained in that kind of thing?

A few minutes later it was Louis' turn to breathe for the patient. It was silent again apart from Louis murmuring to John, just checking his technique was right. Edson stared into the carpet. He still didn't feel tired and his head was still swimming a little. He almost felt like crying. Neil suddenly said, "Do you think we should get some coffees in or something John?"

"That's not a bad idea at all, Neil."

"Er, Oleg," said Neil politely, "Could we all have some coffee?" and he twirled his finger in the air to indicate he meant coffee for everyone. Oleg nodded and rose from his seat with agility.

"Thanks," said Edson as he passed, and, for the first time on the trip, Oleg smiled at someone apart from his colleagues.

"Good idea, Neil," said Dorte. She had slipped past Lotte and now they were both facing in John's direction, and Dorte was resting her head on Lotte's shoulder. They spoke quietly in Danish for a moment. Edson felt a little left out.

After a few minutes Louis finished his shift and Neil took his turn. Louis stood up with John for a while then returned to his seat near Edson. A few more minutes and Oleg returned with seven cups of coffee, he gave them all out and then sat with one himself at Dorte and Lotte's table. The advent of the drinks seemed to break the ice a bit, and Edson said, mainly to Louis, but really to anyone who was listening, "You know, heart attacks run in my family." Lotte turned round and glanced at him for a moment, but it was an uncomfortable position, so she soon turned back again.

"Really?" replied Louis.

"Yeah, well, both my Granddad's died of heart attacks. One had, like, three heart attacks, and the third one killed him . . . obviously. And the other one . . . well, they don't even know how many heart attacks he had, but my Gran said something about one night seeing his chest shoot in the air while they were in bed and he was asleep and the doctors reckoned he might have had up to nine or ten heart attacks. He had a triple-bypass and all sorts, but the ninth or tenth one killed him."

"Shit." murmured Louis.

"I suppose I'll probably die of one too – it's all hereditary, isn't it? The one on my Dad's side, the one that might have had nine or ten of 'em, he actually died laughing!" Edson was smiling at the recollection, but he could feel tears in his eyes, not from sorrow, just perhaps because this was private stuff he wasn't used to revealing. Louis smiled.

"What happened?"

"Well, he and my Gran had some old friends over and they were chatting about the old days, and he was laughing about some remembering or other, and he tilted his head back onto the armchair as if he was just visualising it, but then he just stayed there. He'd just had a heart attack and died right there. Good way to go, I s'pose."

"He probably never even felt it," volunteered John from the other end of the carriage. Lotte turned round and smiled supportively, and Edson could feel a lump in his throat. He tried to swallow it down. He knew he was just over-emotional from the booze, but he couldn't help it.

"And the other one, the one on my Mum's side, well, he was naughty. He refused to take his medication. Maybe he thought he was invincible, I don't know. I wouldn't blame him if he did. Me, my brother and my sister all thought that. He used to spin us all these yarns about the war – you know, stories about a chicken he kept that saved its own neck by always laying eggs for him to eat, and the horse he rode that could negotiate mine fields. He had all these red moles on his huge stomach, and we used to ask him if they were bullet marks from the war. He had a huge belly when he was in his sixties, and because we watched a lot of cartoons it wasn't any kind of leap of faith to believe him when he said they were. We were convinced bullets just bounced off him!" Everyone laughed – even Lotte and Dorte who, Edson thought, must have been struggling to keep up with his speech.

"It's amazing what you believe when you're a little bairn," said Neil, lapsing into a Scottish accent, without anything in the way of explanation as to why, in between his breaths of air.

"What happened to him?" asked Dorte.

"Well, he wouldn't take any medication, and he wasn't well, but he refused to stop work even though he was past retirement age. He used to direct cars where to park at some DIY shop, you know. He just wanted to work, just wanted to keep himself busy. I dunno, maybe he should have done an Open University course or something. Anyway, he was working there directing the cars one day, and he just collapsed. Died in the ambulance." There was silence for a minute. Edson rubbed his right eye vigorously. "And you know what, just by coincidence, my uncle, his son, was in the queue of cars waiting to park there." There was another pause.

"Now there's something to make you believe in a higher being," observed Louis.

"I'm sorry, Ed," intimated Lotte.

"It's okay! It was ages ago! I always thought it was a blessing that he was in the queue, you know, but I asked him, my uncle, about it one day and he said it was horrible. He said, 'Would you like it if you were there to watch your own Dad collapse and die?' I'd never thought of it like that."

"Must've been pretty bad," agreed Louis.

"So I guess one day I'll probably die of a heart attack," Edson said, almost matter-of-factly. He leant forward and sipped his coffee – it was still boiling hot and it burnt his tongue, leaving it tinglingly numb.

Soon it was Lotte's shift. "I've run out of puff," Neil had announced. It seemed strange to say something like that – after all, at least they could all breathe without the aid of a human respirator. Neil and Lotte swapped places wordlessly after that – Neil decided to sit with Dorte rather than on his table perch, and Dorte now rested her head on his shoulder for a moment. A little later she hauled herself onto her feet, edged past Neil and walked down and out of the carriage, mumbling, "I'll be a minute," Lotte lifted her head for a brief pause and watched her leave. After Dorte had gone for a few moments and was clearly out of earshot, Edson said,

"Think she's okay?" Lotte looked up again and nodded slowly, just two bobs of her head. Sure enough, Dorte returned only three or four minutes later.

Instead of sitting down with Neil again, though, she ushered Edson to move up and she sat with him. Then she put a couple of photos on the table. One was a little grainy, a little worn, a little creased even. The colours had faded slightly, too. It was a photo of a man with a small child perched on his shoulders. It was a landscape shot, taken from the man's chest upwards. He had a decent amount of very dark hair, quite wiry with a little curl or two, and an impeccably manicured moustache. The child on his shoulders was gripping gamely to the forefingers of the man as he held them up for her to steady herself with. Both of them were laughing wildly, unaware, perhaps, that the photo was even being taken – they were certainly looking at something to the right of and behind the camera. "Is that you?" Edson asked, pointing at the child.

"Yes."

"And who's that?"

"My Father."

"Nice," said Edson, a little at a loss of what to say. Louis leant over the table to get a more conventional look at the pictures. The second one was clearly more recent. The corners were less dog-eared and the colours were sharper. It was a picture of a man fishing in a river. In his hand was a rod, and strapped to his back Edson thought he could make out a net. He was just entering the river, because he was near the bank, but it looked pretty fast flowing. He wore giant green waders nearly up to his waist and he held his rod high above the water while he looked down, concentrating on his movements. "Is that your Dad, too?"

"Yes, that was about a year ago." Edson could see the resemblance in the two pictures, even though the careful moustache had gone and the hair was greying. Edson now began to wonder why Dorte had retrieved these photos, and as she opened her mouth to speak he suddenly realised, but decided to stay quiet. "He died soon after this. But he was very fit. He did a lot of sports. He played football with Lotte's Father before. Just had a heart attack at work and died . . . Like you say, it's, er, it's in the family." Edson didn't know what else to do, so he stared hard at the pictures and deliberated whether he should squeeze Dorte's thigh or her hand or her arm, or nothing at all. In the end he tentatively reached his hand over and gently squeezed her forearm.

"Come show them to me, Dorte," said Neil. She picked them up and walked over to Neil. John met her there too.

"I remember losing my Father," he said, "It's one of the biggest shocks you can have I think, because you've probably convinced yourself he'll go on forever. I suppose it's the same with Mothers too."

"Great moustache," said Neil, smiling. When Lotte let Edson take over a few minutes later she went over to Dorte and they hugged in the gangway for a while.

The production line continued doggedly over the next hour and a half or so, and from time to time John checked the Chinese man's pulse. Everything seemed to be going to plan. It was a strange atmosphere. Although they were all still feeling the effects of their alcohol intake, the hours when they'd been drinking seemed like days before rather than just a couple of hours previously. Despite the late time of night – whatever that time was – they all appeared incredibly awake. Perhaps it was a particularly strong blend of coffee that Oleg had brewed up. On one occasion the Russian woman from the kitchen strode in to assess the scene. She looked carefully at the man, smiled politely at John who smiled his big, warm, generous smile back, and then she said a few words to Oleg, who shrugged and replied briefly. They both looked over at the patient and then she left again, picking up empty coffee cups as she left.

Later the other waiter, returned and replenished everyone with more cups of coffee. When he handed a cup to John, John started fussing and reaching into his back pocket for his wallet, muttering that "We must pay you for this coffee." The waiter resisted, but John was quite insistent, and in the end Oleg had to come over and reassure John with a, "No, thank you," and John relented.

The train jolted suddenly and then began to slow. Neil was taking his turn at the time, and he fell backwards against the back of the seat, but the Chinese man fortunately remained in position. "Is this the stop?" John asked Oleg.

"Yes, I think so." John's next question was delivered very slowly, "Is the ambulance ready for us?"

"Let me see," and Oleg glided off quickly to find out. John moved forward and checked his pulse again.

"Are you . . . *con*fident, John?" asked Edson, a little anxiously.

"Oh yes, I think we've done the hard bit."

Neil gave way to Lotte who continued giving mouth-to-mouth until the train juddered to a halt. Outside there was the faint flashing of lights, but Edson, looking out the window with his hands shielding the glare from the light inside the carriage, couldn't see the ambulance. He imagined it was parked in the car park. It seemed odd, an ambulance right out here. Did they even *have* car parks in train stations in Russia? He had no idea, and the darkness outside wasn't giving him any further clues. He heard some shouts coming from the train, and then some faint replies from outside. "I wish they'd hurry up," John muttered impatiently.

Edson was straining his eyes through the window to the darkness outside and finally saw some movements. Two paramedics dressed in bright red ran past the window. Moments later they were on board the train and rushing towards the Chinese man, barely acknowledging anyone in their desire to carry out their job as quickly as possible. "The pulse is still there," offered John as he moved away from the scene to allow the two men space in which to work. One of them nodded.

Quickly they strapped an oxygen mask to the Chinese man's face and got him on their stretcher. "Is anyone going to go with him?" asked Dorte.

"I don't know," replied John quickly. "I'm sure none of us can go

. . . well, we're not even *packed*. Maybe one of the staff will go with him?"

"Well someone's got to take his stuff with them to the ambulance," said Louis – and I've got his passport here just in case, and he waved the green document around as if to prove his point. Oleg came up behind them all.

"I will take the bag and the passport," he intimated, and with minimum effort he swung the suitcase off the table and held it simply by the small strap in his right hand. Then he held out his other hand for the passport which Louis handed over.

"Is anyone going with him, Oleg?" asked John slowly.

"No . . . we don't have anyone . . ." At that moment the paramedics were ready to take the stabilised body away, so Oleg turned and quickly led them out of the train.

Everyone stood up in the gangway in the middle of the carriage after they had gone and stooped to try and catch a glimpse of them out the window. Everyone except Neil, anyway, who was back on his perch on the table, his feet on the seat in front of him, his elbows on his knees, and his head bowed down looking at the floor beneath. Edson slumped to his seat and looked away from the window. Lotte, standing near him, put her hand out and massaged gently at his shoulder.

Moments later the carriage door shut again. Oleg walked into the dining car and stood in front of them for a moment. "They think he is okay," he said in his impossibly deep voice, "They say thank you." He smiled and then moved forward and shook hands with John, before turning to everyone else and shaking hands with them silently, each time both participants nodded at each other.

"Thanks for the coffee," John called as Oleg went back to the kitchen. He turned round again, opened his hands out as if to say, 'you're welcome', and then left. Neil spoke up first: "I'm probably going to head off to bed." They all got up at this and silently left the room. "I hope they disinfect that table," said Neil at the last moment.

II

"Uuuhh," murmured Louis. Edson was lying face up, staring at the bottom of the bunk above him with his head resting on his hands.

"You awake?"

"Uuuhh."

"Jesus. I still can't believe last night . . . do you think that guy survived?"

"I dunno. Maybe."

"What if, right, what if he was dead all the time we were resuscitating him, or maybe died during resuscitation at some point, but . . . John wanted to protect us or something, so he just let us believe that he was still alive . . . I mean, can you really breathe for someone for as long as we did?"

"I dunno. I dunno why John would do that, though. We're not little kids."

"Yeah . . . I guess." There was silence again for a few moments. "Did you sleep okay?"

"No, not really. You?"

"No. I've been awake for ages. Got a blahdy headache too."

"Baarh," murmured Louis half-heartedly. He suddenly let his arm dangle down from his bunk. Edson looked at it and imagined hitting it and watching it swing like a pendulum.

"What would we have done if John hadn't been there? He would have died and we wouldn't have been able to do anything."

"Someone would have known something – one of the staff or something."

"Well, where were they? I mean Oleg and the others helped, but they didn't exactly look like they knew what to do."

"Maybe they did, but they saw John had it under control so they sorted the ambulance out, warned the driver, all that stuff."

"I s'pose. But what if it had happened like two minutes later and I went to get John and he was in bed or something, and, you know, he was that much further from the dining car and he'd just arrived too late. I'd've felt terrible . . . I mean, I really had no idea what to do. I hope he's okay. Christ. Imagine what he's going to feel like when he comes round! He'll have no idea what's going on! I bet no-one at the hospital speaks Chinese, and I bet he doesn't speak Russian either. What a nightmare."

"They'll probably get the embassy involved or something."

"But imagine, right. Look how lucky we've been – never had any injuries or illnesses or anything, but what if we did? Neither of us have got much of a clue."

"Remember that time Rowan almost convinced himself he'd contracted some kind of nasty tropical disease after reading about it in the *Lonely*? We told him it was just diarrhea, but he was sure it was some kind of life-threatening thing."

"Yeah – but what if it *had* been that? Look, even now we're laughing about it, but what if it *had* been that? We wouldn't have had a clue."

"Nah, these things always get sorted out in the end."

"They nearly didn't last night."

"But they did, though, didn't they?"

For once they weren't up and getting ready for breakfast straight away. Edson often didn't have much of an appetite in the morning, but today Louis wasn't forcing the issue. They just lay in silence until a little later when Edson said,

"I've just realised it's our last day."

"What a waste of six days," said Louis.

"Well, almost. Last night kind of made it worthwhile, didn't it?"

"What? You mean we finally had a bit of excitement – I'd rather not have had that and the guy not have had a heart attack, mate," replied Louis a touch rakishly.

"Oh, *thanks*. That's *not* what I meant. I just meant that if we hadn't been on here then maybe there wouldn't have been anyone to help the poor guy."

"I see. Well, the *rest* of it was a waste. I've done nothing. I've read a bit of *War and Peace* . . ."

"Have you? How much?"

"Not much."

"Two pages?" Edson asked mischievously.

"Er, four."

"That's good going . . . if you keep going at that rate is it even *poss*ible to finish it before you die?" And then he realised what he'd just said.

"Depends when I die." Edson could hear Louis scrabbling around on his bunk and in a moment he was lowering himself to the floor dressed in jeans and an untucked button-up checked cotton shirt. No socks. "I need a waz."

Edson turned over onto his side so he was in a position to see out of the window. Where had the Chinese man been travelling to? Did he have business in Moscow, or somewhere else in Russia? If so, why didn't he take the 'plane? Perhaps he was scared of flying. That made him think about the Arsenal footballer, Denis Bergkamp – another person afraid of flying. He found people who were afraid of flying enduringly fascinating. He'd been on a 'plane a few times now, and part of this fascination was that each time he boarded a 'plane he was slightly more concerned than the previous time, as if the law of averages were shortening each time.

The first time he'd flown at the age of about ten he was totally fearless, but the last time he flew – the flight to Hong Kong – he could feel a small amount of panic just bubbling under, deep within his gut. He wrenched his mind back from football and 'planes. So how would they get him home? Particularly if he *was* afraid of flying. They surely couldn't put him back on another almost-week-long train journey again. What about his family? Who, if anyone, was going to be waiting for him at the station in Moscow later today, unaware of what's happened? Some business contact who's had confirmation he boarded the train, yet when he's there waiting for him he doesn't see him. He might 'phone China, see what's happened, and even they wouldn't know. The mystery could go on for days. It's at times like these, he supposed, that embassies really come into their own. 'I wonder who invented the idea of an embassy,' he thought, as Louis returned. Louis climbed straight back up to his bed, and Edson saw the bunk take the stress as he slumped down onto his back again.

"So . . . what happens when we get to *Mockba*?" asked Edson after a bit, clearly keen to draw a line under his earlier gaffe.

"Well, the travel company have sorted us out accommodation for the first night which is good."

"I really fancy a long hot shower."

"Yeah, that would be good actually. Still, as long as there's water and it's wet *baaarh*!" Again, his 'baarh' seemed a little half-hearted, a little off-key.

"Hot would be nice though . . . Then what are we doing – we going on to St Petersburg?"

"Yeah, have a look around *Mockba* then head up there for a few days then go to Germany maybe . . . or somewhere else, I dunno."

"Do you think Neil will follow us?" Edson ventured after a brief pause.

"I dunno, it wouldn't be so bad if he came along." Edson, safe in the knowledge that Louis was on the bunk above, screwed his face up at this.

"Maybe." *Maybe*. That was Louis' favourite phrase when someone (Edson) said something he didn't agree with. It was clearly designed to be non-confrontational, but whenever he said 'maybe' it was always followed by 'or we could . . .' 'Maybe' generally meant 'no'. Edson enjoyed saying it to him sometimes. "I think he might be a bit of a nightmare . . ."

"Maybe," replied Louis.

"I don't think I could stand that laugh for much longer – it's like travelling with the bastard son of a hyena that's been shagged by Sid James . . . no offence to Sid James, he was great and I'm sure he didn't go around fucking hyenas, but if he did the result would have a laugh like Neil's."

"I don't think hyenas and humans can interbreed though."

"Well, no, and if they could they probably wouldn't look like Neil. I just meant they'd probably laugh like him."

"Yerrsss," murmured Louis uncertainly. "Right, I'm blahdy starving." Louis swung his feet over the edge of the bunk and jumped down.

"If you wanna go down to the dining car now I'll come when I've got dressed."

"Yeah, okay, see you in a bit then."

Once in the dining car Louis immediately spotted John, Neil and James already nibbling at a bit of breakfast and gingerly drinking their hot coffee. It seemed strange to see James there, Louis had almost forgotten he was still on the train. It was bizarre to think he'd missed such a huge happening. "Morning," he said, surprised that he'd managed to get the first word in before Neil.

"All right, mate?" Neil answered

"Morning Louis," said John.

"They've just been telling me all about it," began James, "I don't know whether I'm pleased I missed it or not . . . it just seems so *surreal* . . . like, I left a party and it turned into *Casualty*."

"Yeah, it was bizarre," agreed Louis as he took the spare seat next to Neil.

"Where's Eddie?" asked Neil.

"He'll be along in a minute – just doing his make-up or something."

"Sounds like you did a great job," said James, "How did you find his cabin? And so quickly?"

"Well me and Edson had seen him doing some kind of slow jog Tai Chi the other day in the morning. Have to admit we took the piss out of him a bit, which I'm not that proud of." John swiftly interrupted here.

"No, we mentioned this last night Louis, you can't think like that. You helped save the man's life."

"Well, *if* we saved it. I mean, we'll never know will we? For sure. We didn't even know his *name*."

"I think we can be confident we did, Louis," replied John encouragingly.

"Yeah, but we'll never know for *one hundred per cent certain*. You know, if I'd've known what to do straight away, if we hadn't had to've run half way along the train to get you back, maybe we'd be absolutely sure now . . . I dunno." Louis rubbed his eyes roughly with the palms of his hands.

"I don't think that would have made a significant difference, Louis. I'm not a doctor, I know, but treatment a few seconds earlier wouldn't necessarily have altered his condition enough to bring him back into total consciousness. Remember that man I told you about who died in the Church? I was right there within seconds and it didn't help him."

"Yeah, I know . . ." Louis drifted off and then smiled slightly at John. "Right. Breakfast."

He looked around for a waiter, and the blond waiter was already gliding towards them. Louis wondered whether train waiters gained some kind of equivalent to sea legs. The waiter smiled – discarding his professional exterior for a rare and welcome moment. Louis appreciated it, smiled warmly back, and nodded his head, unsure of whether to ask after his health or not. The waiter, though, was clearly ready for an order and he looked a little busy, so Louis settled for ordering a double breakfast and, yes, a breakfast for Edson too.

"The great thing about this restaurant," said Louis a few minuteds later, his mouth full of bread, "Is that they never get the order wrong – mainly because they can't because there's no actual choice for the customer to make. Brilliant. You just get your food nice and quick and no arguments." At that moment Edson sauntered in.

"Space for one more?" and he nudged Louis up a bit so he could squeeze on the end of the seat.

"Don't you just love it when you get back from the bathroom and your food's waiting for you?" said Neil in an American drawl.

"Huh?" said Edson, already tucking in. "I haven't been to the bathroom, I was just getting dressed."

"No mate! Don't worry!" laughed Neil in his patronising way. "It was a quote – you know, *Pulp Fiction*? '*Mrs Mia Wallace*'" he said the name in a deep American voice.

"Oh yeah – in the restaurant."

"Yes mate! In . . . the . . . restaurant" he replied slowly, as if it should have been plainly obvious to everyone.

"So, Ed," began James, and Edson looked up from tearing his bread apart in his hands, "You an expert in mouth-to-mouth now then?"

"Well, I wouldn't say expert. How did I do John? I can't have done that badly I suppose."

"You did fine – everyone did. It was pretty impressive, I thought."

"Particularly as we were all drunk as skunks! Hya hya! Well, I wasn't that bad I have to say – takes a bit more than a few small vodka and cokes to get me rat-arsed."

"Yeah, I'd noticed that, Neil," replied James.

"Yeah, funny how we were put in the same cabin but we're complete opposites when it comes to that, isn't it Jim?"

"Yes, I suppose it is . . . a little bit . . . *ironic.*"

A little later, after his fourth cup of coffee (no wonder he's so bloody weird, the amount of caffeine he drinks, thought Edson) Neil announced his upcoming intentions. "Right you lot, I'm off to pay a visit to the Russian Trog . . . I may be some time, hya hya! So no need to send out any search parties after half an hour if I still haven't reappeared. I might give the old toe nails a clip while I'm in there, too."

"TMI, mate," responded James, his eyes squinting in something approaching revulsion.

"TMI?" asked John.

"Too Much Information," replied Neil, and he stalked off down the corridor.

"Well, quite," muttered John.

About five minutes later, timing their run into the carriage as perfectly as a deadly striker into the penalty area – almost *suspiciously* perfectly in fact, Lotte and Dorte arrived for breakfast. "How are you guys this morning?" asked Lotte as she sat down.

"Bit tired," answered Edson.

"Very well thanks," replied John, "And you two? How are you?"

"Okay," said Lotte quietly.

"Okay, thanks," replied Dorte.

"You all right, Dorte?" asked Edson quietly. He just wanted to double check. He would rather have done it privately than in front of everyone else, but he wanted to make sure she knew he had been thinking of her. Dorte smiled through the thin trail of smoke emanating from the end of her skinny rolly.

"Yeah, I'm fine."

"Good," said Edson emphatically, and with a smile.

James suddenly said, "So which table was he lying on then?" Edson, Louis and Dorte were facing towards the table that had made do as a makeshift bed the previous night and they barely needed to move to identify it, but John and Lotte instinctively twisted in their seats to spy on the table. It was about two berths up from their own, and Edson pointed it out. A man and a woman were eating their breakfast of rolls and coffee there. "Didn't anyone consider coming to get me? I'm sure I could've helped out somehow."

"I just don't think we had time to think of it," replied John soothingly.

"It wasn't really very *ex*citing, Jim," added Edson.

"Yeah, that's not what I meant, really . . . I don't know." He took a sip of his coffee.

"It was horrible, James," agreed Lotte as she stubbed her cigarette with authority into the ashtray, "I hardly had any sleep. I kept waking up all night because of dreams."

"I'm sorry, it wasn't supposed to-,"

"I had one where we had all fallen asleep in the carriage and he just died while we were asleep, and one where he came alive while I was breathing for him . . . and another where he fell off the, er," Lotte made an almost frenzied gesture with clenched fists in front of her body and said something in Danish to Dorte.

"Stretcher?"

"Stretcher, yes," affirmed John.

"He fell off it while they carried him and rolled all along the gangway and out the door."

"I'm sorry," pleaded James again. He drank up his coffee and then put down his cup. Fingering in his wallet for some rubles he murmured, "I think I'll go back."

"Why don't you two come and sit over here with us?" suggested John after a moment. The girls nodded and smiled without saying anything and both sat next to each other on John's side of the table.

"I'm sorry," said Lotte, "I just can't stop thinking."

"I know what you mean," agreed Louis who had indeed been pretty quiet, especially for him. Edson couldn't ever recall seeing him so quiet in fact. Apart from early in the mornings, but even then he was always well capable of an amusing comment or put down.

"It's . . . it's difficult to know how to act, isn't it?" suggested Edson after a brief pause.

"How do you mean?" asked John.

"Well, it's weird. I mean, it's a bit like those people who laugh at funerals. They can't help it, it's just a nervous reaction to a sombre occasion, but they're not sure how to act if they can't cry or whatever . . . And now it's kind of like that for us, except worse, because we don't really know what's happened. We don't feel like celebrating because we don't know for sure that he's okay, but we don't exactly want to cry because firstly we don't know him and secondly he might be sitting up in bed eating a fine Russian breakfast as we speak. So what do we do? Is it okay to talk about other stuff? How much do we need to discuss this thing?"

"Maybe we're just all hungover and too tired to decide exactly how to act," suggested Louis.

"Well, it could be that. I know we're not supposed to grieve or anything, but it's like . . . how long do we have to be sad for? Maybe we shouldn't be sad at all. I just think it's a bit confusing," and Edson rolled the warm coffee cup between his palms.

"You're probably right," agreed John, "Maybe I'm just a lot older than the rest of you, but the way I look at it is that we did all we could do under the circumstances, and whether he survived or not, and I'm sure he did, we all did a pretty amazing job there. No-one panicked and no-one got over excited despite the drinks we'd had."

Edson sat uncomfortably. He wanted to ask Dorte about her Dad. Whether she'd been there when it had happened. If she had, the night before must have been pretty harrowing. But he wasn't sure if she would appreciate being asked. But maybe it would be good for her. Maybe, the daytime TV talk show part of his brain told him, she'd actually quite *like* to discuss it with someone other than just Lotte – especially with people who were simultaneously people she might consider her friends, yet who were also almost complete strangers. He knew it wasn't the kind of question Louis would ask, or even the kind of question he'd necessarily even approve of, but where Louis was the master of logic and sound reason ('I'm a pragmatist,' he'd once said to Edson in the middle of a fairly warm debate about market research and whether it stifles creativity), Edson liked to think he was a little more human. A little better at communicating, maybe. A little more personal, perhaps. A little stronger in the department of judging people's feelings. "So, Dorte, your, er, your Father."

"Yes?"

"Were you . . . were you . . . *there* when he, er . . .?" Edson looked over at Louis who was giving him a fiercely puzzled look.

"No. He was at work," damn! Edson suddenly remembered her

stating that the night before. "I was at home studying and then his secretary called saying he was in an ambulance. So when my Mother and I arrived at the hospital he was already dead. I think he had died at the office, really."

"That's really tough," ventured Edson.

"Yeah, it's okay."

"I'm sorry I shouldn't have asked. Stupid."

"No, it's fine. I like to talk about him. Maybe not about that day, but I like to talk about him."

III

A little later Lotte and Dorte said they better go back to make sure they'd packed everything, leaving just John, Louis and Edson at the table.

"You two should definitely come up to visit me in Norfolk," said John.

"That would be great," replied Edson.

"Yes, you know, meet Jennifer, have a bit of dinner and take a look round the village – not as interesting as anywhere you've been over the last few weeks, but still, it would be a nice day."

"No, definitely," said Louis, "What are you up to when you get back?"

"Well, the usual business until Christmas – bit of fundraising and the like for the almshouse, I'm the Church Warden at the local church as well, and there's always meetings to do with St John Ambulance . . . Have you two decided where you're off to next?"

"We think probably St Petersburg and then maybe Germany or the Czech Republic – Edson's keen on Scandinavia, but it's a bit expensive."

"I'm not *that* keen. I was just saying . . ."

"Can I ask you boys something?"

"Yes."

"Why did you come on this train? What I really mean is, why do you think anyone does? In my case I wanted to visit Irkutsk, and this was a novel way of getting there. But what persuaded you to travel for six days on a train – I mean, most people don't even like travelling more than a couple of hours on a train at home."

"I can't remember now," began Edson, "I think Louis suggested and it sounded fantastic, travelling across a vast continent like Asia by train. Why did you think of it, Louis?"

"It just came up when we were deciding what we were going to do. At first we were just going to fly back, but I'd heard that some bloke at

University was going to drive a car from Europe all the way to China, and he was looking for a mechanic to go with him, and that seemed like a fantastic idea."

"Apart from the fact that you have no idea about mechanics."

"Yes, so I couldn't go, but travelling such a distance solely on land sounded like something I'd love to do. We started talking about what we'd do, where we'd go, and then I said that Ed didn't necessarily have to meet me in China – I could travel home, maybe going to Pakistan or India or something on the way back. But then I thought about the Trans-Siberian."

"Yes, but what exactly was it that made it so *appealing*?" John closed his eyes tightly as he tried to force home his question.

"I think it was just something that not many people had done. I didn't know a single person who had done it and whenever I mentioned it people were just really impressed and excited," said Edson, and he sank a gulp of black coffee.

"Yeah – it'll look good on the CV and it's a great story to tell[*] when you get home. I think a lot of people see it as a kind of cruise – they probably think it's all really luxury stuff."

"Yeah – de-luxe cabins and stuff! What do you think of that word, John, 'de-luxe'?"

"I've never really thought about it."

"I just think it's a word so terrible it's almost good, do you know what I mean? I mean what exactly is *de-luxe*? Presumably it's French or something for luxury or whatever, and maybe when it was first said in Britain it sounded quite grand, but now it's the kind of word that they use at rundown holiday camps to try and lure people in, as if that single word will single-handedly mask the fact that the place hasn't been renovated for twenty-five years. It's the kind of word that once upon a time might have sounded really chic, but now it just sounds desperate. It's a word that the bedding industry has tried to monopolise too, I think."

"Yerrrsss," said Louis. "Anyway, I think it's about impressing people, but also maybe it's to impress yourself, you know, to live for six days on a train and cover that amount of ground. I guess it's a little bit like the attitude of Hillary, you know, climbing mountains because they're there, well, we'll travel on this train because it's there and it's an experience that is probably different to any other in the world – although obviously it's a bit easier than climbing Mount Everest without taking extra oxygen."

[*] You'd think so, wouldn't you?

"I agree totally. What's actually surprising is that the train runs at all. You'd think it wouldn't be commercially viable nowadays. Perhaps it's important for people who want to get from one place along the line to another place much further along that maybe aren't serviced by 'planes, but even then surely there could be a more localised service for those people? It seems to me that most people, at least some kind of majority, travel the whole length of the trip in one go – and it can't be cheaper than flying."

"You could never say it ran just for tourists either – there's only a few of us on here that look like tourists, and the tourist numbers must drop right off in the winter," added Edson.

"I'd like to come back and do this again, maybe going in the opposite direction, in about five years time, and see what the differences are – whether there's more Westerners on the train, all that kind of stuff," said Louis.

"I 'd guess that there might well be a lot more Westerners – a lot more youngsters on the train next time. I think more go that way than this way anyway, but I think there'll be more in general because there seems to be big increases in younger people travelling alone in further away and more remote places every year," remarked John.

"You're probably right," agreed Edson, "Since I've been travelling a lot more people seem to be doing it."

"But why?" said John, "Obviously I can see the attraction, but what's happened to make things change so fast?"

"Guide books for student-types, I suppose . . ." said Louis, "They've given more people the confidence to go out and travel to more remote places, because once they've read all the advice in the books it's just like travelling in a more recognisable country, pretty much. I think those studenty books changed a lot of things about the way young people travel. It was out of reach before it came along."

"Yes, but it doesn't exactly make things totally safe, though," argued Edson, "I mean, things change quickly and some of their advice can be out of date . . . stuff like that. I doubt they give advice about how to deal with a heart attack victim on a long distance train journey either!"

"Well, no. But the point is that it gave younger people the confidence to go out and travel to different places – to do something other than," and he turned his nose up as he always did when he said, "Inter-railing." He didn't mean it – but it was the kind of attitude a lot of people who travelled in the East had.

"I think younger people have got a lot more money nowadays," mused John.

"That's part of it too – I don't think my Mum and Dad could ever have afforded to go to the places I've been to – Mum was married by the time she was nineteen for a start," pointed out Edson.

"Exactly, which makes travelling independently a middle and upper class pursuit in the main, don't you think?" asked John.

"Yeah, that's probably fair," replied Louis. Although it's not that expensive – you can go with GAP and people like that and that helps take a lot of the expense away and then once you're in a country like China you can earn plenty of money teaching English on the side."

"But, again, all this is a pretty recent phenomenon. I just wonder . . . if you go back to the sixties and the early seventies a lot of famous people and others too were going to places like India. Now, before that, people didn't go to those kind of places except as part of working for the Empire, and even though there were 'planes around then, people still went to Africa by boat. But in the sixties and seventies people were going to those places to learn about their culture or maybe to visit places that their fathers or mothers had been to as a result of the war or whatever. Now why are people going? They're going to places that no members of their family have ever been to, going to remote places that have barely seen foreigners, and there are more every year, and people seem more desperate to go to the remoter areas, the more dangerous places. It's like some kind of downgraded expedition for some people."

"Well, we've got more money, we like to go on 'planes, and the more people that come back saying what a great time they've had and the more careers advisers advocate it as a way of getting something decent on your CV the more people will get part-time jobs, save up, and go to India or Thailand or Fiji or China or wherever," said Edson.

"But young people seem much more restless to me now. The thing I wonder is that is it because of some kind of feeling of uselessness? If you think back, in the early forties there was conscription for boys your age, so many of them went abroad, if only to Europe, because of that. In those days people just went on holidays within Britain. It was the sons and daughters of that generation that really started to go abroad for holidays, so in some sense they were pioneers of their own. And finally we have your generation who, in the main, have been to France and Holland and Spain and probably Florida. Your parents went abroad to seek the sun and have comfortable holidays different from the ones they had at Southend or Blackpool or Great Yarmouth.

"But you lot, you're different again. You've had a taste. Your grandparents might have some stories about the Far East or Africa. You've got TV showing you pictures from every corner of the world. And just like your parents' backlash against wet weekends in Scarborough, you've rejected warm and easy package trips to the Costa del Sol. You don't need to join the forces, you've been to Spain, 'plane travel can take you virtually anywhere you want, so you need a challenge and that challenge ends up being going to places your parents never went to and at an age they would never would have dreamed of doing it. Do you see what I'm getting at?" Edson and Louis had been nodding away at all this.

"There's definitely competition to do the most outrageous journey or whatever – we were talking about it the other night – trying to decide who'd stayed in the scummiest place," answered Louis. "But I think a lot of parents encourage it."

"And the amount of older people with kids who said to me it was a great idea and to do it now while I still could was amazing. A lot of them regretted not doing something similar when they were younger – a lot of people are putting off marriage and kids to enjoy this kind of thing . . . you only need to look at people like yourself, John, to see why we do it. You're out here doing something that most people in their sixties wouldn't consider now, but thirty odd years ago it would be virtually unheard of. I mean, my parents are in their fifties and they've been to South Africa and Malaysia and places like that, and they don't really do a lot different to us – they just stay in much nicer hotels!" said Edson.

"Yeah," agreed Louis, "It's like they're taking the chance now to do the things they wished they'd done when they were younger. I know my parents were really excited when they came to see me in China."

"It begs the question, though," said Edson, "If this is all broadly right, what is the next generation going to do to distinguish themselves from us?"

"I don't know," answered John.

"Start spending their two week holidays in Redcar and Margate and revitalising our coastal resorts?" laughed Louis. "We'll probably get hammered by the papers in twenty years for not investing in our own towns and spending it abroad instead!"

IV

Back in the cabin things seemed very quiet. "Things seem very quiet, don't they?" said Edson.

"Yes." Edson and Louis were sitting quietly on their bunks, surveying their room, which had become messier and grubbier in the time following the departure of Sasha and Alexander. Their clothes were littered on their own bunks, while on the opposite bunk there were about twelve small empty bottles of Orange Star Cola, a large empty bottle of vodka, an Orange Star Cola stain on one of the now less-than-white pillows, and an empty noodle packet with some shreds of dried noodles lying in the vicinity. On the floor someone had spilt some drink of some sort at some point in the last few days, which fortunately didn't notice against the rug's complicated pattern, but unfortunately did give the cabin the whiff of a living room the morning after a group of sixteen year olds have taken advantage of some absent parents. There was also a fair quantity of jasmine tealeaves that had been ground into the rug – they seemed to get pretty much everywhere, like sand after a visit to the beach.

"I can't be arsed to pack," said Edson.

"Baarh! Come on, get off the pot, get it sorted!" answered Louis in a noticeably weak attempt at his usual army voice.

"All right guys?" James was standing in the doorway.

"All right James, come on in mate," said Edson. James made some space by shifting some Orange Star Cola bottles and sat down on the bunk. "Done your packing, then?"

"Yeah, Neil's still doing his and talking about where he wants to go next so I thought I'd give him some space and come and see you guys."

"Where did he say he was going? Did he mention us?" Edson had been lying down, but was now propping himself up on his elbows doing a bad job at trying not to look too worried.

"Well, yes, he did use the word 'we' and he obviously didn't me because, thank God, I'm flying home tomorrow -" James was interrupted by Louis.

"*If* we arrive before tomorrow," he said, deadpan. James looked worried for a moment.

"Yeah, very funny . . . so he could have meant you I suppose," it was not clear to Edson how serious James was.

"I thought he was going to Kiev, though?" said Louis. "We're going up to St Petersburg first, and even that might depend on the best way to get to Central Europe."

"Well, I asked him casually where he was going because I thought something like this was on the horizon, and his exact words were, 'not sure yet Jimmy-boy, I was well up for Kiev, but it might be a bit pony going it alone, so I'll either convince some of the other guys to come with me or maybe follow them up to St Pete's.'" James shrugged and there was silence for a moment in the cabin.

"We'll just have to tell him," said Edson.

"Tell him what?"

"Well . . . you know, that we've come this far by ourselves and we'd kind of, you know, we'd like to go the rest of the way like that as well – travelling in big groups causes too many problems – remember what it was like in India when there were six of us? It took about an hour to make every single tiny decision!"

"We can't tell him that."

"Why not?"

"He's not that bad-a bloke." Edson and James exchanged glances.

"Look. Jim's been travelling with him now for six days – staying in the same cabin and all that – and he's come to warn us that Neil might wanna tag around with us. Doesn't that tell you something? Jim's not a nasty bloke, but . . . he's clearly a broken man! Look at him!" James did his reluctant best to look broken, which consisted of a soulful, hangdog expression with his shoulders resolutely slumped. "And . . . and, I don't think I can handle him calling me Eddie all the time. It's all right for you – he can't call you Louis-y, can he?"

"Yeah, I s'pose you're right, I just don't see how we can do it without looking like complete wankers – I mean . . . he's not *evil*, is he?"

"Oh no?" said James, "Well look at this!" Louis and Edson both sat up.

"What?" said Edson. There was nothing there.

"Nothing . . . sorry, it just sounded like my cue to produce something proving he was a vampire or something. Sorry."

"Why didn't we suggest that he went with the Chinese guy last night? It would have solved all the problems. He could have helped him out, reported back to us by phone when we got home to England and let us know the outcome of the story, so we wouldn't spend the rest of our lives wondering, and we wouldn't have had to have worried about him following us all around Europe. I bet he'd've done it as well! It would have been just the kind of mad thing he likes to do so he can tell everyone about it afterwards!" cried Edson.

"You're right, he probably would've too."

"Nah, he's all talk," replied Louis, "He'd've found some excuse. It's a dumb idea anyway – wouldn't be much fun sitting around in a hospital hoping someone you've never even spoken to would recover, would it? What could he have done really?"

"I dunno . . . Maybe we could pack up all our stuff now, and then when we arrive in Moscow just leg it to the hostel and hope he doesn't see us! We'll never see him again and we'll never have to face any consequences, hee hee!" Edson's laugh was parodic, mischievous, childlike.

"That won't work," said Louis soberly, "He booked with the same company as us, didn't he? He'll be meeting the same guide we're meeting to get us to the hostel. We'd end up looking really stupid running away only to meet him again immediately afterwards when we find the guide."

"Damn."

IV – The Last Lunch

For the remainder of the morning Louis and Edson tidied their cabin, chucked out the rubbish and packed their decaying clothes into their bulging rucksacks. "I love rucksacks," Louis said for about the fifteenth time on the trip, "There's always room for one more thing, isn't there?" As they packed, James sat cross-legged in the corner of the lower spare bunk, out of the way and conveniently out of sight to certain passers-by. He chattered about how he got into accountancy, how he was desperate for a decent meal of pizza or pasta or fish and chips or McDonalds (he was a big McDonalds fan), and how he was thinking of emigrating. Louis muttered every now and again about going travelling by himself to Nepal without taking any 'poncey guidebooks'.

When they'd finally finished packing the cabin still seemed a real mess. And they could still smell rotting alcohol. "What shall we do with these noodles?" asked Edson. Louis looked round and saw Edson sitting on his bunk with eighteen packets of noodles surrounding him as if he was posing for a publicity shot after winning a year's supply of cheap dried Chinese food in some ridiculous competition.

"Blimey. How much money did we waste on those?"

"'Bout a pound, I think."

"Christ . . . erm, we could offer them round to a few people . . . or . . ."

"Or we could just leave them here and assume that the cleaners will take them home and have a noodle feast for themselves and their extended family and the entire population of their village and the neighbouring village in a massive celebration of noodles and their strange tasting flavour sachet things."

"Deal. Talking of food, is it lunch time yet?"

"More or less," said James.

"Right, let's go, I'm blahdy starving."

"Our last ever bowl of borscht."

"No borscht, eh?" mused Louis five minutes later. The blond waiter shook his head morosely and looked a trifle upset. A trifle! That would have gone down well with the boys. Sorry. The blond waiter stood with his hands behind his back, his head bowed ever so slightly. "What do you have?"

"Bread."

"Ah . . . well, bread it is then, and some of your lovely cola."

"We have no cola."

"Beer?"

"No."

"Oh yeah, I forgot."

"We have *wodka*." All three of them looked at each other with screwed up faces.

"Hmm, just coffee for three, then I think," said Louis finally.

"Jesus, I hope we're not too far away from Moscow," said James, "because when we get there I'm going to go to the first Pizza Hut I can find and order the biggest Meat Feast they've got."

"I want a big lasagne, a really messy one, boiling hot, maybe with a side order of chips," Edson closed his eyes as he thought of it and made puckering shapes with his lips as if he'd be willing to snog the meal before eating it.

"I s'pose that if they've run out of virtually all food and drink it must mean we're fairly close to Moscow, which is good . . . I can almost smell that pizza," said James, wistfully[*], his eyes closed and his nose sniffing the air like a cat in a kitchen when there's a turkey roasting in the oven.

[*] For any fast food company bosses reading this. Here's a tip. Why not hang around outside Moscow Central Station on the day that the Trans-Siberian comes in. Have a lackey there with you – you know, one of those spotty kids like the one in *The Simpsons*, and have him weighed down with ten large pizzas or thirty burgers and fries or whatever, and make gifts of them to everyone who alights the train following their six days of enforced semi-fasting. Then film them tucking in like starving mongrels on the platform. You've got yourself one hell of

a good advert there – just lots of people stuffing glorious fast food into their mouths as if they've never eaten before and absolutely loving your product – and it's all real! And much cheaper than hiring Caprice, or Ryan Stiles, or some footballer who missed a penalty once. Remember me when you do it and sales go sky high, won't you?

"I don't think that's necessarily true, Jim," said Edson sagely, "You know, Russians can live for thirty days on a diet of *wodka* – they store it in a hump on their backs and release some into their body whenever they need the sustenance."

"Aren't you thinking of camels?" asked Louis.

"I could be . . . or am I thinking of dromedaries?"

"Boyzzz!" said a gleefully loud voice. The three of them looked up to see Neil coming down the gangway, his arms outstretched as if he was going to hug all of them at once in a sickening group-hug. "How's it going?"

"Yeah, okay," answered Louis. Neil sat himself down next to Edson and barged him up next to the window.

"Room for a large one! Right, what's on the menu, boys? I could eat a zebra."

"Just bread and coffee," said James quietly.

"Just bread? I don't mind the coffee, I'd never turn down a caffeine shot, but just bread? That's pony. Anyway boys I wanted to speak to you. It's been great travelling with Jimmy-riddle here in our little cabin for nearly a week. I couldn't have asked for a better cabin mate – except for having Lotte and Dorte – now that would be nice, both of them changing at night, eh? Mmm. Those Danish girls!" and he pumped a clenched fist in front of him. "But Jimmy's off, isn't he? Which is a shame, back to the old 9-5 innit? Christ, I'd kill myself if that was me. Anyway, so he's off, and you're still here, and I'm still around, and we get on great and I thought we could all go on together, you know, Kiev, St Petes, wherever. Whaddya think, eh?" Edson didn't know what to say. He was pretty much paralysed – firstly through fear, and secondly because Louis had been the unofficial leader of this whole trip and generally what he said went. He just couldn't stand any length of time with Neil, and it wouldn't be like the train when he could escape to his compartment, he'd be there *all* the time, making *all* the decisions, dominating *all* the conversations . . . describing his . . . *faeces*. He didn't want it. But he might not have any choice. He tried not to look at Neil, but instead focused on Louis who had been listening and nodding away with a smile on his face. Things didn't look good. Louis opened his mouth to answer, but at that moment the blond waiter came back.

"Ah! *Garçon.* It'll be bread and coffee I think!" the waiter nodded and slid off. "Seeing as you haven't got anything else," he sneered once he was out of earshot. "Fucking *pony*, that is."

"Well, how long are you staying in *Mockba* for?" asked Louis. Edson couldn't believe what he was hearing. Well, he could but he didn't like it and he felt his heart speed up with anxiety, which, in turn, made him angry at himself for going over the top on this one.

"I've got to stay for about four days because I'm having some money wired to a bank there from the parents, you know, bit of a birthday present, which is going to come in very Handy Andy."

"It's your birthday soon, mate?" asked James.

"Yeah, in a few days. That's when the money's coming through. I asked if they could do it a bit earlier, but they're funny like that, it has to be actually *on* my birthday."

"How old you gonna be?" said Edson.

"Ah, older than you lot . . . well, maybe not older than Jimmy-boy, eh!" Edson got annoyed easily by people who didn't reveal their age. It's such a trivial thing, but some people like to be coy about it in an effort to appear mysterious or something. In his opinion, it didn't work.

"That's a real shame," said Louis. What was this? "Because we're actually booked on a train to St Petersburg in three days time and we can't really put it off without spending a lot of money – I don't think we can get refunds and we're on a fairly tight schedule as it is." Edson, fighting the instinct to smile and the urge to reach across and shake his trusty old mate, who he never should have doubted, by the hand, managed a surprisingly commendable impression of solemnity.

"Oh, is that in three days? Are you sure?" At this James suddenly seemed to notice his shoe was untied and ducked under the table.

"Yep, definitely."

"Are you sure?" said Neil, "Eddie doesn't seem certain."

"That's because I booked all of our trip, he doesn't really *do* anything. He just follows me around." For once, Edson didn't mind Louis' favourite jibe.

"Well maybe I can catch you up in St Pete's, then?"

"Well, maybe, but we don't want to make any definite arrangements, you know. We might go up to Warsaw or maybe to Scandinavia, or to the Czech Republic, we're not sure. *You* know what it's like," Edson countered, showing as much feeling as he could muster without actually covering Neil's hand with his own and looking into his eyes.

"Yeah, I do. I'd probably change my mind anyway before I went up there and you guys would be waiting for weeks for me to turn up and I'll have probably turned round and gone to Pakistan or something. All right, never mind. Just a thought." Under the table, Edson clenched his fist in victory. Everything was gonna be *aaaalllll* right. "At least we can do the touristy stuff in Moscow, together, though, lads – we've still got three days before we go our separate ways!" Bugger.

Back in the cabin Edson pointed out that they better get those tickets to St Petersburg sorted out. "Yeah, that's not going to be easy when he's probably going to be hanging around with us the whole time. We've got to find out which station the blahdy train leaves from as well, there's probably about six different stations in *Mockba* . . . but if he comes with us to the station where we get tickets from we can just pretend we're picking them up when really we'll be buying them!"

"*You* are a genius."

"Well it's a blahdy good job one of us is."

It had been a strange day. They had woken up thinking about little other than the Chinese man's health, only paying passing thought to the fact that their mammoth journey was almost over. And now, despite the fact that they still hadn't arrived in Moscow, they were already deciding on how they were going to leave the capital. James, who they'd been living with for six days, and John who they'd been living off, almost, for three days, would disappear once they arrived in Moscow and they wouldn't see them again for at the very least a few weeks, if ever. In and out their lives just like that. In a couple more days they'd be shot of Neil. It seemed like time had stood still for six days. It hadn't of course, it had constantly jumped all over the shop, but it had gone so quickly. Edson was at a loss to think where all the time had gone. He'd probably done less in those six days than at any other time of his life since early childhood. Eat, drink, talk, sleep, play cards, even though it's a waste of time, and a very small amount of reading. That was it – at least until the Chinese man had collapsed in front of them. Yet that experience of nothingness prior to the heart attack was somehow an amazing experience in itself, and, apart from the others on the train, no-one else he knew could lay a claim to having felt anything like it.

For the remainder of the journey Louis and Edson lay on their bunks talking occasionally, disturbed only intermittently by various visitors. James popped in every now and again, Neil poked his head round the door, John came to offload more chocolate, Lotte and Dorte came in to say 'hi' and tell them they were staying in the same hostel as them in Moscow. They asked if Neil had booked with the same company and reacted indifferently when they were told the bad news. They smoked a rolly each and then wondered off, Lotte squeezing Edson's forearm as she left so that Edson could have sweet dreams that night. And then, as it got dark, the train stopped for the last time.

Almost in fear that it might immediately drive off again back to Beijing, Edson and Louis jumped off the train, their rucksacks swinging wildly as they struggled to get both arms under the straps. They stood on the platform at Moscow station and gawped at a great big red neon sign saying 'MOCKBA'.

Soon, Edson and Louis were joined by John, Neil, James, Lotte and Dorte and they walked abreast like a human wave into the station. "Just think, James, we're probably only a few minutes way from the nearest McDonalds or Pizza Hut," pointed out Edson.

"Don't get me started, I just wanna get to the hostel, dump my bag and go out for the biggest fast food meal I've ever had, and Mr Credit Card is going to pay for the lot."

"Including mine and Louis' as well, do you mean?"

"Er . . . yeah, why not," replied James a little uncertainly. Edson laughed.

"It's all right mate, I was only joking, I'm sure Louis' got enough money for me and him haven't you, Lou?"

"You can pay for your own blahdy food."

"You wouldn't believe we were best mates, would you? And if you did you'd be wrong because I think he's a tosspot. What time's your flight tomorrow Jim?"

"Ten in the morning so I'll probably be out before you even wake up."

"You saying we're lazy? How you gonna get to the airport?"

"Taxi I guess."

"I think there's a different system here," said John, "I believe anyone can be a taxi if they want to be, so you can just flag down any old car."

"That sounds a bit dangerous," said James. They were nearing the end of the platform now, and they could see a squat man with a messy beard who immediately reminded Edson of the sarcastic comic shop owner out of *The Simpsons*. He had a piece of brown card that he held in front of him. It was just like the kind of sign that grubby hitchhikers hold up in front of cars as they come off roundabouts and onto motorways in Britain. In thick black felt tip it said, 'Moon River'. "That'll be us!" exclaimed Neil.

"Hi guys, hope you all had a good trip," said the man, instantly revealing through his accent that he was American. The only person who hadn't booked with Moon River was John, who was straight off to the airport anyway.

"Well, it was great to meet you all, I've had a fantastic trip!" he said warmly.

"Yeah, it was brilliant meeting you John," said Edson and he stepped forward to shake his hand. "You've got my details and Louis', haven't you?"

"Yes, got all that, I'll be in touch soon." John continued round the rest of the group shaking hands and wishing luck.

"We should get a photo!"

"Do you want me to take it?" said the American guide, with typical American helpfulness.

"Yeah, that'd be great, here's my camera . . . you just need to press that there . . . it's an automatic flash, so . . . Right, er,"

"Gotcha, top button." Everyone got together in an untidy bundle with rucksacks all over the place and the front of the train just behind them. "Okay everyone squeeze in a bit there, after three say 'Vodka'! One, two, three."

"Vodka!"

"Okay, that's great!"

"Wait, can you do one for me," said Lotte.

"Actually, I'd quite like one too," said John and brought out a huge camera with a massive lens. Then everyone stepped forward with all their cameras and there was a cacophony of press thats and switch this-s as the poor American struggled gamely with three around his neck and three more on the floor in front of him. Finally he got to the last one.

"Christ my mouth's aching," said Neil, then he looked around him and said, "Hey! We should have had Dame-o in these, anyone seen him?" But nobody had.